Successful Contract Administration

Successful
Contract
Administration

Tim Boyce MInstPS

HAWKSMERE

© Timothy Boyce 1992

Published by Hawksmere plc
12–18 Grosvenor Gardens
London SW1W 0DH
Tel: 0171-824 8257

Revised reprint
Reprinted 1994, 1995, 1996

British Library Cataloguing in Publication Data

Boyce, Tim
    Successful contract administration.
    I. Title
    692.80941

ISBN 1 85418 090 8

Design and production in association with
Book Production Consultants plc, Cambridge

Typeset by KeyStar, St Ives, Cambridge

Printed in Great Britain by
St Edmundsbury Press Ltd, Bury St Edmunds, Suffolk

I would like to dedicate this book to my sons
Benjamin and Matthew
with love from their Dad.

About the author

Tim Boyce is Commercial Manager at a major electronics company. He is a member of the Institute of Purchasing and Supply and a member of the Institute's National Contract Management Committee. He studied electrical and electronic engineering at London University before joining the Procurement Executive of the Ministry of Defence in 1974. The majority of his six years with MOD were spent in contracts and contracts policy branches.

Since 1980 he has held a number of positions within the electronics industry and has been responsible for the negotiation and administration of many multi-million pound contracts and sub-contracts. These responsibilities continue in his present position.

Since 1986 he has also been a regular and acclaimed speaker at a number of Hawksmere seminars both in the UK and overseas. His published works include his first book published by Hawksmere *The Commercial Engineer*, and he is also a joint author of *Government Procurement and Contracts*.

Contents

Preface

The purpose of this book is to provide practical advice to people whose jobs involve them in the administration or management of business contracts.

Although the title of this book is *Successful Contract Administration*, in the opening sentence of this preface I deliberately add the words 'or management'. In the general sense the words 'administration' and 'management' tend to be almost interchangeable. However, in the business sense managers are usually senior to administrators in most organisations. If that order of precedence is taken to apply also to the function of looking after contracts then I must say that it is not at all clear where the dividing line between contract administration and contract management lies. It is sometimes thought that administrators do the non-thinking, internal paper-processing activity. I would see that as coming under the heading of clerical work. Another common distinction is between the manager who is responsible for people and the administrator who is not. Nevertheless the good 'contracts' person must most certainly have good people skills since the work cannot be done well without sound relationships.

A business or a company is a money machine. If it does not make money it will not survive. It makes money by winning and performing contracts. With no contracts there is no business. Whether the care and custody of the contract once it is won are matters of administration or management I will leave to the reader to decide. The terminology is not important. What is important is that good contract administration is fundamental if the money-making opportunity that the contract represents on the day of its signature is to be converted into good results in the profit and loss account.

This book is aimed at the company employee who is responsible for administration of contracts between his or her company and its business customers or between the company and its suppliers. Its theme is contracts for the sale of goods and it is written in a general sense so as to be an introduction to the principles of contract administration, thus avoiding the particular of individual industries or markets. Certainly I have found that the simple thesis that a contract is a contract regardless of the subject matter holds true. Thus a grasp of good general principles together with the details and nuances applicable to a particular sector will make the contract administrator an expert in his or her own field. Throughout this book I have made use of the word 'he'. This has been for drafting ease only and it is my experience that women and men are equally competent in the role of contract administration.

This idea of a grasp of general principles gave rise to my earlier book *The Commercial Engineer* (Hawksmere Ltd 1990) in which I outlined some underlying commercial principles that should be adopted by all engineers (using the term fairly loosely as a generic title) who, although having no direct responsibility for contract administration, were nevertheless contributing to the commercial success of a business and its contracts. In many ways this book is a development of that theme, and indeed it borrows from and expands upon that earlier work, but it is aimed at the professional contract administrator whose full-time occupation actually is administration of contracts.

There is one question that arises from time to time in connection with contract administration. If the proper formation and performance of contracts is so important (which it is) and if the contract is a legal instrument (which it is), then should not the job of making and administering contracts be left to the lawyers? In the United Kingdom most companies and other organisations, including Government purchasing organisations, leave it to 'enthusiastic amateurs' – a phrase pointed out by Bruce Barton, an acquaintance in MOD. On balance I believe this is right. Provided those in contract administration understand enough of the law to make legally effective agreements, provided they understand enough to identify any legal risks and provided they know enough to know when to seek professional assistance, then all is well. Given these provisos then the advantages of a pragmatic commercial approach, which should be second nature to the contract administrator, outweigh the advantages of a qualified lawyer whose extensive training has been in the strictly correct, rather than in the immediacy and pragmatism of business.

I can find a supporting analogy to this conclusion in the area of personnel management. The employment of people is subject to as much law as is the making of contracts. No one would normally suggest that a company personnel manager should be a lawyer. What is needed is specialist training which embraces an appreciation of relevant law. Exactly the same is true of contract administration.

A major difference though between contract administration and many other business functions is that there is neither any particular training or education process, nor a governing professional body. The practice is that people move into contract administration and hopefully become good at it largely through experience and through *ad hoc* training and education opportunities. Certain business management development programmes such as the MBA touch upon one or two of the relevant topics and of the professional bodies the Institute of Purchasing and Supply (IPS) is the most closely aligned. Indeed the study and examination process leading to membership of the IPS is probably currently the most relevant and useful course to follow apart, of course, from the short courses organised by Hawksmere and similar seminar companies.

In summary, there can be few business management functions as important as contract administration. Despite the lack of formal recognition and absence of traditional-style qualifications, success in it is a matter of dedication and applied professionalism. In its own small way, I hope that this book will contribute to successful contract administration.

Usus promptus facit.

T R Boyce 1992

1

⊚ ⊚ ⊚ ⊚ ⊚ ⊚ ⊚ **C H A P T E R** ⊚ ⊚

Introduction

Champagne corks fly, parties, lunches and launches are organised and everybody heaves an enormous sigh of relief – why?

We've got the contract!

Months of bidding activity, lobbying, marketing and negotiations have finally brought home the contract. Work can start, jobs remain secure, the cash starts to roll and there's the prospect of something to offer the shareholder, the banks and the financial institutions. However, winning is one thing but succeeding is something completely different. To turn the victory in winning the order into a commercial success the contract must be fulfilled in the optimum fashion, with every opportunity to improve the commercial performance identified and exploited to the full.

Success in this endeavour revolves around good sound contract administration. The endeavour can only ever be successful if it is built upon good foundations of pre-contract work in terms of, for example, preparing quotations, drafting Requests For Quotation (RFQs) and contractual documents. Although 'contract administration' is not the most exciting sounding function, without it the chances of success are remote. A more apt slogan would be:

ADMINISTERING FOR PROFIT

This is what this book is about. Its aims can be summarised as follows:

    a)   To promote contract administration as a profession.

b) To propose some different ways of thinking about the contract and its environment.

c) To focus on business commercial objectives.

d) To propose some specific administration techniques.

e) To suggest improvements through enhanced personal skills.

f) To provide through worked case studies instruction on avoiding risks and problems.

These themes flow throughout the book.

2

● ● ● ● ● ● ● ● C H A P T E R ● ●

Professional contract administration

① Introduction

Contract administration is a profession. On the face of it this sounds somewhat odd. There is no obvious educational qualification for it and it would not normally be counted amongst the classical professions of the law, medicine, accountancy and so on. And yet the task must be performed in what can only be described as a professional manner, with individuals displaying high standards of integrity, achieving successful results for the business and at all times representing the status, quality and reputation of the company at the highest standards. For these reasons contract administration will be referred to as a profession and its performers as professionals.

Furthermore it is contended that the role of contract administration is a mainstream business function and that regardless of where it fits into the business organisation it must be fully integrated and subject to modern techniques and theory.

② Total Quality Management

In the late 1980s and into the 1990s Total Quality Management (TQM) has become an accepted piece of management wisdom adopted by many companies.

Total Quality Management is a process that focuses on meeting customer requirements through the quality of *all* the tasks carried out in the Company.

TQM International Ltd

The thesis reminds us of course that companies are in business to satisfy customers without whom there would be no business. But the statement emphasises the word 'all' and this is the essence of TQM. Gone are the days when quality was something to do with a man in a white coat measuring things as they fell off a production line. Today quality is or should be an integral part of every business activity and of the business as a whole.

The question is, how does TQM apply to contract administration?

Let us examine TQM as shown in Figure 2.1 and see how contract administration fits in.

Figure 2.1

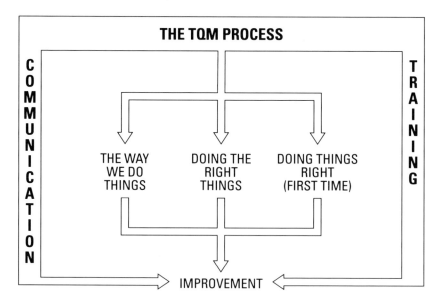

Starting with the outer boxes, we see training and communication. It can be taken as read that the reader in having gone to the trouble of buying or borrowing this book has some commitment to training. Good communication is essential and is a topic to which we will return in later chapters.

Looking at the inner headings, we can find examples to indicate how contract administration is part of this TQM process.

③ Doing things right (first time)

As we shall see in more detail in Chapter 3, it is the job of the contract administrator to make sure that the contract (or quotation, or tender or subcontract etc etc) is accurate. This requires attention to detail, without which mistakes are made, money and time are lost and unfortunate contractual or legal consequences arise.

Simple and common examples where lack of attention to detail causes problems are:

Problem	Consequence
1) Wrong or incomplete part number	a) Item cannot be procured/ supplied
	b) Wrong thing tendered for delivery
	c) Customer rejects delivery
	d) Nugatory cost
	e) Action for breach of contract
	f) Late delivery
	g) Lost customer
	h) Lost reputation
	i) Lost profit
2) Packaging instructions missing or incomplete	a) Delivery delayed
	b) Goods damaged
	c) Payment delayed
3) Invoicing details ignored	a) Invoice sent to wrong address
	b) Supporting paperwork not provided
	c) Payment not made
	d) Payment delayed
	e) Cash flow problems
	f) Financing costs
	g) Bankruptcy

Time spent getting such things right and getting them right first time will pay dividends. An analogy can be found in the carpenter's maxim 'Measure twice, cut once!' Accuracy and checking are at the heart of TQM.

④ Doing the right things

There is a world of difference between doing things right and doing the right things. The former is to do with making sure that all tasks are done accurately and efficiently. There is implicit in this statement a presumption that the tasks need to be done. The latter involves a challenge – a questioning of the need to do certain things or the need to do other things which are not being done.

This concept of making sure the right things are done has in many ways been realised in the issue of BS5750. BS5750 is the British Standard for Quality Systems. In its current form it was introduced in 1987 to provide a model for quality assurance. It is one of a series of three international standards dealing with quality systems that can be used for *external* quality control. The following alternative models represent three distinct forms of functional or organisational capability suitable for two-party *contractual* purposes:

ISO 9001: Quality Systems – model for quality assurance in design/development, production, installation and servicing.

This is for use when conformance to specified requirements is to be assured by the supplier during several stages which may include design/development, production, installation and servicing.

ISO 9002: Quality Systems – model for quality assurance in production and installation.

This is for use when conformance to specified requirements is to be assured by the supplier during production and installation.

ISO 9003: Quality Systems – model for quality assurance in final inspection and test.
This is for use when conformance to specified requirements is to be assured by the supplier solely at final inspection and test.

A review of the BS requirements will show how central good contract administration is to a 'quality company'. In particular certain requirements, such as the need to conduct a contract review meeting upon receipt of a new contract, demonstrates specific actions that should be taken under the auspices of those responsible for contract administration.

It must be understood that the requirements only apply in the strict sense where the contract includes BS5750 or the relevant ISOs or where there is some other contractual requirement for external quality assurance. Indeed the whole principle behind the BS is that companies are encouraged to introduce the principles and apply for national accreditation to the standard. However, it could not be clearer that good, quality contract administration is essential to the success of the company.

5 The way we do things

The third and final leg of TQM is to take the challenge of the second leg even further and question whether the whole approach is the correct one. In contract administration this takes us to the essence of a main theme of this book, namely how we should look at the contract in the first place. The problem in many companies is that traditionally the contract has been compartmentalised, to map on to the organisation of the company, each segment of the contract belonging to one function and each function only interested in one segment, as Figure 2.2 shows.

Figure 2.2

To put it the other way round, look at the building blocks of the company in Figure 2.3.

Both of these charts exaggerate for effect but nevertheless the point is well made that it can be difficult to find someone below the level of managing director who is ostensibly responsible for the whole contract! The compartmentalising happens within the buyer's organisation and in the seller's and it can happen in the tendering phase as well as in contract. So a ludicrous situation can arise as follows:

		Buyer A	Seller B
Q1	Did anybody read the whole ITT before issue?	No	
Q2	Did anybody read the whole ITT on receipt?		No
Q3	Did anybody read the whole tender before despatch?		No
Q4	Did anybody read the whole tender following receipt?	No	
Q5	Did anybody read the whole contract before offer issue?		No
Q6	Did anybody read the whole contract before acceptance?		No

Figure 2.3

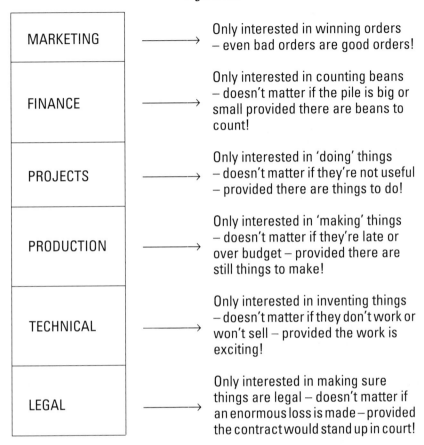

MARKETING	→	Only interested in winning orders – even bad orders are good orders!
FINANCE	→	Only interested in counting beans – doesn't matter if the pile is big or small provided there are beans to count!
PROJECTS	→	Only interested in 'doing' things – doesn't matter if they're not useful – provided there are things to do!
PRODUCTION	→	Only interested in 'making' things – doesn't matter if they're late or over budget – provided there are still things to make!
TECHNICAL	→	Only interested in inventing things – doesn't matter if they don't work or won't sell – provided the work is exciting!
LEGAL	→	Only interested in making sure things are legal – doesn't matter if an enormous loss is made – provided the contract would stand up in court!

No wonder contracting parties so frequently misunderstand one another! Now in practice, in the very large tenders and contracts it may be physically impossible for any one person to read the whole thing but in the many cases where there is no such barrier it is essential that at least one person has read the whole. This task or responsibility should fall to the contract administrator.

6 Business ethics

If the process of contract administration is to be undertaken professionally it is important that the individuals have an ethical framework in which to operate. Business ethics can only ever be a general framework although companies may issue detailed guidelines. Nevertheless the following principles establish this general framework:

6.1 The conduct of the company

6.1.1 AS REGARDS ITS GENERAL CONDUCT
It shall:

a) Comply with the law and applicable codes of practice of any country in which it operates.

b) Do its utmost, within the discharge of its proper obligations, to trade profitably.

6.1.2 AS REGARDS ITS MEMBERS
It shall provide shareholders with adequate and proper information for them to be able to form judgements on the company's activities and prospects, and endeavour to consult its shareholders whenever appropriate.

6.1.3 AS REGARDS ITS CREDITORS
It shall:

a) Observe agreed terms of trade credit.

b) Obtain loans on the basis of current, accurate and complete information.

6.1.4 AS REGARDS ITS SUPPLIERS
It shall:

a) Seek to establish relationships by fairness, integrity and consistency in dealing.

b) Not encourage substantial capital investment without some assurance that the work will not be prematurely or arbitrarily withdrawn.

6.1.5 AS REGARDS ITS CUSTOMERS
It shall:

a) Enter and properly perform commitments with honesty and integrity.

b) Not mislead customers and, if possible, shall seek to prevent them misleading themselves.

6.1.6 AS REGARDS ITS EMPLOYEES
It shall:

a) Seek to foster a genuinely constructive relationship with employees with the aim of establishing wider participation in the process of decision making, and ensuring that employees will have the confidence that their views on matters which affect them are taken fully into account by the company.

b) Uphold the industrial relations code of practice.

6.1.7 AS REGARDS SOCIETY AT LARGE

It shall:

a) Behave as a good corporate citizen, taking account of the interests of others, and seeking to exercise an informed and imaginative ethical judgement in deciding what action should or should not be taken.

b) Within its own field of knowledge, skill, geographical concern and financial capacity, be responsive to the movement of public opinion.

c) Pay proper regard to the environment and social consequences of its business activities.

d) Having knowledge of a potential hazard or critical environmental situation, take all possible remedial measures and inform the responsible authorities.

6.2 The conduct of the individual

6.2.1 AS REGARDS GENERAL CONDUCT

The individual shall:

a) Make proper use of the resources available to him.

b) Appraise his own competence, acknowledge potential weaknesses and seek relevant qualified advice.

c) Take every reasonable opportunity to improve his capabilities.

d) Be objective and constructive when giving advice or guidance in his managerial or professional capacity.

e) Accept accountability for the actions of his subordinates as well as for his own.

f) In pursuing his personal ambitions, take account of the interests of others.

g) Never maliciously injure the reputation or career prospects of others, nor the business of others.

6.2.2 AS REGARDS THE COMPANY

The individual shall:

a) By leadership, co-ordination, personal example and commitment, direct all available efforts towards the success of the enterprise.

b) Apply the lawful policies of the company and carry out its instructions with integrity.

c) Define and maintain an organisation structure, allocate responsibilities and encourage the achievement of objectives, by team work where appropriate.

d) Demonstrate his loyalty to the organisation by promoting its interests and objectives.

e) Advise his superior and/or other responsible person of any action which is, or which he considers to be, an improper business practice.

f) Promote effective communications within the organisation and outside it.

g) Make immediate and full declaration of any personal interests which may conflict with the interests of the company.

h) Refrain from engaging in any activity which impairs his effectiveness as an employee; in any instance of conflict arising from his membership of a trade union, trade association or other body he must act in accordance with his own judgement.

i) Ensure that plant, processes and materials committed to his charge are maintained and operated as efficiently and safely as reasonably practicable.

j) Fully respect the confidentiality of information which comes to him in the course of his duties, and not use that information for personal gain or in a manner which may be detrimental to the company or the organisation for which he has worked.

6.2.3 AS REGARDS OTHERS WHO WORK IN THE COMPANY

The individual shall:

a) Strive to minimise misunderstanding and promote good relations between all who work in the company.

b) Consult and communicate clearly.

c) Take full account of the needs, problems, ideas and suggestions of others.

d) Ensure that all his subordinates are aware of their duties and responsibilities especially in relation to those of others.

e) Encourage the improved performance of his subordinates and the development of their potential, by means of training and in other suitable ways.

f) Be concerned in the working environment for the health, safety, and well-being of all, especially those for whom he is responsible.

g) Promote self-discipline as the best form of discipline both for himself and for his subordinates.

h) Ensure that disciplinary or other corrective action is timely, constructive and respects the dignity of all concerned.

i) Using his judgement, advise senior colleagues in advance of situations in which they are likely to become involved.

6.2.4 AS REGARDS CUSTOMERS AND SUPPLIERS
The individual shall:

a) Ensure that the requirements of customers and suppliers are properly considered.

b) Ensure that terms of each transaction are stated clearly.

c) Ensure that customers and suppliers are informed of any action which may materially affect the terms of transaction and take all reasonable action to minimise risk to the parties involved.

d) Avoid entering into arrangements which unlawfully inhibit the process of open competition or which bring about improper business practices.

e) Respect the confidentiality of any information if so requested by customers and suppliers.

f) Establish and develop with its customers and suppliers a continuing satisfactory relationship leading to mutual confidence.

g) Neither offer nor accept any gift, favour or hospitality intended as, or having the effect of, bribery and corruption.

h) Act with honesty and integrity, and avoid making false or misleading statements or acting with reckless disregard to the facts or circumstances.

i) Accept or deliver the product or service within the quality, quantity, time, price and payment procedures agreed.

j) Ensure that in no circumstances are inherently unsafe goods and services supplied.

k) Ensure that an after sales service is provided commensurate with the kind of product supplied and the price paid.

6.2.5 AS REGARDS THE ENVIRONMENT, NATURAL RESOURCES AND SOCIETY
The individual shall:

a) Recognise the company's obligations to its shareholders, employees, suppliers, customers, users, society and the environment.

b) Make the most effective use of all natural resources and energy sources for the benefit of the company and with the minimum detriment to the public interest.

c) Avoid harmful pollution and, wherever economically possible, reprocess and recycle waste materials.

d) Ensure that all public communications are informative, true and not misleading, taking into account cultural and moral standards in the community and respecting the dignity of the individual.

e) Not make any public statement in his capacity as a manager without making clear, where appropriate, to all concerned his qualifications to make such statements and the capacity in which he is speaking; and without making known to the person(s) to whom his statement is directed any associations he may have with any party which may benefit from his statement.

Overall the individual is of course expected at all times to uphold and promote the reputation of the company.

7 Business awareness

Without contracts there is no business. Without profitable contracts there is no business. It must therefore be a truism that the work of the contract administrator lies at the very heart of the success of the business. To do his job well the professional contract administrator must not sit in isolation concerned only with the papers immediately in front of him. He must be aware in the broad sense. Awareness may be divided into three basic headings: awareness of factors external to the business, awareness of factors internal to the business and general awareness of knowledge relevant to the job of contract administration.

External factors include:

a) The market place: Size
Future
Expanding, static, contracting
Change
Addressability

		Market pull *v* technology push
b)	Customers:	Number, diversity, location, character
		Procurement policies
		Purchasing plans
		Budgeting procedures
		Purse keepers
		Key players
		Future requirements
c)	Competitors:	Number
		Relative positions
		Market strategy
		Bidding tactics
		Product performance
		Takeovers and mergers
d)	Suppliers:	Numbers, location, character
		Performance
		Reliability
		Range of products
		Dependencies
		Competitive prices

Internal factors include:

a) Long term business plan
b) Marketing strategy
c) Budgeting system
d) Product range and performance
e) Private venture developments
f) Organisation and structure
g) Capacity and capability
h) Financial control
i) Management information systems
j) Quality assurance
k) Project management procedures
l) Purchasing policy and procedures

Relevant knowledge includes:

a) Law relating to buying and selling
b) Forms of contract

   c) Negotiation skills

   d) Law relating to intellectual property

   e) Commercial awareness

   f) Communication skills

   g) Personal effectiveness skills

Clearly the external and internal factors are specific to individual companies. The relevant knowledge is of general application and all the topics mentioned are covered later in the book. Beyond these the reader may want to explore other subjects such as accountancy for the non-finance manager, public relations, agency, collaborative deals – the list can be endless. Certainly the more experienced he is about external and internal factors, the broader his relevant knowledge, then the better a contract administrator he will be.

⑧ Summary

Armed with an acknowledgement of how important contract administration is, equipped with an understanding of concepts such as those enshrined in TQM and BS5750, governed by good business ethics and aware of external and internal factors, the contract administrator can use expertise, training and knowledge relevant to his task to effect the most professional approach.

3

Legal environment

1 Introduction

All contracts must be correctly formed so that they will be of legal effect. Needless to say, the professional administrator must see one of his principal responsibilities as making sure that all the contracts for which he is responsible are properly formed. The aim in this chapter is to illustrate the principles and basic legal requirements.

2 Structure of the law

Each country has its own system of law and within each system there are many divisions and subdivisions. In England the law divides into two:

Public law is concerned with the constitution and functions of the many different kinds of governmental organisations, including local authorities, and their legal relationship with the citizen and each other. Public law is also concerned with crime which involves the state's relationship with, and power of control over, the individual.

Private law is concerned with the legal relationships of ordinary persons in everyday transactions. It is also concerned with the legal position of companies. Private law includes contract and commercial law, the law of tort, law relating to family matters and the law of property.

The law in other countries varies dramatically in construction and application compared with our own. Only English law is considered here. Of course companies doing regular business with overseas customers or suppliers should familiarise themselves with the law which is applicable to their particular contracts. However, once one is familiar with the principles of contract formation under English law a commercial assessment of the risks and other implications of a foreign law is easier to make.

Whilst considerations of the law in other countries is outside the scope of the book it is worth mentioning that the choice of law to apply to a particular contract is a matter for agreement between the contracting parties. So as a matter of general advice it can be recommended that a company in the UK should negotiate for English law to apply in an export or import deal. Where the parties disagree the traditional deciding parameter, setting aside the respective bargaining powers, was the location where the work was to be performed. For example, a contract wholly carried out in the UK but where the delivery destination is overseas would be subject to English law. A contract for the erection of a building by a UK company in Saudi Arabia would be subject to Saudi law.

With more and more company mergers and takeovers across national boundaries taking place there has been a development in the thinking to the effect that the law of the country of the company's parent office should be considered. For example, the German-owned British company selling goods to France would argue for the application of German law rather than English. This thinking is developing under EC pressure and may well find enactment on the UK statute books.

The real answer is that it is all up for grabs and to go from the sublime to the ridiculous it would be possible for the French company selling to the USA to select Norwegian law! This is not likely to arise and in any event the parties do not have complete freedom. For example, an English company supplying goods to an English company in England would find it hard to convince a court that the choice of French law was reasonable if an effect was to avoid liabilities or obligations under English law. However, a compromise of this nature does occur frequently where the parties settle upon the law from one of their countries but select a third country in which to prosecute arbitration procedures. It should also be remembered that where the parties agree to refer disputes to arbitration then legal action at large is precluded except to the extent that a court action may be necessary to enforce the findings and decision of the arbitrators. Frequently commercial parties to a contract prefer arbitration for the settlement of disputes as arbitration maintains the privacy of the dealings which a normal court of law could not.

The law as it affects the making and performance of contracts, the duties, undertakings and obligations of the parties to each other and to other third parties is a splendid mixture of common law, contract law, tort law and statutory law. The aim here is to draw attention to some fundamental principles and some terminology.

③ Types of contract

Contracts can be simple or speciality. Speciality contracts are also known as contracts under seal or deeds. This type of contract accounts for a very small proportion of business and is not considered further. Similarly, other types of contractually binding relationships – for example licences, agencies, consortia – are not dealt with in detail. Attention will be given to the type of contract that accounts for the majority of our concern: contracts for the supply of goods or services (being an example of a 'simple contract').

Although the straightforward distinction between speciality and simple (otherwise called 'parol') contracts is the commonest and traditional method of classification there are other expressions which one can come across which may sound very technical and thus off-putting to the contract administrator. This need not be the case as some terminology is quite comprehensible despite the deep legal meaning.

For example, contracts can be divided between bilateral and unilateral contracts. The normal business contract which imposes obligations on both parties which must be discharged is an example of a bilateral contract. On the other hand a unilateral contract has only one half of the obligations that must be performed. The best example of this is the contract a householder makes with an estate agent to sell his house. If he finds a buyer the seller must pay the estate agent his fee. However, if the estate agent does not find a buyer the agent has no liability to the seller. Indeed the agent has no obligation to take any action at all!

Another set of classifications is those of express contracts, implied contracts and quasi-contracts. In an express contract the parties commit the terms of their agreement to writing. In an implied contract it is their conduct and perhaps other relevant circumstances which define the contract. Indeed a contract in practice may be made up of both express and implied terms. A quasi-contract is one in which the law would impose an obligation to make a repayment where the beneficiary would otherwise be unjustly enriched. This is a complicated topic closely linked with the law of restitution and should not normally arise in our business contracts.

There are two other expressions which crop up from time to time. These are executory and executed contracts. An executed contract is one where the contract is fully performed. An executory contract is one which is wholly or partly yet to be performed. In practice lawyers may overlap the expressions but the basic principle is clear enough. Somewhat confusingly a 'completed' contract means only that a contract exists in the sense that an offer of contract has been made and the act of accepting the offer creates or 'completes' the contract. So a completed contract will be either executory or executed.

A final classification of contract types can be found in an analysis of their legal effectiveness. The categories are contracts which are:

a) Valid.
b) Void.
c) Voidable.
d) Unenforceable.
e) Illegal.

3.1. Valid

A valid contract is one which is of full effectiveness. It is not deficient in its construction in any way and is fully enforceable by the law.

3.2. Void

A void contract is the antithesis of the valid contract and logically is a contradiction in terms. A void contract is no contract at all. The drawback is that in practice the parties to the contract may proceed to deal with one another as though the contract were valid probably in naïve ignorance of the void nature of their agreement. In such circumstances a court may try to deduce a contract so that the parties may end up where they intended. Indeed it is probably the case that a proportion of our business 'contracts' are actually void on technical legal grounds albeit that no one notices because the parties achieve their intended aims with no difficulty and the effectiveness of the contract is never examined or tested.

The essence of a void contract or a void contract term is that a court will not enforce it. The parties are free to continue with their arrangements but in the event of dispute concerning or breach of the void term or contract there is no legal enforcement available.

A contract can be void for many reasons of which the following are the main examples:

a) Non-formation. If the contract is not correctly formed through the absence of one or more fundamental criteria (see section 5 below) the contract is void.

b) Public policy. A court will not enforce a 'contract' the purpose of which is against public policy. For example, wagering contracts cannot be enforced.

c) Agreements to oust the jurisdiction of the court. It is fundamental that a party who considers himself aggrieved or injured in some way can appeal to the courts for judgement over a matter concerning his contract. Thus any contract which aims to prevent this will be void. However, it is permissible that the parties may include a contract provision that allows all disputes to be referred to arbitration (Arbitration Act 1979) for settlement with the parties binding themselves in advance to the outcome.

d) Restraint of trade. Many businesses are aware of UK and EC regulations regarding anti-competitive practices and restrictive practices. This is another example where a contract made on this basis would be void.

e) Uncertainty. There can be cases when the agreement that the parties have made is vague or so incomplete that the contract is said to be void for uncertainty. An example of this might be where negotiations are continuing to finalise details of the contract but in practice those incomplete details cover fundamental features so that it is not possible to determine or to be certain what the parties intended ahead of those negotiations reaching a full conclusion. In business contracts, however, the courts are loath to jump to a precipitative conclusion that a contract is void for uncertainty.

Lord Wright[1] has said:

'It is clear that the parties both intended to make a contract and thought they had done so. Business men often record the most important agreements in crude and summary fashion; modes of expression sufficient and clear to them in the course of their business may appear to those unfamiliar with the business far from complete or precise. It is accordingly the duty of the court to construe such documents fairly and broadly, without being too astute or subtle in finding defects; but, on the contrary, the court should seek to apply the old maxim of English law *Verba ita sunt intelligenda ut re magis valeat quam pereat.* That maxim, however, does not mean that a court is to make a contract for the parties, or to go outside the words they have used, except in so far as there are appropriate implications of law, as, for instance, the implication of what is just and reasonable to be ascertained by the court as a matter of machinery where the contractual intention is clear but the contract is silent in some detail. Thus in contracts for future performance over a period the parties may not be able nor may they desire to specify many matters of detail, but leave them to be adjusted in the working out of the contract. Save for the legal implications I have mentioned such contracts might well be incomplete or uncertain; with that implication in reserve they are neither incomplete nor uncertain. As obvious illustrations I may refer to such matters as prices or times of delivery in contracts for the sale of goods or times of loading or discharging in a contract of sea carriage.'

This does raise the question of 'agreements to agree' which are not enforceable. Thus if the parties agree a contract leaving only the price to be negotiated later surely (the consideration is absent rendering the contract void in any event) the courts could not force the parties to come to an agreement. Thus the agreement in the first place is incomplete and thus void for uncertainty. However, in business contracts the courts will generally look to see that the parties attempted to reach agreement perhaps through some pre-scribed process and, if so, the contract would not be void even if the negotiations broke down. If the contract provided for arbitration then ultimately the issue might be resolved by the arbitrators in which case the question of the contract being void should not arise.

On the topic of uncertainty there is case law, examples[2] of which show that an agreement to agree does render the contract void for uncertainty where the parties left the contract with a simple 'price to be agreed' provision. Where there is more substance to the process of future agreement, then case law[3] supports that the contract is not void.

Where the contract is executory the courts would be more ready to find void for uncertainty. Where the contract is wholly or partially executed the preference is to find a binding contract and to imply as necessary any features which appear to be missing.

f) Mistake. A contract may be void for a mistake of fact which is known as an operative mistake. The nature of the mistake is not one of error of judgement where, for example, one side attaches an inaccurate value to some goods that he wishes to buy or sell. It is more of a fundamental failure to understand the nature of the contract or the identity or existence of the subject matter.

A mistake as to the nature of the contract is really referring to the document itself; for instance, to take the definitive case[4] a 78-year-old widow signed a document believing it to be a deed of gift of her house to her nephew but later found it to be an assignment of her leasehold interest in the property. This is an unusual situation in so far as it is normally presumed that the contract document will be read and understood by the person making the agreement. Thus the business person should not expect to find sanctuary in claiming his contract void because he did not understand what he was signing.

Where there is a unilateral and fundamental mistake (made by one side only) the contract will be void if the other side knew or ought to have known of the mistake. If the other side is ignorant of the mistake the contract will be valid.

If both sides make an identical fundamental mistake (a 'common' mistake) the contract is nevertheless valid. If they both make mistakes which are non-identical (a 'mutual' mistake) then the contract will not necessarily be void if the courts can find 'sense of the promise', ie what a reasonable person would have said was the intention of the parties.

As with uncertainty the courts will prefer not to find a contract void if it is wholly or partially executed.

In summary a contract may be void for one or more of the reasons outlined above. However, one or more of the terms of the contract may be void without rendering the whole agreement void. In these circumstances a court would enforce the balance and as necessary deduce terms to fill in for those which are void.

3.3. Voidable

A voidable contract is one in which the contract is valid in the first place but may later be avoided by one party. This is distinct from the contract providing an express right for one party to terminate the contract. The idea here is quite different. If a person were fraudulently induced to make the contract he can later avoid it if he wishes. If he does not so desire he can let the contract stand and it will be valid in the normal way.

3.4. Unenforceable

If a contract which is required by the law to be in writing is not in writing then it is unenforceable. Again, in our business contracts of the simple variety this is not going to be a cause for concern. The definition is given so that the classification list of contract types is complete.

3.5. Illegal

The illegal contract is somewhat similar to the void contract in so far as if the purpose of the contract is criminal in nature or frowned upon by the public interest the contract cannot be effective. The law distinguishes illegal and void contracts because of their different consequences. However, it is presumed that our business contracts are not illegal nor against the public interest and on this presumption the illegal contract is not considered further.

The more recent thinking also takes the classification of contracts beyond strict legal principles into the area of transactions and relations. In a once-and-for-all contract the law sees a simple transaction standing by itself governed by its express terms and within the general framework of contract law. Beyond this and with great relevance to business contracts is the idea of relations between parties who regularly do business, particularly if it is of a complicated or long-term nature.

Atiyah quotes Professor Ian MacNeil[5] when he said:

'In complex relations, obligations, often heavily binding ones, arise simply out of day to day operations, habits, thoughts, customs etc which occur with precious little thought by anyone about the obligations they might entail or about their possible consequences.'

So it can be argued that imputed into the contract are obligations, methods of working, conventions and mutual reasonable expectations which arise through a normal process of trade between contracting parties. However, Lord Jenkinson[6] warns of this importing of custom and practice that:

'An alleged custom can be incorporated into a contract only if there is nothing in the express or necessarily implied terms of the contract to prevent such inclusion and, further, that a custom will only be imported into a contract where it can be so imported consistently with the tenor of the document as a whole.'

So much for types of contract, but what is the nature of a contract in the first place?

Nature of the contract

In the simplest terms a contract is a mutual exchange of promises. The seller promises to supply goods or services and the buyer promises to pay. If certain criteria (explained in section 5 below) are satisfied, this exchange of promises can be enforced in a court of law.

'Contracts when entered into freely and voluntarily shall be held sacred and shall be enforced by courts of justice.'[7]

This ancient statement not only captures the principle of legal enforcement but also illustrates in its use of the phrase 'freely and voluntarily', a fundamental tenet of English law that contracts are made freely and not 'in terrorem'. This means that neither party is forced into the contract by threat or pressure from the other side and furthermore that once in contract, performance relies upon the willingness of the two sides, failing which the courts will decide a remedy. The contract itself may not provide such a remedy if it is of the nature of a penalty. A contract not freely entered into would be voidable and a contract term which creates a penalty for non-performance would be void.

It is a fact of commercial life that the bargaining powers of the two sides to the potential contract will be unequal but commercial pressure of that nature is legitimate. After all the weaker of the two sides is free to decide against entering into the contract. Similarly, the terms of the contract may be quite onerous and that again is fair enough. It is the contractual remedy for failure that must not extend to the point of penalty. It is open to the parties to prescribe what may happen in the event of delayed or poor performance as this both aids certainty and avoids the cost and disruption of a legal battle; however, the not 'in terrorem' rule must be obeyed.

Because of the binding nature of the contract and the consequences of non-performance most companies permit only certain of their employees to sign contracts or to vary the terms once the contract is in place. A normal safeguard is for companies who regularly trade with one another to set out a general set of rules-of-engagement between them so that each may know that only certain persons or functions (eg the chief buyer) possess the necessary authority to make binding commitments. Similarly, the contract may nominate specific persons or functions (eg the contracts manager), in whom is vested authority to vary the contract terms. Indeed this latter concept is of tremendous benefit in business contracts and the principle has been affirmed by the courts:

> 'These (contracts) contain terms which enable the contractor's work to be increased, decreased or varied, perhaps substantially, the period of performance to be extended, again substantially, and the contract price to be recalculated, upwards or downwards, in the light of events occurring during the currency of the contract.'[8]

The danger is that even whilst these safeguards and contract provisions are utilised, custom and practice and carelessness can commit the company in a binding manner. For example, a person not nominated under the contract who nevertheless writes to the other party using company headed paper, signing for the company, referring to the contract and on the face of it varying the terms in accordance with some prescribed procedure will almost certainly have committed the company albeit that he may be in breach of some internal procedure and thus face disciplinary action!

These real-life situations draw us to two concepts which although not at the heart of contract law with its proposition of exchanged promises nevertheless are very material to the principles involved. Firstly, if one person relies upon the words of another and acts accordingly he should not then be let down, and secondly, if in good faith a person acts to some valuable benefit of another then there should be some compensating payment or benefit. This can be a difficult area as it is tempting to say that in the latter case the act in good faith must be with the prior knowledge of the beneficiary. Otherwise it would be possible to earn a good living going around mending people's fences without their knowledge and then expecting to be paid. On the other hand in complicated business contracts it is frequently the case that one side must act expeditiously for the benefit of the other without his prior knowledge or agreement and in such circumstances it is reasonable for some compensation to be agreed.

Key elements of contract formation

In arriving at a contract the parties must exchange their promises. Atiyah quotes Pollock[9] who said:

> 'One party proposes his terms; the other accepts, rejects, or meets them with a counter-proposal; and thus they go on 'till there is a final refusal and breaking-off, or 'till one of them names terms which the other can accept as they stand.'

In business this ideal is frequently not the case and Atiyah says:

> 'Businessmen not uncommonly commence the performance of contracts even while negotiations are still actually going on as to the precise terms of the contract. Such cases show that to insist on the presence of a genuine offer and acceptance in every case is likely to land one in sheer fiction.'

It is not unknown for the parties still to be haggling after the work is complete and payment made. This arises for example where agreement as to residual liabilities (eg for defective work) or benefits (eg rights in Intellectual Property created under the contract) remains to be reached.

The key elements that the contract must have in order to be valid and enforceable are:

a) An offer and an acceptance.

b) An intention by both parties to the contract to create legal relations.

   c) Consideration.

   d) The parties must have the capacity to contract.

   e) The contract must be legal and possible.

5.1. Offer and acceptance

On the face of it, offer and acceptance is simple and straight-forward. A offers to supply 10 widgets to B for £5 each. B accepts and a contract is created. However, if A advertises widgets at £5 each this is not an offer to sell but an invitation to treat. This would mean that B would have to offer to buy at £5 each and A's acceptance would create the contract. It is thus important to be certain when an offer is actually being made. For example, the current practice in buying supermarket vegetables is for the shopper to make his selection and then at the checkout the cashier will say the price. This is the point at which an offer is made.

Acceptance also can have its complications. For the accept-ance to create a contract it must be given without qualifications or conditions since to do so creates a counter offer which itself must be accepted before a contract can come into being. Quite commonly it is the practice for a company to say to a customer 'we accept the contract subject to the following…'. Strictly speaking this is a counter offer and no contract is made until the counter offer has been accepted without qualification. As a matter of custom and practice the two parties to the 'contract' may each proceed with the business of the contract – one to supply goods, the other to make payments – and a court may decide that a contract did indeed exist. The only question to be decided is whether or not *both* parties intended the qualifications given in the initial response to apply. Again this may depend upon the actions of the parties.

For example, if the statement was to the effect that 'we accept the contract but will deliver blue widgets instead of green' and the customer, without having formally confirmed it, accepts deliveries of blue widgets then clearly the qualification was mutually accepted. A factor to be taken into account is where did the matter rest as far as correspondence is concerned? Where a matter has been debated without full resolution whichever party had the final say in corres-pondence may well have the advantage.

This question of the final say is epitomised in the so-called 'battle of the forms'. Atiyah summarises the only full appeal court decision[10] as follows:

'The plaintiffs were manufacturers of machinery, and in response to a query from the defendants, they sent them an offer to supply a certain machine on terms printed on the reverse of their form. The terms included, in particular, a price-variation clause, under which the price to be charged would be subject to increase as a result of increased costs prior to the expected delivery date. The buyers sent in a purported "acceptance" of this offer, but this document also contained various terms and conditions printed on the reverse which were stated to govern the contract, and these terms naturally did not include any price-variation clause. The document also contained a tear-off slip which the sellers were required to complete, acknowledging that the sellers accepted the buyers' terms. The sellers duly sent in the tear-off slip, but they accompanied it with a letter saying that delivery would be made in accordance with their previous quotation. The matter then rested there, the sellers made the machine and it was eventually delivered and accepted by the buyers. The question then arose whether the buyers were bound to pay an extra sum for increased costs arising after the making of the contract, as required by the sellers' original quotation. The Court of Appeal decided that the buyers were not bound to pay the extra. They held that the buyers' purported acceptance was in law a counter-offer, and that the sellers had accepted that counter-offer by sending in the tear-off slip. The reasoning is, however, open to criticism, since the letter accompanying the tear-off slip was probably intended to make it clear that the sellers' original terms were to govern the transactions.'

So here we have neatly set out the situation in which the sides attempt to gain what can only be described as accidental or unconscious acceptance of their terms. In practice it is better to resolve the issues and arrive at a mutually acceptable set of terms which can apply to all future transactions (of substantial similarity) between the buyer and seller.

It is of crucial importance that the offer and acceptance be actually communicated. As far as the offer is concerned, once it has been communicated it must stand until:

a) The offerer revokes it prior to acceptance.
b) The offeree rejects it.
c) The offeree makes a counter offer.
d) The expiry of a specified validity period.
e) The expiry of a reasonable time having regard to the circumstances.

The act of rejection or counter offer by the offeree actually has the effect of cancelling the offer. If the offeree were to make a counter offer, for example, and then have a change of mind, finding the original offer acceptable after all, it would be too late for him to accept that first offer.

As far as both offer and acceptance are concerned the effective moment is that of receipt. The exceptions are that for acceptance by post where the effective moment is that of posting (properly stamped and addressed), regardless of delay or even non-delivery.

In some situations the actions of the offeree may be taken to effect acceptance although there is no formal communication. For example, a buyer taking and accepting deliveries and making use of the goods would have conveyed his acceptance through his actions despite having made no written or oral communication or acceptance.

5.2. Intention to create legal relations

As has already been said, a contract can be enforced by a court if the parties intended their promises to be binding. As a natural consequence of this, the court will provide remedies for the breaking of binding promises – known as breach of contract. In some circumstances it may be that promises made were intended to be kept but no one really expected or wanted a legal remedy for a broken promise – perhaps a cancelled invitation to dinner; in such cases a reasonable person (a standard if somewhat subjective test) would say that there could have been no intention to create legal relations and thus no contract is made.

In some ways the point being examined here is the question of people by their *actions* indicating or not indicating an intention to create legal relations. The whole purpose to professional life is the pursuit of business, the creating of contract. It might be said therefore that there should be no doubt that the intention is to create relations. However, it is frequently just the opposite. Marketing, sales, engineering and projects people will regularly discuss possible transactions with potential customers and suppliers with no intention to create legal relations. It is vital, therefore, that in such matters the purposes of the discussions are clear to all so that relations are not accordingly established. Quite often the contracts person may fire off a letter confirming the discussions but stating that 'the discussions and the letter do not constitute an order or a commitment to place an order with you'. This belt and braces disclaimer points out that not only is no order created but also that no intention to place an order should be construed from the actions and discussions.

Of importance to the individual in this context is that in, say, attending meetings he is representing his company in an official capacity and by his actions he may inadvertently commit the company. Although he may not have authority to make that commitment it may nevertheless stand unless it could be shown that the other side knew him not to have such authority.

The best safeguard in these matters is to use the expression 'subject to contract' which is a recognised expression that excludes legal effectiveness.

5.3. Consideration

Consideration is the legal word for the money that is paid for the supply of the goods. In fact, money is only one example of consideration which has classically been defined as:

> 'some right, interest, profit or benefit accruing to one party, or some forbearance, detriment, loss or responsibility given, suffered or undertaken by the other'.[11]

The principal features of consideration are that:
a) It must be of value to the recipient.
b) It must pass to the recipient.
c) No simple contract can be effective without it.
d) It must be legal.
e) It must not be past – a post-event promise to pay for some

service already completed does not satisfy the consideration criterion.

Curzon says that consideration is executed when the act constituting the consideration is performed: it is said to be executory when it is in the form of promises to be performed at a future date.

Although there can be exceptions it should be taken as a general rule of thumb that consideration cannot be formed of doing that which one was already required to do under some legal obligation or duty. For example, a promise to turn up in court to give evidence under subpoena for which the defendant promises some payment does not constitute consideration and no contract is formed.

In business contracts the question arises whether, if after the contract is made a statutory change imposes greater obligations or costs on the supplier, the supplier can expect additional consideration (most probably an increase in the price) from his customer. For instance, if a change on the statute books under health and safety provisions requires electrical equipment to be triple rather than double insulated, can the supplier put his price up after the date of contract? On the face of it the customer is going to receive a 'better' product and yet the requirement to improve it arises under a general legal obligation and not as a result of the customer changing his requirement. The answer almost certainly is no. However, a precaution that can be taken is to include in the contract an express provision that allows the contract price to be varied in the event of statutory changes which materially affect the product or its cost.

5.4. Capacity

The capacity to contract is fundamental: all adult citizens have the capacity to contract although there are exceptions. For example, there are circumstances in which contracts made by aliens, persons suffering from mental disorder, or drunkards are void. It is important to distinguish between capacity and authority to contract. The former is concerned with the legality; the latter is concerned with permission. In business an individual may have the legal capacity to contract but not the authority of his employer.

5.5. Legal and possible

The contract must not be illegal, that is, for example, a contract to carry out a crime would not be a contract. Also the contract must be capable of performance. There could be no contract to supply a perpetual motion machine for instance.

In some businesses it is customary in urgent situations for a supplier to seek from the prospective buyer an instruction to proceed or letter of intent. The terminology here can be misleading because the fundamental question to be asked is whether the communication from the buyer satisfies the fundamental contract formation requirements such that it can be construed as an offer of contract. If it is an offer the supplier should accept it (if the terms are acceptable to him) and thus complete a contract. If the fundamentals are not satisfied then the communication is not in a legal sense worth the paper upon which it is written. In a practical sense the communication may be of sufficient encouragement that the supplier has the confidence to commence work even at his own risk, particularly if the communication identifies useful features such as an allocated contract or order number. In sending such a communication the buyer should always expressly state if it is intended to be an offer of contract or not, but in any event it is a normal prudent rule that the seller should not expect to rely upon it unless it is clearly an offer.

⑥ Written and oral contracts

Simple contracts of the type being discussed do *not* have to be made in writing. As individuals the majority of contracts we make are oral – whether it be buying a newspaper or purchasing a meal.

Generally, the only contracts that are required to be made in writing are those for the sale of a house, flat, etc; long term leases; those that guarantee another person's debt; hire purchase or consumer credit arrangements.

As a matter of professional necessity companies adopt a practice of committing all contracts to writing. This is for several good reasons including:

a) Unlike the typical consumer purchase the subject matter and rights and obligations of the parties may be extensive in description and definition. This naturally demands commitment to paper.

b) It is vital that both parties are clear and share the same understanding of the contract.

c) As individuals come and go it is important that their successors can establish clearly what is involved.

d) A written contract is a sound baseline for changes in

requirements, rights and obligations which may arise and become contract amendments.

e) In the event of a dispute during or after the completion of the contract the court will be better able to reach a decision based on written evidence.

f) Where many functions within the company will exchange correspondence with their opposite numbers – on project, engineering or marketing networks for example – it is important to know which bits of paper actually constitute the contract.

Although written contracts may be the preferred approach most companies will both place and accept oral contracts where the urgency of the situation demands. The aim will, of course, be to reduce these oral contracts to writing as quickly as possible. Nevertheless, to be valid even oral contracts must satisfy the basic legal requirements described above. Incidentally, written contracts do not have to be 'signed' as such although many institutions prefer to require the formality and ceremony of personal signatures.

Terms and conditions

Terms and conditions is an often heard expression which tends to be dismissed as the 'contractual bit'. The expression itself is to some extent misleading.

The terms of the contract are all of those things which describe all of the rights and obligations of the parties. The terms address, indeed constitute, the entire description of the contract.

Terms are either express or implied. Express terms are those which the parties themselves have established and agreed to. Implied terms are those terms which either:

a) a court will decide may be read into the contract based on what the parties must have intended;

or:

b) arise from a statute.

The best example of statutory implied terms is the famous Sale of Goods Act which, amongst other things, implies terms of fitness for purpose and merchantable quality. This is considered in more detail in later sections.

The terms of the contract are also sub-divided into conditions and warranties. Not all of the obligations created by a contract are of equal importance and this is recognised by the law which has applied

a special terminology to contractual terms to distinguish the vital or
fundamental obligations from the less vital. The word 'condition'
applies to the former and 'warranty' to the latter. 'Warranty' in this
sense should not be confused with the common usage relating to a
supplier's guarantee. This is considered in more detail later.

Smith and Keenan describe the difference thus:

> 'A condition is a vital term which goes to the root of the
> contract. It is an obligation which goes directly to the sub-
> stance of the contract, or is so essential to its very nature that
> its non-performance may be considered by the other party as
> a substantial failure to perform the contract at all.
>
> A warranty, on the other hand, is subsidiary to the main
> purpose, and there is no right in the injured party to repudiate
> the contract; there is only an action for damages. A warranty
> has been variously defined, but it may be said to be an
> obligation which, though it must be performed, is not so vital
> that a failure to perform it goes to the substance of the
> contract.'

To put this into context in the supply of goods the principal
condition with which the supplier must comply is the requirement
to actually supply the goods. The principal condition with which the
buyer must comply is the requirement to pay the agreed price. By
comparison, an obligation on the supplier to provide the buyer with
progress reports against the contract would normally be construed
as a warranty.

In practice many purchasers will refer simply to the 'conditions of contract' implying that all terms are fundamental. This would
not necessarily be upheld by a court.

It can be seen from the definitions of conditions and warranties that a crucial difference is in the remedy available for non-
performance. Non-performance of a condition entitles the injured
party to repudiate the contract and sue for damages. Non-performance of a warranty only carries the right to sue for damages, that is,
the injured party must continue with the contract. Sitting behind this
is the principle that the parties should have prior knowledge as to the
consequences for non-performance of a particular contract requirement. Breach of a condition gives the injured party the right to
terminate; breach of a warranty does not – it is as simple as that. The

consequence is that the only dispute that could come before a court is whether (if it was not clear in the contract, a common situation) the parties intended the requirement to be a condition or a warranty. In this case the court would resolve the question by examining the words and deeds of the parties (to determine the intent at the time of the contract being agreed) and not the consequences of the breach.

The absurdity here is that the consequences of breach of a condition might be trivial but the (lightly) injured party could terminate the contract, possibly to the severe detriment of the other side. Conversely the consequences of breach of a warranty may be very serious but the (badly) injured party has to continue with the contract.

Arising from this is the idea of a contract term which is neither a condition nor a warranty but a so-called 'intermediate' term where the remedy available will depend upon the actual consequences of breach rather than the predicted consequences as seen by the parties at the date of the contract.

However, this concept of intermediate terms should not be seen as an automatic or universally available alternative to the traditional black-and-white perception of conditions and warranties as the courts still prefer that in business transactions the parties have certainty at the outset regarding the consequence of their actions and inactions.

8 Breach, termination and damages

Unless the contract provides for one side to unilaterally prematurely end the contract – for example under a cancellation for convenience arrangement as described in Chapter 6 – then both sides must see the deal through to its natural conclusion. If however the contract is improperly formed, through for example pre-contract fraud, then the injured party may rescind the contract. This has the effect of retrospectively undoing all that has been done and the objective is to return the parties to their respective positions before the contract was made.

Where the contract is valid but is not performed or is repudi-ated then if the non-performance is sufficiently serious the innocent party may terminate the contract. The effect, however, is not necessarily fully retrospective as with recision. Any obligation fully performed to the date of termination cannot be retrospectively undone. Only the unperformed balance can be so treated. Non-performance and repudiation are similar in appearance and identical in effect. If one side has not performed its obligations the other side can determine this even though the defaulter may be silent. In repudiation the defaulter indicates his intention not to continue with the contract. If he does so in advance of performance being due then this is known as anticipatory breach.

This means that non-performance is breach of contract allowing the right of termination.

The expression 'non-performance' can mean that the entire contract is unperformed or that part of it is unperformed or that the performance is defective in the sense that the work is unsatisfactory in not meeting the requirements of the contract.

The principal remedies available to the innocent party are recision or termination and damages. The availability of these remedies depends upon the nature of the fault. Generally damages are not available where a contract is rescinded but are always available if a contract is terminated for breach. In the former case the principal exception is that damages may be available against a contract which is rescinded for misrepresentation.

In the case of breach of contract the right to terminate would arise for breach of a condition, but not of a warranty. Termination for breach of an intermediate term would depend on the severity of the consequences of the breach. The right to terminate would arise for breach of a promissory representation depending on whether it was implied into the contract as a condition, warranty or intermediate term as described earlier.

Breach of a warranty does allow the right to damages but not, as has been said, to termination.

An important feature of both recision and termination is that the innocent party must act to affirm them, without which act his right may disappear. For example, if a supplier of goods is late in delivery then the buyer has the right to terminate for the breach. However, if he does not so act then he is deemed to have waived his right and must continue with the contract.

In the event of breach of contract the injured party's reaction is not usually one of wishing to immediately terminate the contract.

If the buyer prefers to force the defaulting supplier to perform the contract he can apply to the courts for a decree of specific performance. It is a discretionary matter for the courts whether to grant such a decree or not but the option is certainly there for the injured side to exercise. If the goods were readily available elsewhere, or if checking compliance with a decree of specific performance was impossible or required constant supervision by the courts, then a decree would not be granted.

So where, for example, the goods are available elsewhere no decree would be issued, the contract would be considered terminated and if the goods bought elsewhere were of a higher price, then the buyer would have a right to damages from the defaulting supplier.

Following from this last example is the concept that in contract law the right to damages is limited to financial loss. Breach of contract has this direct relationship to financial loss and there is no concept of damages being awarded where there is no such loss (except perhaps nominal damages) nor of punitive damages which are elsewhere used as a form of punishment to express the community's distaste at the deed.

In business contracts it is commonly the practice to make an advance assessment of the level of financial damage that late or non-performance would cause to the buyer and thus include a contract provision that allows the buyer to recover such a sum from the seller in the event of delay. These so-called liquidated damages clauses are discussed in Chapter 6.

Having seen that damages must be representative of financial loss, the question arises as to how that loss might be valued and what limitations may apply. In answering the first question a distinction needs to be made between 'expectation' damages and 'reliance' damages. The difference can best be seen through examples. If in a simple contract for the sale of goods the buyer refuses to take delivery, the supplier is entitled to sue for his expected profits on the sale, ie his lost expectation. Loss of profits damages are commonly awarded although the seller must have taken all reasonable steps to mitigate his loss. In the example this would be based upon his attempting to sell the goods elsewhere. Indeed if the goods are sold elsewhere at no lower price then the claim for expectation damages would fail, although the additional costs of marketing or selling expenses would be recoverable.

Reliance damages are somewhat different and are derived from costs actually incurred by the injured party through relying on the contract. In one case[12] a marine salvage contractor purchased a wreck said to be lying on a particular reef. As it turned out the wreck did not exist but in relying on the contract the salvagers incurred substantial expenditure equipping a survey expedition. All these nugatory expenses were recovered as reliance damages. Expectation damages – in this example the profits would have been the salvage value of the wreck less the salvage costs – were not awarded as the salvage value was too speculative.

So a difference can be seen between expectation and reliance damages. In addition to these there is the concept of restitution damages where a defaulting party would otherwise benefit from his own breach. An example would be where a buyer has made an advance payment to a defaulting supplier. Clearly for the advance not to be returned following the supplier's breach would be wrong, the damages claim here being restitutionary.

Over and above these concepts is the question of limitation of damages in the sense of how far the defaulter should be held liable for the consequences of his default. The test is one of foreseeability. It is expected that the parties in the normal course of events can foresee the likely results of their actions or inactions. If they can, then they are liable for the result. If the damage is so remote as not to be reasonably foreseeable then there is no liability.

Of course it is open in business contracts for the parties to provide for liability for consequential damages and it is not uncommon for the buyer in a superior bargaining position to insist that the supplier carries express liability for consequential damages. Needless to say the supplier of horseshoe nails would not want to be liable for the consequences of a battle being lost!

As far as late payment of money is concerned it is interesting that it is assumed that the consequences of non-payment are not foreseeable. So the supplier who goes bankrupt as a result of debtors who do not pay cannot sue for the real financial loss as it is considered not foreseeable. Indeed it is not always safe to assume that a court would allow a claim for interest on overdue debts as part of a claim for damages.

In the UK contracting parties tend to the view that both sides have lost if their problem ends up in court and for the most part every effort will be made to settle the difficulty by sensible negotiation. At the end of the day the buyer wants his goods and the seller wants his money, neither side believing that this aim will necessarily be achieved where there is the potential cost and delay of legal action to contend with.

Furthermore a supplier will be most unwilling to cause upset to his customer by taking him to court (or even threatening or suggesting this would happen) unless there really is no other option.

Indeed the contract may set out extensive procedures for handling disputes whether of a technical or commercial nature. This may include a mechanism for negotiation which, if unsuccessful within a specified period of time, will allow the two sides to elevate the problem within their own organisations until a level is found at which settlement can be reached. In some cases one side can reserve the right to a conclusive say on a particular aspect – interpretation of technical specification for example.

Between the processes of full legal action through the courts and a disputes procedure written into the contract lies the process of arbitration.

The sensible and pragmatic use of the law followed in this country contrasts dramatically with the practices in other countries where use of litigation in commerce is far more commonplace.

(9) Statutory requirements

In addition to the general requirements of contract law there are specific requirements, obligations and limitations which Parliament has decreed should apply to contracts. The principal statutory requirements are:

   a) The Unfair Contract Terms Act 1977.
   b) The Sale of Goods Act 1979.
   c) The Supply of Goods and Services Act 1982.
   d) The Consumer Protection Act 1987.

9.1. The Unfair Contract Terms Act

Traditional contract law denies the possibility of contracts which are 'unfair' in their outcome. The conventional wisdom is that the provisions of contract law are a set of procedural rules which ensures that the parties make their agreement on the proverbial level playing field. If one participant is better than the other, the deal is likely to prove in its outcome more beneficial to him than to the other party. Thus contract law exists to provide a framework of fair rules and not to ensure that the result of each game is more or less a draw.

Developments over the past decade or so show, however, that the courts in some circumstances are prepared to take an interest in the fairness of the outcome and to set aside obligations or duties which would otherwise cause a significantly unfair outcome. It is not the intention to explore these developments here, but rather to point out the rigour of conventional theory which must, from a pragmatic point of view, continue to be taken as the working assumption by business people making commercial contracts.

That said, it is the case that as part of the process of establishing fair rules, the UCTA has been brought into being to cover the particular area of exemption clauses. It is important to emphasise that the UCTA, rather like the Sale of Goods Act, came into being primarily to protect the consumer in consumer transactions. Both Acts consolidated earlier statutes as well as introducing new measures. The application of both to non-consumer transactions has some flexibility for the parties to decide.

The principal provision of the UCTA is that it is not permissible under contract to exclude liability for personal injury or death. Exemption clauses of this nature would be void, leaving the balance of the contract unchanged.

Further, the UCTA prohibits clauses which exclude liability for the supply of defective goods. This is closely linked to the Sale of Goods Act which lays down the binding precepts of merchantable quality and fitness for purpose. However, where the prohibition of exclusion clauses on injury and death is absolute, this prohibition on defective goods is only absolute in consumer transactions. In business transactions the parties may include clauses excluding such liabilities. In the absence of an express provision of exclusion the provisions of the Acts would apply. On the face of it it seems odd that any company would agree to exclude its rights to statutory obligations regarding merchantability and fitness for purpose but in some circumstances it can seem a logical thing to do. For example where the contract contains detailed statements of performance specifications, methods of testing, criteria for contractual acceptance and post-acceptance liabilities under some express warranty, then it is logical for the supplier to argue that his total responsibility has been fully and thoroughly defined and thus it is unfair for the buyer to potentially be able to rely also on the fairly vague concepts of merchantability and fitness for purpose. The supplier can argue that his price is precisely linked to his express responsibilities and liabilities and that importing the uncertainty of statutory obligations must of necessity increase his price.

Also the UCTA requires the test of reasonableness to be applied to all exemption clauses. An unreasonable clause would be void. This is fraught with the usual difficulties of assessing reasonableness but, for instance, it would normally be assumed that excluding liability for negligence is unreasonable. Taken into account though, would be the terms of the contract, the bargaining powers of the two sides and the extent to which one side derives some benefit from agreeing to exclude a right it would otherwise have. If the buyer overtly has the choice between a price for which all statutory rights are available and a second lower price in which some rights are excluded, then if he opts for the lower price it would patently be wrong for the exemption later to be made void.

9.2. Sale of Goods and Supply of Goods and Services

It is well beyond the scope of this book to describe in detail the provisions of the various statutes but rather it is the aim here to give a general flavour of the obligations and limitations imposed under these provisions. This is particularly so with the Sale of Goods Act and with the Supply of Goods and Services Act as in both cases the statutes themselves are fairly voluminous and in both books and other reference works, lawyers will themselves resort to much case law by way of describing the provisions and distinctions. Nevertheless further reading is advised and recommendations can be found at the end of this chapter.

Under these provisions the seller or supplier of goods has strict duties regarding the quality (using the term in a very general sense) of the goods whereas the provider of a service has to exercise only a duty of care. The distinction between goods and services is not always as clear as one might expect. Case law shows a restaurant meal to be a sale of goods and the supply and installation of roofing tiles a service. The difference appears to hinge on the standard nature of the product, which as such is deemed goods. The essence of the roofing work was the application of skill to a 'non-standard' roof and hence was deemed a service. However, also taken into account would be the comparative value of the skill with the value of the materials.

The Sale of Goods Act implies undertakings on the seller. The careful use of the word 'undertaking' should be noted. The point is that whether the undertakings can individually be construed as conditions or warranties will depend upon the construction of the contract of sale. Further the Act prescribes that conditions can be waived, or treated as warranties, and conversely that a warranty so-called can be treated as a condition.

The main implied undertakings are:

a) Where goods are sold by description there is an implied condition that the goods shall correspond with the description.

b) That the seller owns the goods to be sold, that he is free to sell them and will be at the time of contract performance.

c) That the seller will deliver the goods.

d) That the buyer will accept and pay for the goods.

e) The goods shall be of merchantable quality and fit for purpose.

Item (a) can for these purposes be taken at face value and items (b) – (d) are dealt with in later chapters.

The merchantable quality and fitness for purpose undertakings move us away from the ancient concept of 'caveat emptor' or Let the Buyer Beware. However, the principle is preserved in so far as it is made clear that except for the specific obligations implied by the Act no other obligations of this nature can be implied. It should be pointed out that the obligations are implied where the seller makes the contract in the course of business. That is, the private sale of a secondhand car provides for no such obligations on the seller. Since this book is only concerned with business contracts this point will not be considered further. Also, and to reiterate an earlier point, in business contracts the obligations may be expressly excluded and hence in this part of the discussion it is only those contracts where no such exclusion applies which are being addressed.

The 1979 Act says that:

'Goods of any kind are of merchantable quality … if they are as fit for the purpose or purposes for which goods of that kind are commonly bought as it is reasonable to expect having regard to any description applied to them, the price (if relevant) and all the other relevant circumstances.'

and goes on to say that:

'Where the seller sells goods in the course of a business and the buyer expressly or by implication makes known to the seller any particular purpose for which the goods are being bought, there is an implied condition that the goods supplied under the contract are reasonably fit for that purpose, whether or not that is a purpose for which such goods are commonly supplied, except where the circumstances show that the buyer does not rely, or that it is unreasonable for him to rely, on the skill or judgement of the seller.'

Thus it can readily be seen that the two provisions rather go hand in hand albeit that each raises some interesting points. The reference to purpose or purposes under merchantable quality invites the question as to whether the goods must be suitable for one purpose or all purposes. On balance the answer is not at either of those extremes but that the suitability must be across a normal range of purposes. There is also the issue of comparison with the common purpose which is a rule extraordinarily hard to apply where goods are customised or designed especially for the buyer. Quite clearly though, the price and other relevant factors such as description will be material to a test of merchantability. Further – and even more so with fitness for purpose – we are drawn into the need for the buyer to describe his purpose or intent as regards the goods. This wisdom (from the buyer's point of view) sits happily with the principle of drawing to the seller's attention the potential consequences of a contractual breach such that the seller would have difficulty in relying upon the unforeseeability and remoteness defences against consequential damages.

If the buyer plays his cards right it is almost a case of Let the Seller Beware! An absolutely important caveat for the seller to observe is that if he brings defects to the attention of the buyer then there is no obligation of merchantable quality nor similarly so where the buyer fails to notice a defect upon his examination of the goods where reasonably he should have done so. However, the avoidance only applies where these events took place prior to the making of the contract. This is another conflict for the seller who naturally enough does not wish to prejudice his chance of a sale.

9.3. The Consumer Protection Act

The Consumer Protection Act 1987 is in three parts:

PART I: Covering civil liability for defective products.
PART II: Covering criminal liability for unsafe goods.
PART III: Covering misleading price indications.

It is Part I which is of greatest interest in business contracts. It enacts European Community Directives concerned with product liability. Its purpose is to place a strict liability where goods cause to the buyer, or to a third party, injury, death or any loss or damage to property. Pure financial loss is excluded, as is damage to or loss of the product itself.

Until the arrival of the 1987 Act it had been necessary to show that the damage was caused through negligence. The Act reversed this and the liability is now strict, that is, not only is there no requirement for the injured to prove negligence but there need not have been any negligent act or omission for the liability to fall. The injured only has to show that the product was defective. The Act defines a defect where:

'... if the safety of the product is not such as persons generally are entitled to expect; and for those purposes "safety" in relation to a product, shall include safety with respect to products comprised in that product and safety in the context of risks of damage to property, as well as in the context of risks of death or personal injury.'

Also relevant is the use to which the product is expected to be put. There is a presumption of reasonable foreseeability regarding what will be done with the product including some degree of predictable misuse, including misuse by children. Of great importance, therefore, is the creation of adequate instruction manuals and hazard warnings although the existence of these would not in itself necessarily provide a full defence against defect liability.

There are some defences against the strict liability under the Act including arguments based upon the state of scientific and technical knowledge at the relevant time.

The question is whether the business contract gets caught in this minefield of liabilities concerned only with protecting the consumer. The answer is that the liability is intended to lie with the 'producer' of the defective product rather than the 'supplier'. The term 'producer' embraces not only the manufacturer but also an 'own brander' (someone who holds himself out as the producer by putting his own trademarks on the product) or an 'importer' (here meaning someone importing from outside the EC). The supplier may in some circumstances be liable but the normal expectation is that the liability can be passed up the line to the producer. So the danger exists where goods produced and sold under a business contract are sold on to, or incorporated into other goods for onward sale to the consumer.

Returning to the distinction between goods and services it is presently the case that the supplier of goods is strictly liable if they cause injury or other damage regardless of whether there was any negligence or fault on his part. Conversely the supplier of the services, such as a car repairer, only owes the buyer a duty of reasonable skill and care. If damage arises through a faulty repair the injured party has to prove negligence in this duty on the part of the supplier. However, there is in the EC growing pressure to bring the strict liability concept to bear on services as well as goods.

10   Contract negotiation

It is all very well to describe the legal principles surrounding the formation of the contract but in practice many business contracts are arrived at through the process of negotiation or at least some discussion between the parties. So it would be incomplete to leave this introduction of contract law without some discussion as to the legal obligations carried by the contract negotiators.

The first principle is that in ordinary commercial relations there is no obligation on the parties to disclose facts to one another. However, in some cases it has been construed that the parties have a general duty of care. For example, in *Crossman* v *Ward Bracewell*[13], a solicitor was held liable for negligently failing to advise a possible client that his insurance company would probably pay his legal costs, in the absence of which advice the client decided not to instruct the solicitor at all. The relationship of experts providing professional advice to their clients is beyond the scope of this book but clearly there is a risk to be wary of. Insurance, contracts of partnership and the trustee/beneficiary relationships are situations in which duties to disclose material facts may arise, but our common business contracts are covered by the general and ancient theme of English law that the two parties are free to use their best skills and information to negotiate the best deal possible.

A second important principle is that the negotiating parties owe each other the obligation to treat one another's information in confidence. Once a contract is agreed information exchanged must in any event be held in confidence and a precaution is to include an express term to this effect. In the pre-contract stages it is as well to set up a contractually binding confidentiality agreement; however, even in the absence of such an agreement this duty of confidentiality exists. This may be particularly important where the negotiations fail to reach a conclusion and no contract is ever made. In these circumstances it is important that neither party should go off to make use of information received during the failed negotiations. In *Seagor* v *Copydex Ltd* Seagor obtained damages from Copydex[14] who marketed a new type of carpet grip making use (without realising it, so it seems) of ideas proposed by Seagor to Copydex in earlier negotiations which had not reached a conclusion.

From the point of view of the contract administrator an interesting point is that this question of a duty of care is a matter of the law of tort and this question of confidentiality is a matter of the law of equity. So it can be seen that our dealings are not limited to the framework of contract law as such, but also to many other parts of the law.

It must be stressed that in the process of negotiation and agreement it is fundamental that between the parties there is:
   a) No fraud.
   b) No coercion, duress or undue influence.
   c) No misrepresentation.

To get at misrepresentation it is necessary first to describe representation. In the process of negotiation the parties will say different things which are intended to influence the outcome. In broad terms it might be said that the sayings of the two sides can be divided between that which they intend to be legally binding – promises to be incorporated in the contract – and other apparently factual statements which are intended to influence but not be incorporated. However, this latter category are known as representations and can have legal effect. They are impliedly incorporated and referred to as 'promissory representations'. Pre-contract representations which a reasonable person would know to be 'non-promissory' such as advertising puffery (the estate agent's over zealous property description, for example) are excluded.

The converse of a representation is a misrepresentation which Curzon defines as:

> 'A false statement which misrepresents a material fact; which is made before the conclusion of a contract with a view to inducing another to enter that contract.'

Or as Lord Denning[15] put it:

> 'In my opinion any behaviour, by words or conduct, is sufficient to be a misrepresentation if it is such as to mislead the other party. If it conveys a false impression, that is enough.'

The law here is governed by the Misrepresentation Act 1967. Misrepresentation comes in three varieties, defined by Curzon as:

FRAUDULENT: 'A false representation made knowingly or without belief in its truth or recklessly, careless whether it be true or false.'

INNOCENT: 'A misrepresentation in which there is no element of fault, ie fraud or negligence.'

NEGLIGENT: 'A false statement made by a person who has no reasonable grounds for believing that statement to be true.'

If a contract is concluded following misrepresentation then the innocent party is entitled to rescind the contract and to pursue the other side for damages. If promissory representations are made but then not performed the injured party will have available his normal rights for breach of contract.

References and further reading

In this chapter the following main references are used:

Atiyah: *An Introduction to the Law of Contract*, 4th Edition, P S Atiyah, Oxford University Press, 1989

Smith and Keenan: *English Law*, 5th Edition, Kenneth Smith & Denis J Keenan, Pitman Publishing, 1975

Curzon: *Dictionary of Law*, 3rd Edition, L B Curzon, Pitman Publishing, 1988

Davies: *Sale and Supply of Goods*, 1st Edition, Dr Irwan Davies, Longman, 1990

Atiyah, Smith and Keenan, and Davies are highly recommended as further reading matter.

Other references

1) *Hillas & Co* v *Accos Ltd* [1932] All ER Rep 494
2) *Courtney & Fairbairn* v *Toulaini Bros (Hotels) Ltd* [1975] 1 WLR 297
3) *Foley* v *Classique Coaches* [1934] 2 KB 1
4) *Saunders* v *Anglia Building Society* [1970] 3 All ER 961
5) *Relational Contract: What We Do and Do Not Know* (1985) Wisconsin Law
6) *London Export Corp* v *Jubilee Coffee Roasting Co* [1958] 2 All ER 411
7) *Printing and Numerical Registering Co* v *Sampson* [1875] LR 19 Eq462
8) *Ashwill Investments Ltd* v *Elmer Contractors Ltd* [1988] 2 All ER 577, 591
9) *Principles of Contract*, 13th Edition, London, 1950
10) *Butler Machine Tool Co* v *Ex-Cell-O-Corp* [1979] WLR 401
11) *Currie* v *Misa* [1875] LR 10 Ex153
12) *McRae* v *Commonwealth Disposals Commission* [1950] 84 CLR 377
13) *Crossman* v *Ward Bracewell* [1986] 136 New LJ 849
14) *Seagor* v *Copydex Ltd* [1967] 1 WLR 923 and [1969] 1 WLR 809
15) *Curtis* v *Chemical Cleaning and Dyeing Co Ltd* [1951] 1 KB 805

4

⦿ ⦿ ⦿ ⦿ ⦿ ⦿ ⦿ Ⓒ Ⓗ Ⓐ Ⓟ Ⓣ Ⓔ Ⓡ ⦿ ⦿

Drafting skills

① Introduction

The importance of sound drafting skills cannot be overstated. The fortunes of the enterprise revolve around the work of the contract administrator. Whether the particular activity is in:

- a) letter writing
- b) drafting documents
- c) drafting clauses
- d) drafting contract amendments
- e) formulating estimates and quotations
- f) preparing reports
- g) drafting subcontracts

the need to 'get it right' is paramount.

The fundamental objective is that all such material must be:

Clear
Concise
Precise
Accurate
Complete
Relevant

and written in good, unambiguous English. There is no need for legalistic terminology or Latin phrases although, to be pedantic, it is important that what is said is legally effective.

For any document of a contractual nature to be effective it must be *clear*. Without clarity there is uncertainty as to the intentions of the parties which in the extreme can cause the contract to be void.

Similarly the wording must be *concise*. This may appear to contradict with the apparent length of some sentences that arise in contract documents. However, a well-constructed lengthy sentence in practice can convey the meaning far more concisely than a rambling paragraph or two of briefer sentences.

The wording must also be *precise* if doubt is to be avoided.

Finally, the drafting must be *accurate* and *complete*. This is for a number of reasons. Firstly, if the drafting is inaccurate it may accidentally contain falsehoods or it may mislead. This exposes the risk of illegal sins of misrepresentation or fraud. Secondly, inaccuracy may lead to misunderstanding or incompleteness. The classic example was the contract for:

'10,000 army boots'

which whilst accurate in itself was incomplete and thus nobody should have been surprised when the supplier delivered 10,000 left boots. In this case there was inevitably an argument as to whether the customer was at fault in failing to accurately specify his requirement or whether the supplier was at fault in failing to supply in accordance with the established convention – it being the custom and practice that soldiers have a right foot as well as a left.

In many ways this example sums up the intent of this book: it is not so much about the legal arguments and niceties of who might be in the right in a contract dispute, but the fact that better drafting skills would have prevented the dispute from arising. Beyond this, the legal position was of interest to the lawyers, but commercially the contract was a disaster:

The customer failed to get the goods he thought he had ordered and might have to pay for the matching rights.

AND

The supplier at worst faced the cost of supplying the right boot and at best had a very dissatisfied customer.

all through poor drafting in the first place.

An additional point is that all this *clear, concise, precise, accurate* and *complete* wordology must be *relevant* to the topic in question.

These basic skills are essential to success.

Figure 4.1: The Hexagon Principle

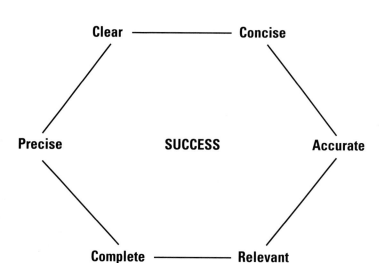

2   Letter writing

The Hexagon Principle (Figure 4.1) rules apply to the drafting of commercial letters as much as to the drafting of contract documents. The topic of letter writing has been put before the drafting of contract clauses or contract documents because correspondence frequently precedes the formalisation of a contract. Certainly correspondence exchanged throughout the life of a contract can, in practice, have an importance almost equal to that of the contract itself. If there should be a dispute or doubt as to the intention of the parties, an arbitrator or court will look to the relevant correspondence for an indication or corroboration of the intentions.

Let us look at examples of a letter between two companies.

Example A

Williams-Hanks Ltd plc   P J Wolfe & Sons
Derby   Friars House
Lancs   Wilkenthorpe Road
                                             Basingstoke
FAO Mr W Williams   Hampshire

Dear Bill

Widgets

I am very disappointed. It was only last month you promised
me the order would be delivered on time and most of them
don't work. It is disgraceful and my quality people don't know
how you make them at all. It's not the first time and I want to
know what on earth you think I am going to do about it.

Yours faithfully

John Wolfe

It is not difficult to list the shortcomings of this letter:

1) *The addressee's address is incomplete.*

This may sound trivial but the letter concerns a problem about
which Wolfe & Sons feel very strongly and apparently an urgent
resolution is needed. The last thing wanted is for the letter to be lost
or delayed in the post. If the Williams-Hanks site is a large one or if
the company is distributed across several sites in the Derby area
then the letter may not find its correct destination quickly. The
address is also incorrect in itself – Derby is not in Lancashire!

2) *The addressor's address is incomplete.*

Again, the absence of the postcode may be trivial but including
it is an example of the self-discipline that is required in writing
material which is both accurate and complete.

3) *The date is missing.*

This is not just to make the obvious point about sloppiness. In the heat of the moment the date can be forgotten but later the letter could be vital in establishing the intentions of the parties, or the time at which a claim was lodged or the time at which the seller was notified of non-performance.

4) *The form of address is informal.*

The contract is a legally binding agreement between two parties. Here, the parties are the corporate bodies of the two companies. The contract is not between individuals. It is preferable therefore – particularly where the subject matter is contentious – that the form of address is formal, ie Dear Sirs and not Dear Bill, Dear Mr Owen or even Dear Sir, which again is individual.

5) *The title is incomplete.*

The individuals – Bill Williams and John Wolfe – probably know what they are talking about, but their colleagues, heirs, successors and – if it comes to it – arbitrators or lawyers, may be uncertain with the vague title of 'Widgets'.

If the correspondence relates to a contract then the contract number (or other unique identifier) must be included.

6) *The first sentence is irrelevant.*

It may be a statement of fact but it adds nothing to the substantive message of the letter. If the conveyance of a sentiment is thought to add weight to the letter it is usually best left to the end or if included as the beginning, it should sit alone in its paragraph by way of context or scene setting.

7) *The second sentence is unclear and imprecise.*

It is unclear in the sense that the real message is obscure and imprecise. The reference to 'last month' is imprecise and suggests that no record of the conversation was kept and that the writer has impatiently cobbled this letter together.

It is not entirely clear whether the grievance is late delivery or faulty goods or both. There is no information specifying how late the delivery is alleged to be, nor precisely how many didn't work nor precisely what is wrong with them.

8) *The third sentence is probably irrelevant.*

Probably irrelevant, but not certainly, because the point of mentioning quality is not clear. Perhaps there is a separate concern about the quality standard or standard of testing. Perhaps the failed units have something to do with poor quality (the two are not necessarily synonymous).

9) *The final sentence is unclear.*

Again the point of this is not clear. Is the angry writer just venting his spleen or is 'not the first time' relevant? Does 'first time' relate to earlier breaking of promises? earlier delivery problems? earlier fault problems? earlier quality problems? Does it relate to just the contract apparently in question, or other contracts as well?

Is the final question serious or is it rhetorical? If it's serious, surely the injured writer should be saying what *he* wants done? If it's rhetorical then the letter has ended with no conclusion.

10) *The signature block is deficient.*

The contract is between the companies. Therefore the letter should be signed by the company, ie by including the words 'for P J Wolfe & Sons plc'.

Although of relatively minor importance it is helpful for the job title of the sender to be included as it helps for a reply to find its destination. Also the proper close for an informal letter is 'Yours sincerely'. (However, the letter should have been addressed formally, in which case 'Yours faithfully' would be correct.)

11) *The letter contains no reference number.*

For the sake of avoiding future doubt and for ease of reference, letters should always be given a unique reference number.

Compare Example A with Example B.

This letter corrects all the straightforward errors (missing date, etc) and conveys its message following the Hexagon Principles.

The opening paragraph sets the scene with accurate factual information (the recipient should, of course, check that the information is correct).

The second paragraph introduces the problem, again with factual information. There is no doubt here at all as to the deficiencies – a precise statement of lateness of the delivery and a precise statement regarding the failures. The final two sentences are important not so much in what they say but the way in which they say it. They could be omitted altogether. The symptom of the failure – not working when plugged in – is enough to justify rejection. Pointing to a possible cause is not necessary but may be helpful to the supplier

Example B

Williams-Hanks Ltd   P J Wolfe & Sons plc
St Andrews Road   Friars House
DERBY   Wilkenthorpe Road
Derbyshire   Basingstoke
D28 4JA   Hampshire BA43 2RC
FAO Mr W Williams
10 June 1992

Dear Sirs
WIDGETS   Your Ref: 2133/WW/BT
ORDER NO 21469/ST   Our Ref: A/Wid/JW/281

Under the above order a quantity of 100 widgets was due for delivery on 3 June. In the telephone conversation (Williams/Wolfe) of 20 May you confirmed that delivery would be effected on time.

We must point out that delivery did not take place until 8 June. Further we have discovered that 25 of the units failed to operate when connected to their power supply. It would appear that this is due to a quality problem as the connectors appear to be corroded. This is only an opinion and is offered without liability or prejudice.

As regards the 75 units which appear to be satisfactory we reserve our rights as regards the lateness of delivery. You are hereby advised that the 25 failed units are rejected. Please arrange to collect them and supply replacement units in accordance with condition 15 of the order.

We must express our extreme disappointment in that the order has been delivered late – with a 25% failure rate – against the background of a confirmatory promise to deliver on time.

Yours faithfully
for P J Wolfe & Sons plc

John Wolfe
Commercial Administrator

in identifying and rectifying the problem. There is no reason not to be helpful. After all the buyer's interest is in getting working goods, not in causing trouble for the supplier. However, if the opinion is to be included then it should be stated as such with the rider that it is without liability or prejudice. This means the supplier remains fully responsible for correcting the fault and cannot use the buyer's opinion of the cause as a reason or excuse to avoid this responsibility.

The third paragraph is crucial. The first sentence contains two key principles. Firstly, it uses the expression 'which appear to be satisfactory' rather than 'which are satisfactory'. To use the latter would be construed as conveying acceptance of the 75 units. The buyer is using a more cautious phraseology as he has reason to suspect the quality of the goods. Secondly, the buyer reserves his right to sue the supplier for any damages that he may incur through the order being late.

The final two sentences are complete, clear and precise. The formality of rejection is conveyed and the required remedy is stated clearly.

The closing sentence expresses sufficient sentiment without bordering upon the abusive. Abuse rarely achieves anything in such matters as it tends to provoke negative reaction where a real remedy – perhaps with an apology – is the objective.

③ Commercial objectives

The Hexagon Principle is fair enough by way of setting out the manner of drafting letters but it does not encapsulate the commercial objectives in writing the letter. These objectives are:

To maximise profit
To optimise cash flow
To secure further orders
To protect ideas
To minimise risk

For the buyer and the seller these are potentially conflicting aims. The seller's profit is increased by a higher price to the buyer whose cost is thereby increased to the detriment of his profit.

Similarly the seller's cash flow is enhanced by early or quick payment to the disadvantage of the buyer, and vice versa.

To protect future business the seller wishes to keep his own ideas – his intellectual property – to himself. This may cause difficulties for the buyer, depending on the nature of the work.

In some ways the essence of all business is risk management. Risk management means identifying risk, eliminating or containing it, or at best giving it to someone else. Thus the buyer wants the supplier to carry all risks and the supplier wants shot of the risk as soon as possible.

Only in securing further orders do the two sides have overlapping interests.

So as well as the Hexagon Principle there is also the Pentagon Objective shown in Figure 4.2.

Figure 4.2: The Pentagon Objective

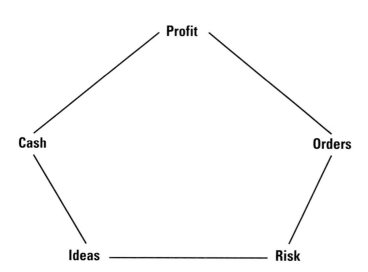

The Pentagon Objective encapsulates the key commercial objectives of the business and with some of these objectives in mind the correspondence on widgets might continue.

Example C

P J Wolfe & Sons plc
Friars House
Wilkenthorpe Road
BASINGSTOKE
Hampshire
BA43 2RC

William-Hanks Ltd
St Andrews Road
DERBY
Derbyshire
D28 4JA

14 June 1992

Your Ref: A/Wid/JW/281
Our Ref: 2124/WW/BT

Dear Sirs

WIDGETS
ORDER NO 21469/ST

Thank you for your letter reference A/Wid/JW/281 dated 10 June 1990.

We regret that you have experienced difficulty with 25 of the units. If you wipe the connectors with the standard 4121 cleaning fluid before connection to the power supply there should be no further difficulty.

We apologise for the late delivery, this being due to industrial action at Customs which was completely beyond our control.

Although we consider that we are not at fault we would be prepared – without prejudice – to offer you a 5% discount on our quoted price against your next order, provided this can be placed by 31 August 1992.

In the meantime we enclose our invoice for the 100 units under this order and request payment within the next seven days.

Yours faithfully

for William-Hanks Ltd

Enc

In this, an objective is to defuse the situation over the failed units. The sentence is carefully worded to avoid arguing over the formality of rejection/acceptance. The aim is to put the ball back into the other court. If the buyer acts on this advice and it works, the seller has solved 'the problem' at no cost to himself (thereby preserving his profit) and if the buyer then accepts the goods the risk of a further problem has transferred to the buyer. The buyer will need to consider all this very carefully, and ask himself a number of questions.

– Is it reasonable that pre-connection cleaning is necessary?
– How often are the units unconnected and re-connected?
– Is this a short term solution to a more serious problem?
– Are maintenance procedures affected?

That is to say, in examining this suggestion the buyer is weighing up possible future costs and risks against the immediate problems of non-utilisation.

In the third paragraph the supplier apologises for the lateness. He has clearly decided that as a matter of fact he was late and an apology may help to placate the buyer. However, he takes the precaution of stating that he himself was not the cause of the delay. This may be of assistance if the contract contains a 'force majeure' condition or it may help him in negotiations with the buyer.

The next paragraph states that the supplier considers himself blameless and by careful drafting and construction of the letter embraces both the 'quality problem' and the lateness in this dis- claimer. Here he offers an inducement – the price discount – to the buyer to place a further order. The inducement is time limited to increase the pressure on the buyer.

The final paragraph attempts to wrap up the whole matter with a request for quick payment for the total quantity. This may or may not work but at least the seller has remembered to ask for his money.

The Hexagon Principle describes how to write material while the Pentagon Objective describes the underlying commercial con- cerns. However, the overriding questions that the drafter must ask himself are these:

a) Does this letter harm me in any way?
b) Have I said anything that might work against me later?
c) Have I considered the reaction that the letter might pro- duce? Am I happy that the likely reaction is what I want? Have I built

in counters to what would otherwise be undesirable reactions?

In other words, the Hexagon Principle may be couched in cautious and non-committal terms.

Factuality should not be confused with Firmness.

For example, rather than state:
'The free issue material was received three weeks late but we can still achieve the delivery programme.'

it is much better to say:
'The free issue material was received three weeks late. The full impact upon our work has not yet been assessed but we will use our best endeavours to maintain the delivery programme.'

In these two statements the factual content ('three weeks late') is identical but the firmness of the conclusion is entirely different. Even if the lateness has no real impact it nevertheless may provide a convenient 'smokescreen' to cover later delays the causes behind which have yet to emerge.

Similarly, avoid:
'We regret to announce a price rise of 25%.'

when softening the blow and explaining costs nothing:
'You will be aware of the recent sharp rises in the import prices of untreated copper oxide. Across the board these represent an increase of 35% but we have been able to secure undertakings so that our present supply prices will be maintained for a further six months. This means that in the next year we are able to limit our own price rises to 25%.'

This predicts the customer's reaction and counters it with both an explanation and an attempt to show what measures have already been taken to contain the problem.

A summary of the things to bear in mind when drafting a commercial letter is included as a checklist in Appendix 1, List A.

One final point is that there really is no need to use Latin expressions although they do crop up from time to time and occasionally it does add something to the text. A list of the more common expressions is provided at the end of this chapter.

(4) Contract documents

Drafting an entire contract document is not as difficult as it may sound. There are two schools of thought as to where to begin in drafting a contract from scratch:

Photocopy the most similar document you can find and work from there;

or:

A blank sheet of paper.

Theoretically you must start from a blank sheet of paper. The reasons for this are surely obvious:

Every contract *is* different;

and:

Simple repetition breeds mistakes.

There is a lot of truth in this. To do the job properly it is necessary for every clause, every paragraph, every sentence and every word to be properly thought out and constructed intelligently and specifically for the purpose in hand. In particular the previous or other apparently similar document may be the result of a negotiation. To this extent the wording may be a mixture both of compromises and of material drafted by the two sides.

Each of these possibilities gives rise to its own problems. Clearly if the draft of a new contract is taken from a previous compromise agreement then on the new occasion the draughtsman's side is starting with what previously has been its finishing position – which is not too good an idea if negotiation is expected before a new agreement can be reached. On the other hand there is a certain logic in saying that where two parties regularly do business then why waste everybody's time in repeating arguments over and over again when an acceptable compromise has already once been reached. From this logic derives the idea of standard contract conditions, model conditions or conditions customary in the trade, of which more later.

Using a previous contract (where at the end of the day the

wording was a mixture of several persons' drafting) means that it is likely that style and elegance will have been lost. Although these are peripheral considerations – they do not appear in the Hexagon Principle – they have a level of importance. Contract drafting is a valuable skill and it must be done well. If from the outset the draughtsman adopts a professional approach and aims to accomplish both style and elegance in his work, the result will be that much better, 'better' being defined for these purposes as legally more sound and effective.

Conceptually the objectives in drafting a contract can be reduced to the three principles shown in Figure 4.3.

Figure 4.3: The Triangle Concept

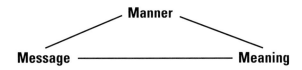

The adoption of this geometric shape, just as with the Hexagon Principle and the Pentagon Objective, is simply intended as a memory aid.

The *manner* is common to all commercial drafting, ie the Hexagon Principle in Figure 4.1.

In contract drafting these six aspirations must reach their zenith. In writing a commercial letter there can be room for and purpose in embellishment, exaggeration or extended explanation. For example, if the particular purpose of the letter is to provide a basis for negotiation then embellishment, exaggeration and extended explanation are perfectly permissible. However, they have no place in a contract document. The content and purpose of each statement within the contract must stand in its own right, conditioned only by the rest of the document, and no other explanation (of the content or purpose) should be necessary either within or outside of the contract. This can be more difficult than it sounds, as complex thoughts can be hard to articulate and even more difficult to commit to writing if the Hexagon Principle is to be followed.

The *message* in the contract is comprised of six features which might be paraphrased as follows:

The WHAT	:	definition and specification.
The WHEN	:	timescale and timing of contract performance.
The WHERE	:	destination.
The HOW	:	method of delivery.
The WHAT ELSE	:	dependencies.
The HOW MUCH	:	price and payment.

The message is the conveyance of the objective of the contract, that is it deals with the real substance of the contract, ie what goods or services, at what price, delivered where and when, by what method and when paid for. If the *message* can be conveyed in the prescribed *manner* then we are two-thirds of the way to formulating a well thought out contract document.

The final third to be put in place is the *meaning*. What is intended here is that reduced to its simplest, the contract is a collection of benefits and obligations. Although in a typical and straightforward contract for the supply of goods the primary benefits and obligations are obvious, there is nevertheless the question of risk. Virtually nothing in life and certainly nothing at all in terms of a business transaction is free of risk. Therefore the *meaning* in the contract is that both sides are exposed to risks of a variety of different types. If the *meaning* is to be clear then who is carrying which risks must be clear.

The drafting of individual clauses designed to convey the message and meaning in the correct manner is covered in the next section. Before that it is worth considering the structure of the contract.

There is no legal or other requirement for the basic structure of the contract provided that it satisfies the basic principles described in Chapter 1. A useful structure to adopt in practice is as follows:

SECTION 1:	Priced schedule of requirements.
SECTION 2:	Contract conditions.
SECTION 3:	Statement of work.
SECTION 4:	Specifications.
SECTION 5:	Payment plan.
SECTION 6:	Definition of deliverable articles.
SECTION 7:	Definition of deliverable data.
SECTION 8:	Programme plan.

Not all of these sections may be applicable and, indeed, additional ones may be necessary. A lot depends on the type of work, but this list should provide a basic framework from which to work. The monetary value of the contract is not necessarily a determining factor as, for example, a contract for a million pounds for the supply of standard products at list prices to standard contract conditions may be a far simpler document than that describing a £50,000 contract for research into nuclear power generation.

4.1.   Priced schedule of requirements

The priced schedule of requirements is essentially a list of 'line items' of work and provides at the start of the contract document a summary of the message of the contract. It may appear as shown in Figure 4.4.

Figure 4.4: Schedule of requirements

Item No	Part No	Description	Quantity	Price
1	1234/ABC	Design and develop an electric motor	–	£200,000
2	To be inserted	Supply of electric motors as designed and developed under Item 1	5000	£250 each
3	Not applicable	Supply of data as described at section 7	Three sets	£100 per set

This is a summary of the message and is certainly written out in the manner of the Hexagon Principle. However, it is not necessarily complete and without completeness the Hexagon is broken. Section 2 of the contract will link each of the items to a fuller description. Moreover, where the schedule is obviously incomplete – absent part numbers or phrases such as 'not applicable' are examples – the balance of the document must provide somewhere an explanation so that there is no doubt as to the parties' intentions.

4.2. Contract conditions

The purpose of the contract conditions is to encapsulate both the message and the meaning of the contract. The six aspects which comprise the message can each be included in the contract conditions or made into a separate section or annexe to the contract dependent upon the space that each description will take. The contract conditions – which may be referred to as the body of the contract – are more readable if, for example, large specification documents are annexed rather than written out in full within the body of the contract. Thus, following the stylised structure proposed above, the six features of the message can be reduced in the example of the electric motor contract to the first few conditions of the contract in the following manner:

Condition 1: (The WHAT)	The seller shall supply the items described in the schedule in accordance with the statement of work at Section 3 of the contract.
Condition 2: (The WHEN)	The seller shall perform the contract in accordance with the programme of work at Section 8 of the contract.
Condition 3: (The WHERE)	The seller shall deliver the goods to the buyer's premises at Milton Lane.
Condition 4: (The HOW)	The seller shall deliver the goods CIF under Incoterms 1980.
Condition 5: (The WHAT ELSE)	The buyer shall provide the seller with packaging materials and crates.
Condition 6: (The CONSIDERATION)	The buyer shall make payment of the contract prices in accordance with the stage payment scheme at Section 5 of the contract.

So here in the first six conditions of the contract the message is captured. The wording of the conditions used above is designed to convey only the principle of what is being said. In practice the wording of these conditions needs to be more detailed and this is explored in the next section.

The conditions section of the contract must also embrace the meaning. Risks, responsibilities and liabilities must be set out and commonly some such matters will have been reduced to standard conditions. Thus the meaning element of the contract conditions usually comprises both standard conditions which may be called up by reference and conditions written specifically for the individual contract. Typically the risks, responsibilities and liabilities to be covered include:

Late delivery
Loss or damage to the goods
Transit risks
Injury or death
Loss or damage to property
Third parties
Acceptance and rejection
Warranties
Intellectual property rights
Bonds and guarantees

Where standard conditions are incorporated it is necessary to consider each one to ensure its suitability and applicability.

So in some ways it can be said that the contract conditions are like the hub of a wheel – they encapsulate the entirety but link out to elements, such as the statement of work, which require copious and voluminous description.

4.3. Statement of work

The statement of work, or SOW to use its common acronym, is the section of the contract which in some ways is the most pragmatic and practical element of the lot. It should be the section in which is described what the supplier actually has to *do* and therefore embraces not only the principal objective of the contract but also the peripheral matters as well. If the contract for the design and supply of the electric motors is taken as an example then in *summary* form the SOW may be constructed as follows:

Example D

Paragraph 1:   The supplier shall design Item 1 of the contract to meet the requirements of the specifications referred to at paragraphs 1, 12, 13 and 26 of Section 4 of the contract.

Paragraph 2:   Resulting from paragraph 1 the supplier shall create a manufacturing drawing package in respect of Item 2 of the contract that meets the requirements of paragraphs 3, 4, 5 and 6 of Section 4 of the contract.

Paragraph 3:   The supplier shall manufacture and supply Item 2 of the contract in accordance with the drawing package referred to at paragraph 2 above.

Paragraph 4:   The supplier shall provide data packs under Item 3 of the contract in line with the requirements detailed at Section 7 of the contract.

Paragraph 5:   The supplier shall support meetings with the customer in the following manner:
a)   Attendance at six-monthly senior level steering committees.
b)   Attendance at monthly progress meetings. Such meetings being at the customer's premises.
In such meetings the supplier shall provide a secretary and two representatives. Minutes of the meetings shall be issued by the seller within ten days of the date of the relevant meeting.

Paragraph 6:   The supplier shall provide monthly technical, progress and financial reports in triplicate no later than fifteen days before the due date of the progress meeting referred to at paragraph 5(b) above.

Paragraph 7:   Within three months of the date of contract the supplier shall provide a draft quality plan in accordance with paragraph 18 of Section 4 of the contract.

The entire contents of the SOW requires considerable thought and attention to detail but as the example shows its two purposes are:

a) to link the summary message provided in the schedule of requirements with detailed definitions provided elsewhere – for example in the list of specifications, ie

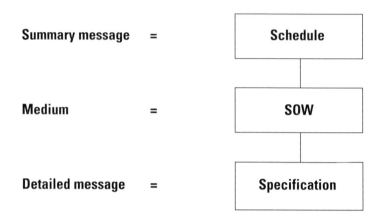

and

b) to set out those things over and above the message which are a key ingredient in the work being performed in practice.

It is in the SOW that the contract draughtsman and the technical manager have to work most closely together if the contract is to have genuine purpose insofar as the Hexagon Principle is concerned.

4.4. Specifications

Where the contract is complex or lengthy in the definition of the technical requirement it is usual to construct such a definition by the inclusion of, or by reference to, 'specifications'. This generic heading covers a multiplicity of different documents:

Procurement specification
Functional specification
Technical specification
Requirement specification
Performance specification
Test specification
Acceptance specification

Process specification
Interface specification
Reliability specification
Maintainability specification
Availability specification
Durability specification
Quality standards
Design standards
Manufacturing standards
Material standards
Building standards
International standards
Safety standards

The list is endless and even this list is only a list of headings. As the meaning of each of these phrases can differ between industries and technologies, individual definitions are not attempted here. This section of the contract is usually prepared by a technical person and the most the contract administrator can reasonably do is, in discussion with the technical people, to:

a) Ensure that the Hexagon Principle is followed.

b) Consider how the various specifications form part of the message and the meaning.

c) Check that a sensible order of precedence is provided.

Quite often technical people, if left to themselves, will *not* follow the Hexagon Principle. A favourite habit is to include within the specifications a list of 'related' documents. This offends virtually every corner of the hexagon. The term 'related' documents does not mean anything in a contractual sense. One way or another the relevant specifications are there to provide a part of the definition of the message and thus will be used as a measure of contract performance. 'Related' documents have no part in this and are therefore irrelevant and should not be included.

As has been said, anything included in the specifications section is in some way a part of the message. Thus they must not only be relevant but the contract must explain *how* they are relevant. For example, they must be expressly cross-related to an item in the schedule of requirements or to an item or paragraph number in the statement of work.

If the specifications section is to be formulated wholly in line with the Hexagon Principle then there should be a sensible order of precedence of the documents. The concept of order of precedence is a subject of some debate and the arguments are examined later in this chapter.

4.5. Payment plan

Not all contracts require a detailed payment plan. In the simple case where the contract is for 10,000 widgets at £100 each and the supplier has the ability to fund work in progress, then £100 will be payable on the delivery of each article and the details of the payment arrangement are reduced to the procedures and paperwork that this entails. Where life is more complicated than this then it is as well to have the payment plan set out and recorded in detail in its own right within the contract. In this the Hexagon Principle is of paramount importance. Any technical defect in the description or method of the payment scheme will undoubtedly cause payments to be delayed incurring unattractive penalties in terms of cash flow.

4.6. Definition of deliverable articles

With more complex products it is desirable to set out a detailed definition of the so-called deliverable article. As well as aiding clarity it is of enormous practical benefit both in terms of:

a) Specifying what is actually deliverable – for example, if a development contract intrinsically includes the provision of 'B Models', are these models ultimately deliverable to the customer or are they retained by the designer for disposal at his discretion?

And

b) Saying in clear terms what the deliverable article *is*. For example, it may be accurate to say that the article to be delivered is a widget that confirms with drawing number 414/69/213/02 but it is far more helpful to say that the deliverable article comprises:

Widget	:	414/69/213/02
Power supply	:	414/69/212/08
Mounting bracket	:	414/69/828/01
Test software	:	414/70/000/04
Operating manual	:	414/00/121/00

With this approach, both sides to the contract are absolutely clear in real terms about what is intended and the formality of delivery and acceptance should be facilitated.

4.7. Definition of deliverable data

Many contracts embrace a requirement for data or documentation to be delivered. This must be seen as being of equal importance to the physical delivery of hardware. It may be that in the real world a court would construe the delivery of the hardware as a condition (ie fundamental) and the delivery of data/documentation as a warranty (ie of secondary nature) but in practice if deliverable data/documentation is missing then almost certainly final payment is at risk as well as the good relationship between the two parties. All things considered, if the contract includes the delivery of data/documentation then it is as well for this to be spelt out in detail. This falls into two categories:

    a) What is to be delivered.

    b) The format in which the delivery must be made.

The former can be referred to as the CDRL (pronounced 'seedral'), being the 'Contract Data Requirements List' as defined in detail by the DID, being the 'Data Item Description'. For example, the CDRL may say 'Implementation Software' and the DID will go on to define this as 'Implementation software in source code on 4" floppy disc in accordance with specification XXX as described in paragraph 38 of Section 4 to the contract'.

4.8. Programme plan

In the example given, Section 8 of the contract is the programme plan which may be comprised of a PERT network, a bar chart or simply a list of dates against key events. The programme plan is an example of an aspect of the contract which may or may not be important enough to warrant a detailed separate section in the contract. Whether this is so depends upon the nature of the contract, the particular importance which the customer attaches to the individual features and, of course, whether the supplier feels willing to provide the customer with that level of visibility. Thus conceptually the Section 8 and onwards parts of the contract are tailor-made to the individual circumstances. Thus Section 8 onwards may include, for example:

Quality plan
Purchasing plan
Manufacturing plan
Development plan
Test plan
Acceptance plan

In this part of this chapter consideration has been given to how the:

MANNER
MESSAGE
MEANING

may be enshrined in the contract using an idealised – but stylised – structure. It is not the intention that everyone should slavishly follow this structure (because it is so case-by-case dependent) but only that a *structure* should be evolved in all cases to ensure that the *message* and the *meaning* have been captured in the prescribed *manner*. A checklist is provided in Appendix 1, List B covering these principles. The details to be covered within individual contract conditions and clauses are discussed below.

---

(5) Contract clauses

The heading for this section is somewhat misleading insofar as it uses the word 'clauses'. This usage has been adopted because in common parlance the parts of the body of the contract are often referred to as this 'clause' or that 'clause'. Strictly speaking the contract should be clearly divided into conditions and warranties (Chapter 3) but in practice this is rarely the case and given the emergence of the intermediate term it may be as well to avoid such a division. More commonly the reference is only to the 'conditions' (or terms and conditions – not a helpful heading) leaving the true distinction between the conditions and warranties to be determined by the individual wording. Thus if a correct nomenclature for the structure of the contract is to be adopted it should be as follows:

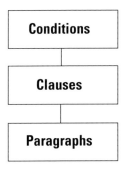

For example, the payments provisions may be enshrined in Condition 14 of which Clause 2 describes the invoicing arrangements of which paragraph 3 describes the dates at which invoices may be submitted.

Thus in practice this section looks at the drafting of contract conditions rather than of contract clauses.

By now it should not be necessary to repeat that the drafting of clauses must follow the Hexagon Principle.

That said, the aim of this section is to look at each of the typical contract conditions mentioned in the previous section and to provide a checklist of the things to be borne in mind when drafting each of these conditions, and, beyond that, to provide some examples of good draughtsmanship to compare with poor draughtsmanship.

The checklist is provided in Appendix 1, List C.

It is not the intention to provide an example of a contract condition to cover each of the topics listed in the checklist. This would be largely valueless as all contracts and their conditions require tailoring to the specific circumstances to a lesser or greater extent. Indeed the purpose of this book is to assist the contract administrator to acquire the skills required for drafting and not to do the job for him. The formula for how to draft contract conditions could be described as shown in Figure 4.5.

Included in Chapter 5 is the contents page from the IMechE/ IEE (Institute of Mechanical Engineers/Institute of Electrical Engineers) Model Form of Contract Conditions (MFI) for building contracts. This is not only a good example of structure being given to the conditions section of the contract, but it also demonstrates that each industry needs its own special set of conditions. Thus the

Figure 4.5

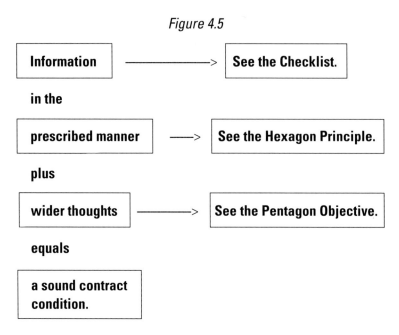

checklist can only provide a good working document from which to develop a unique set of conditions tailored to the particular requirements. Also, a brief glance at this contents list shows just how much space and time may be devoted to the 'Meaning', ie what can go wrong and who carries the liability and risk. Some of the conditions can be examined as examples of draughtsmanship (Example E).

In the first paragraph of Clause 1 the opening sentence provides a clear statement of the requirement. It is concise and also complete, ie the words 'for the due performance of the Contract' complete the requirement insofar as without them there would be ambiguity as to what the bond or guarantee is to cover. The paragraph also conveys precision in describing (by reference) the form of the bond or guarantee to be provided.

The second paragraph covers the key issue of who is to pay for the bond or guarantee, so there is an express provision for this and absolute certainty. It sounds foolish, but often there is argument about the principles or detailed wording of a condition such as this, whilst the most important thing (who pays) is overlooked.

The third paragraph deals with the detail and in four brief lines addresses five important issues.

Clause 2 is a good example of remembering to legislate for what to do if the event in question does not happen. Enshrined in

Example E

8.1 Performance Bond or Guarantee

If required by the Purchaser the Contractor shall provide the bond or guarantee of an insurance company, a bank or other surety for the due performance of the Contract. Unless otherwise specified in the Special Conditions, the terms of the bond or guarantee shall be in the form annexed to these General Conditions.

Unless otherwise specified in the Contract the Contractor shall provide the bond or guarantee at his own Cost.

The amount of the bond, the period of its validity, the procedure to be followed for its forfeiture, the arrangements for its release and the currency of any monetary transactions involved shall be stated in the Special Conditions.

8.2 Failure to Provide Bond or Guarantee

If the Contractor shall have failed to provide the bond or guarantee within 30 days after the date of the Letter of Acceptance or within such further period as may be advised by the Purchaser, the Purchaser shall be entitled to terminate the Contract by seven days' notice to the Contractor. In the event of termination under this Clause the Contractor shall have no liability to the Purchaser other than to repay to the Purchaser all Costs properly incurred by the Purchaser incidental to the obtaining of new tenders.

these few lines is also an expression of how fundamental is the bond or guarantee, ie if it is not provided as required then the purchaser has the right to terminate the contract.

In Example F the draughtsman can be seen exercising his craft carefully and diligently and in this condition he covers some important principles:

a) Mitigation of loss

Where one party may be liable to the other for costs associated with some loss it is only fair that the injured party has a duty to use

Example F

Limitations of Liability

44.1   Mitigation of Loss

In all cases the party establishing or alleging a breach of contract or a right to be indemnified in accordance with the Contract shall be under a duty to take all necessary measures to mitigate the loss which has occurred provided that he can do so without unreasonable inconvenience or cost.

44.2   Indirect or Consequential Damage

Except as expressly provided in Sub-Clauses 34.1 (Delay in Completion) and 35.8 (Consequences of Failure to Pass Performance Tests) for the payment or deduction of liquidated damages for delay or failure to achieve performance and except for those provisions of these Conditions whereby under Sub-Clause 41.2 (Allowance for Profit on Claims) the Contractor is expressly stated to be entitled to receive profit, neither the Contractor nor the Purchaser shall be liable to the other by way of indemnity or by reason of any breach of the Contract or of statutory duty or by reason of tort (including but not limited to negligence) for any loss of profit, loss of use, loss of production, loss of contracts or for any financial or economic loss or for any indirect or consequential damage whatsoever that may be suffered by the other.

44.3   Limitation of Contractor's Liability

In no circumstances whatsoever shall the liability of the Contractor to the Purchaser under these Conditions for any one act or default exceed the sum stated in the Appendix or if no sum is so stated, the Contract Price.

The Contractor shall have no liability to the Purchaser for or in respect of any consequence of any loss or damage to the Purchaser's property which shall occur after the expiration of the Defects Liability Period except as stated in Sub-Clause 36.10 (Latent Defects).

44.4 Exclusive Remedies

The Purchaser and the Contractor intend that their respective rights, obligations and liabilities as provided for in these Conditions shall be exhaustive of the rights, obligations and liabilities of each of them to the other arising out of, under or in connection with the Contract or the Works, whether such rights, obligations and liabilities arise in respect or in consequence of a breach of contract or of statutory duty or a tortious or negligent act or omission which gives rise to a remedy at common law. Accordingly, except as expressly provided for in these Conditions, neither party shall be obligated or liable to the other in respect of any damages or losses suffered by the other which arise out of, under or in connection with the Contract or the Works, whether by reason or in consequence of any breach of contract or of statutory duty or tortious or negligent act or omission.

reasonable endeavours to mitigate the loss. It would be unreasonable for him to allow the value of the loss to continue to accumulate (if it is within his power to stop or reduce it) simply because someone else is liable. On the other hand it would be unfair to expect him to go to extraordinary lengths to mitigate the loss when it is not his fault in the first place.

b) Indirect or consequential damage

As a general legal principle where there is breach of contract the injured party may only pursue the defaulter for direct damages and not for indirect or consequential damages unless the contract expressly permits it. Here the contract is making it absolutely clear that there is *no* right of redress for indirect or consequential damages. The distinction between the direct and other forms of damages can be difficult to perceive. It is a question of foreseeability and remoteness as explained in Chapter 3.

c) Limitation of contractor's liability

This type of provision is included as a matter of custom and practice depending upon the particular industry. It is clearly beneficial to the seller who knows what his maximum liability may be. In

Example G

Vesting of Plant and Contractor's Equipment

37.1 Ownership of Plant

Plant to be supplied pursuant to the Contract shall become the property of the Purchaser at whichever is the earlier of the following times:

a) when Plant is delivered pursuant to the Contract
b) when the Contractor becomes entitled to have the Contract Value of the Plant in question included in an interim certificate of payment.

37.2 Marking of Plant

Where, prior to delivery, the property in Plant passes to the Purchaser, the Contractor shall, so far as is practicable, set the Plant aside and mark it as the Purchaser's property in a manner reasonably required by the Engineer.

Until the Plant has been so set aside and marked the Engineer shall be entitled to withhold any interim certificate of payment to which the Contractor might otherwise be entitled.

The Contractor shall permit the Engineer at any time upon reasonable notice to inspect any Plant which has become the property of the Purchaser and shall grant the Engineer or procure the grant of access to the Contractor's premises for such purposes or any other premises where such Plant may be located.

All such Plant shall be in the care and possession of the Contractor solely for the purposes of the Contract and shall not be within the ownership or disposition of the Contractor.

No interim certificate of payment issued by the Engineer shall prejudice his right to reject Plant which is not in accordance with the Contract. Upon any such rejection the property in the rejected Plant shall immediately revert to the Contractor.

the example given this is a limitation per incident. In some sectors it is conventional to state the contract price or some multiple of it as being the total maximum liability.

d) Exclusive remedies

This is an interesting clause. It is saying that the contract has set out in full the rights, liabilities and remedies each party enjoys and having done so there can be no other grounds ('breach of contract or of statutory duty, or tortious or negligent act or omission') for an action. This exclusion of other remedies is permissible although some statutory obligations – for example those related to causing personal injury or death – cannot be limited or excluded by the words of a contract. Some statutory obligations, such as those provided by the Sale of Goods Act, can be excluded in business (but not consumer) transactions provided that the contract effects such exclusion. The condition is interesting insofar as both sides take the gamble that the provisions that they have made will prove to be adequate should there be a problem.

The purpose in the two clauses of Example G is fairly clear. It is a good example of where the draughtsman has followed the Hexagon Principle. In 37.1 the point is not just the transfer of property but *also* the when of it. It is noticeable in good drafting how often the word 'and' appears. The good draughtsman writes down the requirements or provision and then thinks 'and...', ie:

What else?

What have I forgotten?

What are the consequences if this doesn't happen?

In drafting contract conditions there are a few other basic ideas which help:

a) **Examples**. Using examples to help draft is a valuable aid in achieving the Hexagon Principle. If the draughtsman sets his mind to collecting examples – not just of contracts but also of individual conditions – he will quickly develop a data bank of material to help him. Once done, it is surprising how similar many examples of particular conditions are. In this way it is easy and quick to pick the best version or indeed to draft his own, combining the best features from a range of examples.

b) Paragraph structure. Remember:

Contracts have conditions.

Conditions have clauses.

Clauses have paragraphs.

Paragraphs have sub-paragraphs.

c) Grammatical precision and consistency. In general terms use the word 'shall' when drafting, eg:

The seller *shall* supply the goods.

The buyer *shall* pay.

Do not alternate between 'shall' and 'will' unless there is a clear distinction between them, eg:

'Shall means a requirement that demonstrably must happen during contract performance.'

'Will means a requirement that does not actually require demonstration during contract performance.'

Use the word 'may' only in the situation where an option exists, eg:

'In the event that the seller shall have failed to provide the data the buyer may terminate the contract.'

This gives the buyer the option to cancel which can be exercised at his discretion. Equally effective, though, would have been to say 'shall have the right to terminate'.

Words such as 'would', 'could', 'should', 'might', 'try', and 'attempt', have no place at all in a contract condition.

d) Order of precedence. There are two schools of thought on order of precedence. Firstly, that the concept is meaningless because the contract is *not* of a hierarchical nature but should be seen as a homogeneous whole. Secondly, that some features of the contract naturally have greater importance than others and therefore it aids clarity and mutual understanding. The author tends to the latter view as in larger contracts – despite the best endeavours to adhere strictly to the Hexagon Principle – it can be virtually impossible to guarantee that there are no accidentally built-in conflicts between various provisions of the contract. An order of precedence does at least provide some assistance in resolving any such conflicts.

e) Avoidance of doubt. It can be helpful to refer to documents outside of the contract for the purposes of avoiding doubt. The important thing to remember here is that there is a potential ambiguity which must be avoided. That is, it should be clear whether reference to other documents is intended to:

    a) enhance the overall description of the requirement so that the chance of there being doubt is minimised;

    or

    b) occur *only* if doubt *does* arise from within the contract.

Finally, an important point to remember is that the clarity of many contracts can be enhanced if there is a complete set of definitions included. Again the IMechE Model provides a good example as shown below.

Example H

GENERAL CONDITIONS
Definitions and Interpretations

Definitions

    1.1 In construing the Contract the following words and expressions shall have the following meanings hereby assigned to them.

    1.1a 'Purchaser' means the person named as such in the Special Conditions and the legal successors in title to the Purchaser but not (except with the consent of the Contractor) any assignee of the Purchaser.

    1.1b 'Contractor' means the tenderer whose Tender has been accepted by the Purchaser and the legal successors in title to the Contractor but not any assignee of the Contractor.

    1.1c 'Sub-Contractor' means the person (other than the Contractor) named in the Contract for any part of the Works or any person to whom any part of the Contract has been sub-let with the consent in writing of the Engineer, and the Sub-Contractor's legal successors in title, but not any assignee of the Sub-Contractor.

    1.1d 'Engineer' means the person appointed by the Purchaser to act as Engineer for the purposes of the Contract and designated as such in the Special Conditions or, in default of any appointment, the Purchaser.

    1.1e 'Engineer's Representative' means any assistant of the Engineer appointed from time to time to perform the duties delegated to him under Clause 2 (Engineer and Engineer's Representative) hereof.

1.1f 'The Conditions' means these Conditions and the Special Conditions.

1.1g 'Contract' means the agreement between the Purchaser and the Contractor (howsoever made) for the execution of the Works including the Letter of Acceptance, the Conditions, Specification and the drawings (if any) annexed thereto and such schedules as are referred to therein and the Tender.

1.1h 'Contract Price' means the sum stated in the Contract as the price payable to the Contractor for the execution of the Works.

1.1i 'Contract Value' means such part of the Contract Price, adjusted to give effect to such additions or deductions as are provided for in the Contract, other than under Sub-Clause 6.2 (Labour, Materials and Transport), as is properly apportionable to the Plant or work in question. In determining Contract Value the state, condition and topographical location of the Plant, the amount of work done and all other relevant circumstances shall be taken into account.

1.1j 'Cost' means all expenses and costs incurred including overhead and financing charges properly allocatable thereto with no allowance for profit.

1.1k 'Tender' means the Contractor's priced offer to the Purchaser for the execution of the Works.

1.1l 'Letter of Acceptance' means the formal acceptance by the Purchaser of the Tender incorporating any amendments or variations to the Tender agreed by the Purchaser and Contractor.

1.1m 'Time for Completion' means the period of time for Completion of the Works or any Section thereof as stated in the Contract or as extended under Sub-Clause 33.1 (Extension of Time for Completion) calculated from whichever is the later of:

a) the date specified in the Contract as the date for commencement of the Works;

b) the date of receipt of such payment in advance of the commencement of the Works as may be specified in the Contract;

c) the date any necessary legal, financial or administrative requirements specified in the Contract as conditions precedent to commencement have been fulfilled.

1.1n 'Contractor's Equipment' means all appliances or things of whatsoever nature required for the purposes of the Works but does not include Plant, materials or other things intended to form or forming part of the Works.

1.1o 'Plant' means machinery, computer hardware and software, apparatus, materials and things of all kinds to be provided under the Contract other than Contractor's Equipment.

1.1p 'Works' means all Plant to be provided and work to be done by the Contractor under the Contract.

1.1q 'Section of the Works' or 'Section' means the parts into which the Works are divided by the Specification.

1.1r 'Programme' means the programme referred to in Clause 14 (Programme).

1.1s 'Specification' means the specification of the Works annexed to or included in the Contract including any modifications thereof under Clause 27 (Variations).

1.1t The 'Special Conditions' means the alterations to these General Conditions specified and identified as the Special Conditions in the Contract.

1.1u 'Site' means the actual place or places, provided or made available by the Purchaser, to which Plant is to be delivered or where work is to be done by the Contractor, together with so much of the area surrounding the same as the Contractor shall with the consent of the Purchaser actually use in connection with the Works otherwise than merely for the purposes of access.

1.1v 'Tests on Completion' means the tests specified in the Contract (or otherwise agreed by the Purchaser and the Contractor) which are to be made by the Contractor upon completion of erection and/or installation before the Works are taken over by the Purchaser.

1.1w 'Performance Tests' means the tests (if any) detailed in the Specification or in a performance test schedule otherwise agreed between the Purchaser and the Contractor, to be made after the Works have been taken over to demonstrate the performance of the Works.

1.1x 'Defects Liability Period' has the meaning assigned to Clause 36.1 (Defects Liability).

1.1y 'Purchaser's Risks' has the meaning assigned by Clause 45.1 (Purchaser's Risks).

1.1z 'Force Majeure' has the meaning assigned by Clause 46 (Force Majeure).

1.1aa 'Appendix' means the Appendix to these General Conditions.

1.1bb 'Writing' means any handwritten, typewritten or printed statement.

1.1cc 'Day' means Calendar day.

1.1dd 'Week' means any period of 7 days.

1.1ee 'Month' means Calendar month.

Interpretation

1.2   Words importing persons or parties shall include firms, corporations and any organisation having legal capacity.

Singular and Plural

1.3   Words importing the singular only also include the plural and Vice Versa where the context requires.

Notices and Consents

1.4   Wherever in these Conditions provision is made for the giving of the notice or consent by any person, unless otherwise specified such notice or consent shall be in writing and the word 'notify' shall be construed accordingly. Any consent required of a party or the Engineer shall not be unreasonably withheld.

Headings and Marginal Notes

1.5   The headings or marginal notes in the Conditions shall not be deemed part thereof or be taken into consideration in the interpretation or construction thereof or of the Contract.

6 Contract amendments

An amendment to a contract has the effect of creating a new contract and so the most critical thing about a contract amendment is that it complies with all the prerequisites of a contract and that in practice all aspects of the contract which are not being amended are clearly stated as continuing to apply. In this regard the golden rule (so that the draughtsman *thinks* about what he is doing) is:

> **Don't assume that the rest of the contract can continue unchanged: read the rest of it and make all necessary amendments.**

Example I

B J Buxton Ltd   P J Perkins
4 Williams House   98 Wallings Avenue
London   London
EC4 3AT   WC3 5XZ

FAO Mr J Smith – Contracts Officer
15 July 1992

Dear Sirs

**CONTRACT NUMBER 14AJ/301 – AMENDMENT
NO 28
SUPPLY OF MK 28 WIDGETS**

Following our discussion regarding additional quantities and
other changes we are pleased to propose the following amendment to the Contract.

Schedule of Requirements
Quantity : Delete '5000'.
                    Insert '6000'.

Price
Delete: 'The price each shall be £100'.
Insert: 'The price each for the first 5000 off shall be £100 and
for the balance of 1000 shall be £120 each'.

Delivery Programme
Delete: the existing Annex 3 – Delivery Programme.
Insert: the attached new Annex 3 – Delivery Programme dated
3 July 1992.

   All other terms and conditions of the Contract remain
unchanged.
   Please confirm your acceptance of this amendment.

Yours faithfully

J K Franklyn

For example, if the delivery schedule is being amended then perhaps the stage payment scheme may need adjustment as well.

It is important to remember that a contract amendment is not legally effective until it has been accepted and it is important to prompt the recipient to reply with an acceptance.

For convenience, contract amendments should have a unique serial number and date.

If the amendment arises out of some discussion or for whatever reason, it is conventional and helpful to set this out as a precursor but if this is done then care must be taken to ensure that there is no confusion or overlap between the explanation and the body of the amendment itself.

Above all, the amendment must follow the Hexagon Principle.

An example of a contract amendment is given on the previous page and there is a checklist in Appendix 1, List J. Note from the example the precision of the way in which each segment of the amendment is described – giving not only new wording but the exact words which are being replaced. All this serves to ensure clarity.

(7) Commercial reports

Amongst the categories of written material that a contract administrator should be expected to produce is that of reports. Here, as elsewhere, the Hexagon Principle applies. Commercial reporting is a key function of effective liaison. This subject is covered in Chapter 9.

(8) Estimates, quotations and tenders

A contract is comprised of an offer and an acceptance. The document committing this exchange of promises to writing can be voluminous. A quotation is *not* just an indication of price associated with a job of work, it is an offer of contract. It could be argued, therefore, that the quotation should be as voluminous as the contract document. Put another way, the quotation should be constructed as a contract and offered precisely as such. This is the approach which is adopted in full tendering procedures where both the request for tenders and the tender submitted in response are presented in the form of contract.

Example J

F W Smith
14 Friars Way
Basingstoke
Hampshire
B12 4DA

G A Walker plc
Walker House
Southampton
Hampshire
SO14 0HS

FAO Mr A Ladd – Buyer
23 November 1992

Dear Sirs

QUOTATION

Enquiry No: FWS/4374/2 dated 1.11.92
Quotation No: GAW/JG/281

Thank you for your enquiry to which we are pleased to provide this quotation.

Item: Mk 14 Widget Part No: 138/492/01.
Quantity: 1500.
Delivery: 150/month commencing 2 weeks from receipt of order.

Price: £125 each ex-works plus VAT at rate prevailing at date of invoice. The price is firm and not subject to variation.
Payment: 28 days from date of invoice subject to 2.5% discount for payment within 5 days.
Packaging: Trade standard marked for your Friars Way site.
Terms: G A Walker Standard Conditions of Sale (UK) in your possession.
Validity: 22 December 1992.
Assumptions/Exclusions: None.
Please contact the undersigned with any queries. We look forward to receiving your order.

Yours faithfully

R A Brown
Sales Officer

Example K

F W Smith   G A Walker plc
14 Friars Way   Walker House
Basingstoke   Southampton
Hampshire B12 4DA,   Hampshire SO14 0HS

FAO Mr A Ladd – Buyer
23 November 1992

Dear Sirs
BUDGETARY ESTIMATE
Enquiry No: FWS/4374/5 dated 29 September 1992.
Budgetary Estimate No: GAW/LMB/4969.

Thank you for your enquiry to which we are pleased to provide this *Budgetary* estimate.

Work: Design and supply approximately 100 off widget replacements generally in line with draft specification 491/PWT/43.

Budgetary Estimate: £500,000 at September 1992 economics base excluding VAT.

Likely Timeframe: Approximately 18 months' work which would commence 2 months from date of an effective contract.

Terms: To be negotiated but generally in line with previous Contract No A81/432 including interim payments. All IPR to vest in us.

Assumptions/Exclusions: The draft specification must be finalised by no later than 2 weeks prior to contract start.

We stress that this is the budgetary estimate only and is not intended to be an offer of contract.

We trust this is attractive to you and if you have any technical queries please contact Mr Crane on extension 1234 and the undersigned for any other queries.

Yours faithfully

R A Brown
Sales Officer

Thus the checklist for items to include in a tender is precisely the same as those items to be considered in drafting a contract and its conditions *plus* those things which apply only to the pre-contract phase. (Such a checklist is provided in Appendix 1, List D.) Very often there is no full invitation to tender and the value and complexity of the work warrants a summary form of quotation. However, even in a summary form it is vital to capture all the key features that will comprise the contract. An example of this is given on page 97 and a checklist in Appendix 1, List E.

Estimates or budgetary quotations are not binding (ie not offered for acceptance in the contractual sense) and are of necessity less precise. The two important things are:

a) To make the quotation as helpful as possible.

b) To make it absolutely clear that no formal offer is being made.

An example is given on page 98 and there is a checklist in Appendix 1, List F.

9 Requests for quotation, etc

Requests to another party for a proposal are known by many different acronyms:

RFQ : Request for Quotation.
RFP : Request for Proposal.
ITT : Invitation to Tender.
IFB : Invitation for Bids.

Frequently the above documents are prepared and issued by other than the contract administration department. For example, where engineers are producing estimates that include bought out elements they phone or write to suppliers asking for prices. This is fraught with danger and nobody should be surprised that when the response arrives it is less than helpful.

The principle is that an RFQ is a request for somebody to make an offer of contract. Therefore if the offer is to match what is wanted then the RFQ must spell out its requirements in detail. Thus the same set of items must be addressed as for preparing tenders *plus* those things which the requestee is to take into account in preparing his reply. A checklist of these items is provided in Appendix 1, List G.

Again, following the ideas of the previous section, in many instances the nature of the work or its value may not justify a full blown RFQ or it may be that only budgetary information is required. For these situations, shortform RFQs and Budgetary Requests are provided and examples of these are given below. Checklists are given in Appendix 1, Lists H and I.

Example L

G A Walker   F W Smith
Walker House   14 Friars Way
Southampton   Basingstoke
Hampshire   Hampshire
SO14 0HS   B12 4DA

FAO Mr R A Brown – Sales Officer
1 November 1992

Our Ref: FWS/4374/2

Dear Sirs

REQUEST FOR QUOTATION

Please provide your firm unit price (not variable) ex works including VAT quotation for the following:

Item: MK 14 Widget Part No 138/492/01.
Quantity: 1500.
Delivery: Please specify best delivery.
Packaging: Trade standard.
Terms: G A Walker Standard Conditions of Sale (UK).

Please provide a validity to 22 December 1992 and reply in writing by 24 November 1992.

This is an enquiry only and does not imply any commitment to place an order.

Yours faithfully

A F Ladd
Buyer

Example M

G A Walker   F W Smith
Walker House   14 Friars Way
Southampton   Hampshire
Hampshire   B12 4DA
SO14 0HS

FAO Mr J D Williams – Contracts Officer
29 September 1992

Our Ref: FWS/4374/5

Dear Sirs

REQUEST FOR BUDGETARY ESTIMATE

Please provide your budgetary estimate for the following:

Work: Design and supply approximately 100 off widget re-placements generally in line with draft specification 491/PWT/43.

Likely timeframe: Please provide an outline proposal.

Terms: Generally in line with contract no A81/432.

Please reply by 20 November 1992.

Yours faithfully

A F Ladd
Buyer

In both cases, if the examples of request and response are examined a very close correlation can be seen with a lot of words/phrases actually repeated – this is exactly how it should be.

10 Subcontracts

The topic of drafting subcontracts has been left to the very end of this chapter because by now it can be seen that the technique for drafting subcontracts is no different to drafting any form of contract and thus the checklists B and C in Appendix 1 are to be followed.

Beyond this the following general advice can be given on what to include:

a) Virtually all of the prime contract conditions whether or not flow down is mandatory.

b) The right of access to the subcontractor's premises for the purposes of inspection, quality assurance and general monitoring of the progress of work.

c) The free right to copy, use and modify subcontractor intellectual property.

d) The right not to pay the subcontractor until payment has been received from the customer.

e) The right under contract to claim all damages including special and consequential damages from the subcontractor in the event of delay or default.

f) The right to delivery penalties – but phrased carefully under the heading of liquidated damages to satisfy the requirements of English law – whether or not these apply in the main contract.

g) The right to withhold or recover payment in the event of delay.

h) Extended warranty to cover any prime contract warranty period.

To put this into context the subcontractor may respond in the following terms:

a) Only the main contract conditions which are required to be passed on to subcontractors should be included.

b) Right of access is limited by commercial security considerations.

c) Intellectual property can only be used for the purposes of the main contract.

d) Payment must be made within X days whether or not the main contractor has been paid.

e) Liability for damages should be limited to a specific sum not exceeding the value of the subcontract.

f) Force majeure protection against delays.

g) A period of cure and consultation before any withholding or recovery of payment.

h) Extra price for non-standard warranty.

The final piece of advice is that in flowing down the main

contract conditions some interpretation is required particularly in the case of standard conditions which are incorporated by reference only.

Typically the approach to this is limited to including a condition as follows:

The standard conditions listed shall apply except that:

a) 'Contract' shall mean 'subcontract'.
b) 'Contractor' shall mean 'subcontractor'.
c) 'Contract price' shall mean 'subcontract price'.

Except where the context otherwise permits.

This is not really good enough as the caveat at the end imparts uncertainty and the potential for future dispute. It is far better to take the time to do one of two things:

a) Work through the conditions one by one, writing out specific interpretations or translations.

or

b) Word process the conditions from scratch, building in the interpretations as you go.

The result is a document which can be used time and time again and included by reference into subcontracts. Thus sets of model standard subcontract conditions develop which can be tailored to individual companies, products, services or technologies and combinations thereof.

Latin expressions

Although there is no need for Latin expressions, they occasionally crop up and can be mystifying if the translation is not obvious. One or two (such as 'Mutatis mutandis') are useful because they capture a concept briefly which in English would become longer and somewhat clumsy.

'Ad eundem gradum'	–	To the same degree.
'Ad interim'	–	In the meantime.
'Ad rem'	–	To the matter in hand.
'Ad verbum'	–	Verbatim.
'A posteriori'	–	From effect to cause.

'A priori'	–	From what is already known.
'Ceteris paribus'	–	Other things being equal.
'Causa sine qua non'	–	A necessary condition.
'De facto'	–	In reality.
'Exempli gratia'	–	For instance (eg).
'Idem'	–	The same.
'Id est'	–	That is (ie).
'Inter alia'	–	Among other things.
'Mutatis mutandis'	–	After making the necessary changes.
'Non sequitur'	–	It does not follow.
'Per diem'	–	Daily.
'Per se'	–	Intrinsically.
'Post hoc, ergo propter hoc'	–	After this, therefore because of this.
'Prima facie'	–	At first sight.
'Quantum'	–	As much.
'Quod erat demonstrandum'	–	Which was to be demonstrated (QED).
'Sine qua non'	–	An indispensable condition.
'Telum imbelle sine ictu'	–	An ineffectual argument.
'Videlicet'	–	Namely (viz).

5

● ● ● ● ● ● ● ● **C** **H** **A** **P** **T** **E** **R** ● ●

Types of contract

① Introduction

In his career the contract administrator will come across many different types of contract. Each in its own way will provide some challenge perhaps as a drafting exercise or in pursuance of the Pentagon Objectives.

In this chapter we will look at some basic types of contract:

a) Contracts under standard conditions.
b) Contracts under model conditions.
c) Negotiated contracts.
d) Contracts of different price type.

② Contracts under standard conditions

The use of standard conditions as the basis for the contract has many advantages. Both buyer and seller will be familiar with them and this aids mutual understanding and commonality of purpose. The preparation of tender and contract documents is reduced. Disputes are minimised as custom and practice develops the interpretation of the conditions.

However, standard conditions also have disadvantages. Because they are easy to use they might be used where they are not appropriate. Because they are pre-prepared they might be used unintelligently with no review of individual conditions. Custom and practice can negate the effectiveness of particular conditions which will prove to be disastrous on that one occasion when reliance upon the condition would otherwise have been vital.

This means that standard conditions must be used with care

if their advantages are to be realised.

Standard conditions of purchase and sale are those prepared either by the buyer or the seller respectively. To state the obvious, the former favour the buyer and the latter favour the seller, and yet this essential difference is not always realised. People jump to the conclusion that sets of purchase conditions and sets of sale conditions must be almost identical as they must cover the same ground. Whilst it is true that the same topics must be covered – delivery, acceptance, payment, warranty, etc – the way in which the two sides would prefer to treat them are quite different.

The following pages give real examples of standard conditions of sale and purchase, and a comparison between them. The sale standard conditions are export based, and the purchase conditions UK based. This in itself serves to show that in the key areas of making a contract all the principles are the same.

However, a comparison is a very good technique for highlighting the key points in any contractual document. Points which are innocuous or which need to be even handed will appear similarly worded but the difference in wording on essentials as drafted by the buyer and seller is quite marked.

Usually, standard contract conditions are pre-printed in a very pale colour, in fine print on the reverse side of other documents (eg quotations, purchase orders). This makes them difficult to read and easy to ignore or miss: this is done at great peril. The comparison shows just how great the difference is, depending on whether the drafting is left to the buyer or the seller.

Example A: Standard conditions of sale

GENERAL CONDITIONS OF EXPORT SALE FROM THE UNITED KINGDOM

1. EFFECT
These Conditions are subject to any special stipulations set out by Supplier in the Contract documents. The said Conditions and stipulations shall prevail over any put forward by the Buyer unless it is otherwise agreed in writing.

2. PRICES
The prices stated are for delivery FOB (as defined in INCOTERMS 1980) and include for packing to Supplier's normal export standards but are exclusive of V.A.T. if any chargeable in the U.K. or any taxes, duties or charges levied in the country of destination in respect of the goods or their use. Any such taxes, duties or charges shall be payable by Buyer. Buyer shall not be entitled to these prices where Supplier agrees to vary quantities or delivery rates from those specified. While Supplier will endeavour to maintain prices quoted he reserves the right to increase them proportionately to increases in cost of labour and/or materials taking effect between quotation and delivery.

3. STORAGE
If Supplier is unable to despatch the goods within 30 days following notification to Buyer that they are ready for despatch, by reason of lack of adequate forwarding instructions, or if by the end of that period Buyer has not obtained the necessary export-import documents and consents or has not made payment arrangement which it is his duty to obtain or make, Supplier will arrange storage which shall be at Buyer's risk except for damage due to Supplier's negligence. Any charges for such storage or demurrage shall be paid by Buyer. Should such storage continue for a period exceeding six months and Buyer not have made payment in accordance with 4(c) Supplier shall have the right to the sum payable by Buyer. Nothing in this Condition shall prejudice any other rights and remedies of Supplier in respect of delays on Buyer's part.

4. DELIVERY
(a) Time shall not be of the essence in relation to delivery and Supplier shall not be required to commence performance until all payment documentation (including any confirmation or guarantee) has been where appropriate established in favour and to the satisfaction of Supplier and placed at his disposal in the United Kingdom. Subject to the foregoing and to (b) below, should there be serious delay in delivery Buyer may give notice to Supplier to deliver within a reasonable period and should Supplier fail so to deliver Buyer shall have the right to terminate the Contract and Supplier's liability shall be limited to damages other than for loss of use, contracts of profit and not exceeding the contract value of the delayed goods.

(b) Should delivery be delayed by industrial dispute or any circumstance beyond Supplier's reasonable control then the period(s) for delivery shall be extended by such period(s) as is/are reasonable in the circumstances. Should such delay continue for a period exceeding six months then unless the parties agree to the contrary the Contract shall be deemed to be terminated without compensation.

(c) In cases where Buyer is obliged to make a ship or other vessel available for the export of goods from Supplier's country and he does not do so within 30 days next following the date of Supplier's notice to him that goods are ready for dispatch, then Buyer shall become liable forthwith on expiration of that period to pay Supplier for those goods at the Contract rate.

5. CONSENTS
Buyer shall furnish such documents as may be necessary to enable Supplier to obtain any authorisation required by the United Kingdom authorities and shall also obtain any authorisations required by the authorities of the countries of destination and transit outside the U.K. and shall furnish details thereof to Supplier. Supplier shall not be obliged to commence performance until he has obtained such authorisations and Buyer has obtained and given Supplier particulars of the other authorisations aforesaid.

6. TITLE AND RISK

Unless otherwise agreed in writing, title and risk shall pass to Buyer upon delivery FOB as defined in INCOTERMS 1980.

7. EXPORT/IMPORT RESTRICTIONS

Notwithstanding any stipulation in the Contract documents to the contrary. Buyer shall be liable to pay at the Contract rate for all goods delivered and services rendered to him or his order in part performance of the Contract by Supplier, notwithstanding that subsequent export or import restrictions or the cancellation withdrawal or non-renewal of export or import licences prevents further performance of the Contract in whole or in part and no part of any payment already made for goods or services already so delivered or rendered shall be payable by Supplier PROVIDED that Buyer shall have credit for any advance payments made for goods or services still to be delivered or rendered.

8. DRAWINGS ETC.

Buyer shall make good to Supplier any loss on account of delay by Buyer in furnishing adequate and suitable specifications, drawings, tools, parts or materials required to enable Supplier to proceed. Descriptive and shipping specifications and particulars of weight and dimensions furnished to Buyer are approximate only and descriptions and illustrations in Supplier's trade literature are intended to give only a general idea of the goods and none of these shall form part of the Contract.

9. SHORTAGE OR DAMAGE

No claim for non-delivery, shortage or damage will be considered unless received in writing by Supplier and also by any carrier known by Buyer to be concerned within 40 days next after the date on which the goods are ready for despatch from Supplier's factory or (if appropriate) the warehouse plus reasonable air or sea stage transit time.

10. EQUIPMENT WARRANTY

Supplier undertakes to replace or (at his option) repair any goods proved to his reasonable satisfaction to have failed within twelve months next after the date on which they are ready for despatch from his factory by reason of faulty materials or workmanship used in their manufacture or (if in Supplier's opinion such replacement or repair is impracticable) to refund any price paid for the failed goods PROVIDED:

(a) this undertaking shall not extend to failures not reported to Supplier within the period mentioned in 9 above where such failures result from defects which ought reasonably to have been discovered if inspection and/or test of the goods had been practicable;

(b) Buyer informs Supplier promptly on discovery of the alleged failure and promptly returns to goods carriage paid with full written report on the failure, unless Supplier agrees to inspect and replace or repair in situ;

(c) the goods have been stored, installed, maintained and used properly having regard in particular to Supplier's and other agreed applicable specifications and instructions;

(d) this undertaking shall not apply to any goods or parts thereof obtained by Supplier from another;

(e) Buyer shall refund to Supplier the cost to Supplier of any replacement, repair or redelivery of the goods affected by the Supplier where the failure is not within the scope of this undertaking.

Buyer shall have no right to reject later than the end of the period mentioned in 9. Any liability howsoever arising whether in contract or in tort or under statute in respect of quality, fitness, condition, use, trade description, specification or representations of or relating to the goods supplied is hereby excluded and Buyer shall have no rights other than as stated in this Condition in respect of goods which have failed after delivery.

11. TERRITORIAL RESTRICTIONS

Buyer shall not without express written approval of Supplier (which shall not be unreasonably withheld) export or use the goods, or sell or hire them to a person who to his knowledge intends to export or use them, outside the country of declared first destination except as parts of larger assemblies previously exported from such country. This restriction shall not however prevent export, use, sale or hire of the goods to or within any country of the EEC.

12. PATENTS ETC. INFRINGEMENT

Notwithstanding any approval under 11 Supplier shall (in lieu of all all other liability to Buyer for loss where patents, registered designs and similar rights have been infringed by use of the goods) indemnify Buyer against claims (including the costs thereof) by owners or licensees of patents and registered designs of the country of declared first destination of the goods granted at the date hereof for infringement thereof by use or sale of the goods, PROVIDED:

(a) this Indemnity shall not extend to infringements resulting from use by Supplier of Buyer's parts, designs or specific instructions or from use or sale in combination with other items where infringements would not have otherwise occurred;

(b) Buyer shall immediately inform Supplier of claims, shall make no settlement or admission and shall permit Supplier alone (and at Supplier's expense) to deal with claims;

(c) Supplier's liability under this Condition 12 is limited to the amount of royalties or payments in lieu thereof ordered or agreed to be paid to the owner and/or licensee or the patent or design.

13. COPYRIGHT AND CONFIDENTIALITY

The copyright in all Supplier's documents (including drawings) furnished to Buyer for the purposes of this Contract shall at all times remain vested in Supplier and neither they nor their contents shall be used without Supplier's express written consent for any purpose other than that for which they were furnished.

14. TOOLS, DIES, MOULDS, ETC.

Any tools, dies, moulds etc. used by the Supplier for the purpose of his performance of this Contract will be charged at part cost only and will remain the property of the Supplier.

15. SPECIFICATIONS

(a) Buyer accepts responsibility for the goods (and all combinations of the goods with services, software or other goods) achieving Buyer's intended results and for the selection of and results obtained from any services,

software or other goods with which the goods are used in combination.

(b) Supplier does not warrant that the goods are of any particular quality or conform to any particular specification other than the contractual specification.

16. SOFTWARE

Unless otherwise stipulated by Supplier all software supplied in whatever form is supplied under licence and not by way of sale and is subject in the case of Supplier's software to Supplier's relevant terms and conditions of licence and in the case of other software to terms and conditions equivalent to those agreed between Supplier and Supplier's licensor.

17. DETERMINATION OF CONTRACT

If Buyer shall break any provision of this or any other Contract with Supplier, or suffer distress or execution or commit an act of bankruptcy, make arrangement with creditors or go into liquidation (except for amalgamation or reconstruction) or have a receiver appointed, Supplier may (without prejudice to any other claim or remedy) suspend performance of, or determine, this or any other such Contract by written notice and shall be entitled to payments for the goods already delivered, work in progress and tooling costs under the Contract in question at the Contract rate, or (if none) at a rate reasonably based on the price in question.

18. LAW

The Contract shall be governed by English Law and the English Courts shall have exclusive jurisdiction over any matter arising out of the Contract. The Uniform Law on the International Sale of Goods shall not apply.

19. INTERNATIONAL CHAMBER OF COMMERCE ARBITRATION

All disputes arising in connection with this Contract shall be finally settled under the Rules of Conciliation and Arbitration of the International Chamber of Commerce by one or more arbitrators appointed in accordance with the Rules.

Example B: Standard conditions of purchase

TERMS AND CONDITIONS

1. The acceptance of this order involves the acceptance of the conditions under which it is placed. These will not be deemed to have been varied unless our written confirmation of such variation is obtained.

2. (1) No goods will be paid for by us, or any variation of this order recognised, unless ordered or confirmed on our official printed form, duly signed.

   (2) In paying any one or more of your invoices for the items included in this or any future order placed by us we may recover by deduction:

       (a) the unit price (for a reasonable proportion of the contract price), plus the cost of return to you, for any defective item properly rejected by us; and/or

       (b) any amounts payable to us at due payment date of any such invoice for supplies or services by us to you.

       "We" and "you" in this Condition 2(2) shall be deemed to include references respectively to our and your holding subsidiary and other associated companies and "our" and "your" shall be construed accordingly.

3. Time of delivery of the essence of this Contract, such time of delivery being stated on the face of this order hereof or as otherwise agreed by us in writing. Late delivery will signify non performance of the Contract and we reserve the right to cancel the order at our option without cost, for such late delivery.

4. We reserve the right to reject and return at your expense the whole or part of any materials or goods which are faulty in design, quality or construction or which do not come up to sample or standard specified.

5. In the event of orders being placed on "price to be agreed basis" quotations must be submitted AND OUR OFFICIAL AMENDMENT CONFIRMING THE PRICE MUST BE IN YOUR POSSESSION BEFORE THE GOODS ARE INVOICED.

6. BREAK CLAUSE

   (1) We shall in addition to our power to terminate our liability under this order in case of default by you, have power to terminate our liability thereunder at any time by giving one month's notice in writing to you of our desire to do so.

   (2) In the event of such notice being given, we shall be entitled to exercise the following powers or any of them:

       (a) To direct you to complete in accordance with the order all or any of the articles in course of manufacture at the expiration of the notice and to deliver the same at such rate as may be mutually agreed on or in default of agreement at the rate specified in the order.

       All articles delivered by you in accordance with such directions and accepted shall be paid for at a fair and reasonable price.

       (b) To direct you to cease manufacture wholly or partially at the expiration of the said notice.

       (c) To require you as soon as may be reasonable practicable after the receipt of the notice of termination:

           (i) to take such steps as will ensure that the production rate of the articles specified in the order is reduced as rapidly as possible

           (ii) as far as possible consistent with (i) above to concentrate work on the completion of parts already in a semi-manufactured state

(iii) to terminate on the best possible terms such orders for materials and parts bought out in a semi-manufactured or wholly manufactured state, as have not been completed, observing in this connection the requirements of (i) and (ii) above so far as this may be possible

(3) In the event of such notice being given and of you having reasonably performed all the provisions of the order binding upon you down to the date of notice:

(a) We shall take over from you at the cost price thereof plus a reasonable allowance for handling charges all material and bought-out components in your possession at the termination of the notice properly provided by or supplied to you for the performance of the order and unused owing to the exercise of the power of termination unless you shall, with our concurrence, elect to retain such materials and components.

(b) We shall indemnify you against any commitments, liabilities or expenditure which in our opinion have been reasonably and properly incurred by you in connection with the order, to the extent to which such commitments, liabilities or expenditure are in our opinion of no value to you by reason of the termination of the order.

(c) Unless you shall, with our concurrence, elect to retain such articles, we shall take over from you all articles in course of manufacture at the expiration of the notice which you shall not be directed to complete as aforesaid and will pay a fair and reasonable price therefor.

(4) You shall prepare and deliver to us within an agreed period, or in default of agreement within such a period as we may specify, a list of all unused and damaged materials bought-out components and articles in course of manufacture liable to be taken over by or previously belonging to us and shall deliver such materials and things in accordance with our directions and we shall pay you fair and reasonable charges incurred in complying with such directions.

(5) If in any particular cases hardship to you should arise from the operation of this condition, it shall be open to you to refer the circumstances to us and, on being satisfied that such hardship exists, we shall make such allowance, if any, as in our opinion is reasonable.

(6) Any dispute under this condition shall be referred to an arbitrator or arbitrators, selected by us from a panel of arbitrators to be agreed upon mutually or in default of agreement to be appointed by the President of the Law Society.

7. You will be held responsible for loss or damage however occurring to our property in you possession.

8. All information supplied in connection with this order is confidential and is not to be disclosed or used otherwise than for the purpose of this order.

9. No part of this order is to be sub-let without our authority. (Other than such details as are usually sub-let in the class of work involved).

10. You are to indemnify us against all loss, claims, costs, expenses or damages which we may sustain or for which we may be liable by reason of the user of disposition of the goods the subject of this order constituting a violation of any Letters Patent.

11. Advice Notes must be sent on the day that the goods are despatched and priced invoices within three days. Invoices will not be passed for payment unless our order number and the advice note number are shown. We decline responsibility for goods sent without advice notes and/or invoices. Invoices must state address at which goods were delivered.

12. Reasonable care will be exercised in returning empties but not packing or package charge will be accepted. Any memorandum statements of returnable packings must be rendered separately.

13. Terms to be less 2.5% monthly account unless otherwise stated on the front of this order.

14. This Contract shall be construed and interpreted in accordance with English Law and English Courts shall have jurisdiction over the Contract. These Terms and Conditions do not derogate from our Statutory and Common Law rights and are in addition to these rights and not in substitution for them.

15. It is a condition of this order that you will at all times comply with all legislations and regulations (including but not by way of limitation the Factories Act 1961 and the Health and Safety at Work etc. Act 1974) relevant to the goods and/or services covered by this order and will indemnify us against any liability costs losses and expenses we may sustain if you fail to do so.

16. If so indicated on the face hereof, this Order is placed on behalf of the Secretary of State for Defence and is subject to Ministry of Defence regulations including but not necessarily limited to security regulations and the Official Secrets Acts. Acceptance of this order signifies acceptance of such regulations.

17. Suppliers Representatives on our Premises.
    Should your obligations under this order require the attendance of your employees, agents, servants or sub-contractors on our premises, the following conditions shall apply:
    (1) You shall retain in force during the whole period of your performance of this order employers liability insurance in the form of an unlimited indemnity against claims made by or n behalf of your employees, agents, servants or sub-contractors for death or personal injury to such employees, agents, servants or sub-contractors.
    (2) You shall retain in force during the whole period of your performance of this order third party liability insurance in the form of an indemnity of at least £1,000,000 covering loss or damage and an unlimited indemnity covering death or personal injury arising from or relating directly or indirectly to your negligence in the performance of your obligations or otherwise under the order.
    (3) We reserve the right to refuse at our discretion entry to our premises to any of your employees, agents, servants or sub-contractors for any reason and we shall suffer no penalty under any of the Terms and Conditions of the order should we so exercise that right.

Difference analysis

Topic	Buyer condition	Commentary	Seller condition	Commentary
Ts & Cs	1	Order acceptance conveys agreement to Ts and Cs. No variation without buyer's written agreement.	1	Supplier conditions prevail over buyer.
Rejects	2.2	Unilateral right to decide and recover monetary sums for rejected items. No time limit.	—	Seller does not offer this right to the buyer!
Delivery	3	Of the essence. Right of summary cancellation. No 'force majeure'.	4	Exactly the opposite.
Warranty	4	In effect an unlimited warranty on design and manufacture.	10	A precisely defined and time limited warranty which also excludes all other liabilities.
'Break'	6	Cancellation for convenience at one month's notice available to buyer.	—	Seller does not offer this right to the buyer.
Determination	—	Buyer does not offer this right to the seller!	17	Seller has the right to cancel if buyer is bankrupt, etc.
Loss/damage	7	Seller liable in respect of buyer's property.	—	Seller does not offer this benefit to buyer!
Confidential information	8	Buyer's information is confidential.	13	Seller's information is confidential.
Patents etc.	10	Seller indemnifies buyer.	12	This is offered to the buyer but is limited, detailed and excludes other liabilities.
Terms	13	A discount is demanded for prompt payment.	—	Seller does not offer this benefit to the buyer.
Specification	—	Buyer does not provide seller with this indemnity.	15	Buyer has the risk that the goods suit his purpose.

Example C: Model Conditions

MODEL FORM OF

GENERAL CONDITIONS OF CONTRACT

INCLUDING FORMS OF TENDER,
AGREEMENT, SUB-CONTRACT
and PERFORMANCE BOND

RECOMMENDED BY

THE INSTITUTION OF MECHANICAL ENGINEERS
THE INSTITUTION OF ELECTRICAL ENGINEERS

AND

THE ASSOCIATION OF CONSULTING ENGINEERS

FOR USE IN CONNECTION WITH

HOME OR OVERSEAS CONTRACTS – WITH ERECTION

1988 EDITION

Published for the Joint IMechE/IEE Committee on
Model Forms of General Conditions of Contract
and obtainable from

THE INSTITUTION OF ELECTRICAL ENGINEERS
Publication Sales Department, P.O. Box 26, Hitchin,
Herts SG5 1SA
or to Callers, at the Reception Desk, Savoy Place
or from

THE INSTITUTION OF MECHANICAL ENGINEERS
Publications Sales Department, P.O. Box 24, Northgate
Avenue, Bury St Edmunds, Suffolk IP32 6BW
or to Callers, at the Reception Desk,
Birdcage Walk, London
or from

THE ASSOCIATION OF CONSULTING ENGINEERS
Alliance House, 12 Caxton Street, London SW1H 0QL

It can be seen from this example that even standard conditions contain risks and liabilities and therefore the golden rule must be never to accept the other side's standard conditions without a careful review.

③ Contracts under model conditions

The difference between standard conditions and model conditions is that standard conditions are produced unilaterally by one side to the potential contract whereas model conditions are produced by an outside agency and the parties may elect to settle on one model or another.

Many trade associations and professional institutes or other bodies produce several sets of model conditions from which the parties can choose. The following BEAMA (British Electrotechnical and Allied Manufacturers' Association) list gives an idea of the range available:

- For Machinery & Equipment (Excluding Erection) UK
- For Machinery & Equipment (Including Erection) UK
- For Repair of Machinery & Equipment UK
- For Stock & Catalogue Articles UK
- For Erection of Electrical Plant & Machinery (Home or Export)
- For Electronic Equipment Including Installation UK
- For Machinery & Equipment (Excluding Erection) Export: FOB, FOR, FOT
- For Machinery & Equipment (Excluding Erection) Export: CIF & F&F
- For Machinery & Equipment (Including Erection) Export: FOB
- For Repair of Machinery & Equipment Export: FOB
- For Stock & Contents Articles Export: FOB
- For Commissioning Electronic Equipment UK

A main advantage of using model conditions is that they can be very thorough and comprehensive as shown by just the contents list from the IMechE/IEE Model Form of General Conditions of Contract (MF/1):

TABLE OF CONTENTS

General Conditions
Definitions and Interpretations

Clause   **Page**

The principal disadvantages with using model conditions are not only that there is a tendency to use them blindly but also, because they are produced by an independent third party, they are even handed. This may be no bad thing if both sides are content to agree to use them with no negotiation. On the other hand if the contract is to be negotiated it is usually not a good idea to start with a proposal which of itself is already something of a compromise.

4 Negotiated contracts

Once it is decided that a contract is to be drafted from scratch then frequently once it is prepared and sent to the other side, the recipient can usually find something he does not like about every sentence.

Appendix 5 shows a straightforward contract and the sort of analysis that the other side should do.

5 Contracts of different price types

There would be an almost infinite number of ways of segregating categories of contract into different types, eg by:

    a) Value.
    b) Duration.
    c) Product.
    d) Technology.
    e) Phase.
    f) Customer.
    g) Market.
    h) Territory.

However, from a commercial point of view it can be more helpful to categorise by reference to the means by which a price is agreed for the contract.

5.1. Firm price

This is the most common type of price – a price which is agreed by whatever means by the two parties to the contract to be the price for all of the work under the contract, regardless of the difficulties and extraneous factors which the manufacturer/supplier may encounter. It is a price which will not vary from the time it is agreed for any reason. That is, the price for the defined and specified work requirement will not vary. However if that work requirement is changed by the customer, then the supplier is entitled to change the price and indeed the time allowed for performance of the contract.

Throughout this explanation of contract price types it is assumed that the content of the work is not varied by the customer. In the case of the firm price contract therefore the price also does not vary. However whilst the price is not permitted to vary, the cost to the supplier of undertaking the work may indeed alter to a degree outside of his contemplation.

Within his contemplation may be uncertainty over the

Figure 5.1: Firm price contract

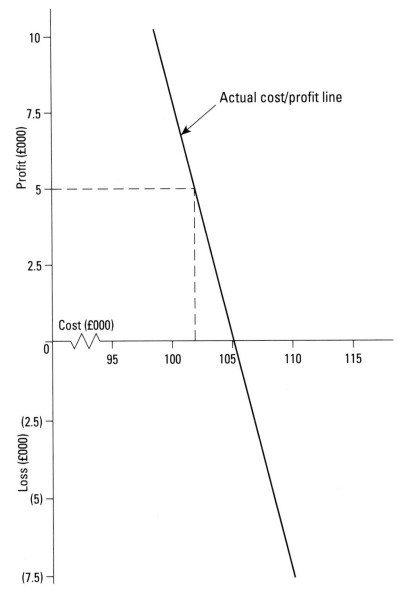

Firm price is £105,000

Effects:
1) If costs are £100,000, profit is £5,000.
2) Break-even point is £105,000.
3) All costs above £105,000 result in a loss.
4) All savings against the estimated cost of £100,000 will be added to the profit.

accuracy of cost estimating and he may make an estimating allowance for this in the price, based on previous experience. He may also consider that this cost may be affected by general inflation and he may make a contingency allowance for this in his price. However, the actual incidence of these known but unpredictable events and also the incidence of unknown events such as subcontractor industrial strike action may cause his costs to prove to be highly under-estim-ated or highly overestimated. In the former case the difference between estimated and actual costs will be an erosion of profit or even a loss and in the latter case the difference between estimated and actual costs will become additional profit. This relationship between cost and profit can be seen in Figure 5.1.

Clearly in a firm price environment the accuracy of cost estimating and the efficiency of contract performance is most vital. The seller is at maximum risk as he must absorb any and all cost overruns.

5.2. Fixed price

Fixed price contracts are very similar to firm price contracts except that the price is variable based on movements in some factor that influences contract costs. For example, the contract price may be linked to inflation indices recording the change in labour and/or material costs or both. One disadvantage here is that published indices relate to sectors of industry as a whole and the environment in which a particular firm operates may cause it to be more adversely affected by inflation than is suggested by the relevant indices. Another varying cost to which the price may be linked is currency exchange rates. A supplier offering goods or services including a significant foreign content in respect of which he must pay in the foreign currencies will be at risk if his customer wishes to agree the price in sterling only. An element of this risk can be passed on to the customer if he is prepared to include an exchange rate variation clause.

A typical variation of price ('VOP') clause covering inflationary effects would be expressed by a mathematical formula of the following type:

$$P_f = 0.1 P_o + P_o \left(0.6 \frac{L_f}{L_o} + 0.3 \frac{M_f}{M_o} \right)$$

where P_f =   Final price
          P_o =   Basic price for VOP purposes
          L_f =   Final labour index
          L_o =   Initial labour index
          M_f =   Final material index
          M_o =   Initial labour index.

In such a formula there is usually an element (here 10%) of the basic price which is not subject to VOP adjustment and a split (here 2:1 making up the balance of 90%) between labour and material indices to recognise that the movement of inflation in each may be different and that the content of the work may not be evenly divided between the two elements.

The initial indices may be chosen as those applying at the date of price quotation or at some earlier or later time. For example, a firm using September as its economics base-date may offer a quotation subject to VOP where the initial indices are those applying in September although the quotation may be dated December. The final indices may be chosen as those applying at the date of final delivery or at some mid-point if delivery is spread over a significant period of time. Both the initial and final index dates may be different between the labour and material elements to recognise that labour will be deployed over a different time-frame to that in which materials are bought.

The relationship between cost and profit in a fixed price contract is identical to that in the firm price contract (Figure 5.1) albeit that the supplier is at somewhat lesser risk, having passed some element(s) of risk on to the customer. In practice, though, the entire risk in relation to that feature may not have been passed on either because there is a non-variable proportion of the price or because the indices on which the VOP formula depends do not fully reflect the effect on the individual firm.

Where the price is adjusted by a VOP clause the operation of the clause can be implemented in a number of ways depending upon whether payments are being made in advance of delivery or on/ following delivery only. If interim payments are being made on a stage-payment arrangement, where the values of stages are percent-

Figure 5.2: Cost plus percentage fee contract

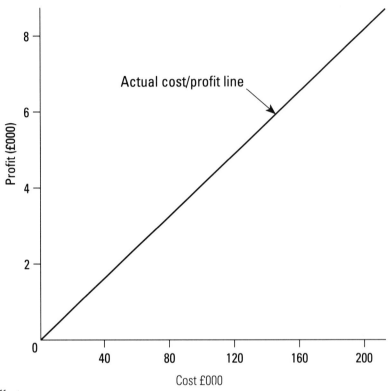

Effect:
The seller always earns a profit at a predetermined percentage of cost, irrespective of the level of cost.

ages of the total price, then the price and thus the stage values may be adjusted as each stage-payment becomes due. Alternatively, where payment is on final completion then there will be one single adjustment of the price and one single 'VOP' payment. As one example, the formula can be repeated with some real values:

$$P_f = 0.1\,P_o + P_o\left(0.6\,\frac{L_f}{L_o} + 0.3\,\frac{M_f}{M_o}\right)$$

where
$$P_o = £100,000$$
$$L_f = 180$$
$$L_o = 100$$
$$M_f = 130$$
$$M_o = 100.$$

Figure 5.3: Cost plus fixed fee contract

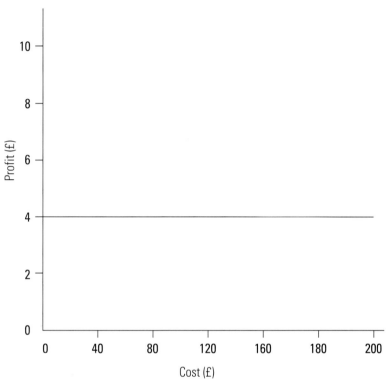

Effect:
1. Regardless of cost the seller is guaranteed a predetermined fixed sum for profit

The P_f = £157,000, and thus the VOP has added £57,000 to the price.

These general principles applying to VOP in relation to inflation also apply to other variable parameters such as exchange rate variation.

It should be emphasised that the foregoing definitions of firm and fixed price contracts are not universal. Sometimes the reverse definitions apply and occasionally the expressions are combined as in a 'firm fixed price' or 'fixed and firm price'. This just serves to confuse and should be avoided. It is most important that the contract, quotation or request for quotation is clear on the definition of the price type.

5.3. Cost plus

Quite simply a so-called cost plus contract is a contract in which the customer pays the seller all his actual incurred costs plus something for profit. The something for profit is either a predetermined and agreed sum of money or a predetermined percentage of the actual costs. In neither case is the seller at any risk as he is guaranteed to recover all of his own costs no matter what happens in the execution of the contract, provided, of course, that he meets the requirements of the contract. Where the profit is a predetermined sum of money the supplier's profit rate as a percentage return on cost reduces as costs increase. Where it is a predetermined percentage then his absolute profit increases as costs increase. These relationships can be seen in Figures 5.2 and 5.3. Neither type of cost plus contract is inducive to efficiency, cost reduction or timely performance and is usually avoided by customers although in some situations of high risk or uncertain work specification they are obviously beneficial to the seller.

5.4. Incentive contracts

Incentive contracts, as the name suggests, are designed to put pressure on the seller to strive for efficient performance whether in terms of cost, timescale, technical performance or combinations of these. In a firm price or fixed price arrangement the pressure is on the seller to perform well, but to do so is in direct terms to his sole advantage. That is, the customer derives no benefit from efficient performance on a fixed or firm price contract. He was, after all, entitled to timely delivery of the correct product. In a cost plus contract there is no pressure on the seller to perform efficiently, in fact quite the opposite, to the customer's clear disadvantage. The purpose behind an incentive contract is to create this pressure on the seller but at the same time to allow the customer some concrete benefit from the seller's efficiency. This arrangement, which is essentially a compromise between the firm price and cost plus arrangements, is useful where neither side is able or willing to take the risk in the outcome of costs in high risk or poorly defined work.

The most common form of incentive contract is that related to cost only. The customer and seller agree a target cost for the work and agree how each will take a share of any savings or contribute to any overspends against that target. Additionally they will establish

Figure 5.4: Target cost incentive fee contract

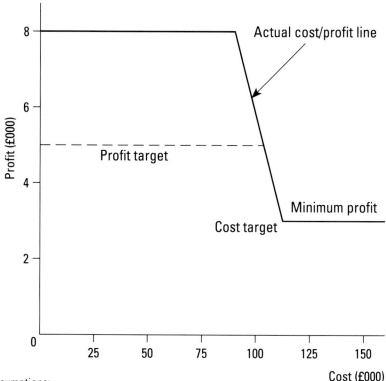

Assumptions:
1)   Cost target is £100,000 with 5% profit rate.
2)   Overspends or underspends are shared in the proportion 80/20.
3)   Maximum profit is £8,000 and minimum profit is £3,000.

Effects:
1)   If cost is less than £85,000, all savings accrue to buyer.
2)   If costs exceed £110,000, the overspend is borne by buyer.

a target fee – that is, the sum for profit which the seller will earn if the actual cost exactly equals the target cost.

In such an arrangement, therefore, the customer is agreeing to pay the supplier his actual costs plus the target fee which shall be increased or decreased against the target cost, their respective shares in either case being known as the share ratio and agreed in negotiation. Conventionally the customer will take the lion's share of any overspends. A typical example of a target cost incentive fee contract is illustrated in Figure 5.4. This demonstrates the 'cost

Figure 5.5: Fixed price incentive contract

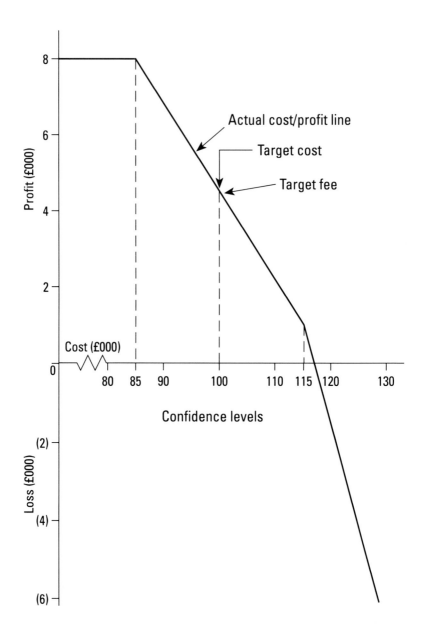

incentive range', being the span of cost between the most optimistic cost and the most pessimistic cost, two figures also agreed in negotiation between the two parties. In this example it can be seen that the seller can earn unlimited profit on the underrun side. Countering this, on the overrun side is the maximum price feature, that is, the extrapolation of the share line beyond the most pessimistic cost shown, the erosion of the seller's fee on a 0/100 ratio until excess costs have eliminated all profit and the seller goes into a loss.

It is open to the parties to negotiate different incentive schemes. An alternative called the cost plus incentive fee contract is shown in Figure 5.5. In this situation there is no maximum price, which has the effect of saying that no matter what the costs are, the seller will receive a minimum fee. The quid pro quo for this is that there is a limitation on the maximum fee that the seller can earn.

In addition to benefits to both sides relating to the seller's performance in meeting or bettering the target cost, the parties may agree that the seller can earn an additional – ie over and above the target fee and shared cost savings – fee for early delivery or improved technical performance. As far as delivery is concerned the scheme may be quite simple, eg he shall earn the sum of £X for each week that delivery is achieved ahead of schedule. This is relatively straightforward to plan and monitor. Technical performance incentives in quality standards, reliability or specific features such as power-to-weight ratio are more difficult to achieve and measure.

In a mixed incentive scheme there is a complicated trade-off analysis to calculate. Extra cost means less savings to be shared but may allow higher technical performance which will earn its own enhanced profit. Early delivery may bring extra profit but at the sacrifice of not introducing performance improvements, thus missing other profit opportunities.

Assumptions:
1)   Target cost is £100,000 with fee of £5,000.
2)   Upper and lower confidence levels are £115,000 and £85,000.
3)   Overspends or underspends within the confidence levels will be shared in the proportion 80/20.
4)   Maximum price is £117,000 with a fee of £2,000.

Effects:
1)   For each £5,000 saving against target, seller's profit increases by £1,000, e.g. at £90,000 cost he earns £7,000 profit.
2)   All costs above £117,000 result in a loss.

6

Key features

① Introduction

In this chapter a close look will be taken at some of the key features that are expressed or implied in a typical contract.

② Possession, ownership and risk

2.1. Definitions

Possession, ownership and risk of loss or damage to the goods are bound up together. Let us consider the definitions:

a) **Possession** is concerned with the physical location of the goods. Does the buyer or seller or a third party actually hold the goods?

b) **Ownership**, in legal terms, is known as property (as in 'the property in the goods vests in X') or title (as in 'X has title to the goods'). Property and title can have different meanings but for these purposes it is adequate to consider them as having the same meaning.

c) **Risk** is concerned with who is liable for loss or damage to the goods. It is worth mentioning the distinction between liability and responsibility. If the goods are stolen the seller might be liable to the customer for their replacement albeit that the thief was responsible for the loss.

Before developing the relationship between possession, ownership and risk it is necessary to explain two important background principles. Firstly, it is not possible to sell things that do not belong to you unless you are acting as agent for the owner. Thus a 'buyer' of stolen property gains no ownership of the goods as the 'contract' of sale is not enforceable. Secondly, it is also presumed that the seller is entirely free to sell the goods. The innocent buyer will not be aware of the existence or details of any other contract that the seller holds, any of which may entitle another customer to have a legal claim on the seller's property which could include the goods that the buyer believes are for him. So for the purposes of this discussion it is assumed that the seller owns the goods he intends to sell and that there is no legal encumbrance to prevent him from so doing.

2.2. Delivery

It might be thought that the definitions given above should have included a definition of delivery. Unfortunately it is not possible to come up with a general definition. Commonly, delivery is concerned with:

a) The timing of the goods being available to pass into the buyer's possession.

b) The place where the buyer will take possession.

c) Any necessary paperwork.

It would be pleasantly simple to define delivery as the event by which the buyer concurrently takes possession, acquires ownership and accepts liability for loss or damage. However, very frequently these three events do not happen concurrently.

The Sale of Goods Act 1979 recognises this situation where it says that:

> 'Unless otherwise agreed, the goods remain at the seller's risk until the property in them is transferred to the buyer, but when the property is then transferred to the buyer the goods are at the buyer's risk whether delivery has been made or not.'

2.3. Acceptance and rejection

There is one other factor to consider in this subject and that is acceptance/rejection. There is a point when the buyer, whether by his actions or by compliance with a requirement of the contract, must have accepted that the goods are what he wanted and that his right to reject the goods for not being what he wanted has disappeared. In practice, 'what he wanted' means that for which he contracted and the two may not be synonymous. In practice, the period available to the buyer to reject goods can be a specific number of days or weeks or, if none is specified, then a reasonable time having regard to all the circumstances. If the contract includes detailed arrangements and procedures for the goods to be accepted then there can be no right of rejection once the acceptance procedures are satisfactorily completed.

2.4. Buyer and seller

As regards ownership and risk the positions of the buyer and seller are diametrically opposed. The buyer will want to acquire ownership as early as possible and risk as late as possible. Generally the seller will wish to retain ownership until the last possible moment but to pass the risk to the buyer as quickly as possible. There are two general observations that can be made:

a) Ownership will pass to the buyer when payment is made. Thus if payment is made on physical delivery, ownership passes on delivery. It is, however, open to the parties to agree that ownership can pass at different times. For example, if the buyer makes advance or stage payments prior to deliveries being made, the ownership can pass prior to delivery. If payment is due on delivery but in practice is delayed because some other procedural aspect of the contract has not been satisfied – perhaps where payments are made once a month only on a predetermined day – then ownership may nevertheless pass on delivery. Thus the aim is to have ownership pass on delivery but in practice regard will be had to the timing of payment. Again, the principle is that delivery does not have to be concurrent with the buyer taking physical possession. Deliveries can be made on a 'self-to-self' basis with ownership passing to the buyer but the goods remaining with the seller to hold for collection or perhaps to utilise on some other contract with the buyer – embodiment into other goods for example.

b) Risk will pass when the parties agree. Trading practices exist on which the parties may rely. For example, contracts may be 'ex-works', 'Free on Board (FOB)', 'Cost Insurance Freight (CIF)' which have generally accepted meanings, of which more later. Clearly again the question of possession is important but not invariably so. The party with possession may be best placed to take care of the goods and therefore to assume liability for loss or damage. However, if the buyer rejects the goods after taking possession he may not wish to carry this liability as the goods are no longer of any interest to him. Similarly, if the goods are found to be defective and the seller is liable under warranty, the buyer may not acknowledge a contractual liability to take the risk of further loss or damage.

2.5. Delivery terms

The consideration of possession, ownership, risk, rejection, acceptance, and warranty can be seen in Figure 6.1. As far as delivery is concerned, the point at which risk passes depends on the type of contract. The types range from 'ex-works' where the responsibility of the seller is limited to making the goods available at his premises for collection by the buyer to 'delivered duty paid' where the seller is responsible for delivering the goods overseas to the ultimate destination with all costs and duties paid by the seller (but included in the selling price, of course). The former type is minimum risk to the seller and maximum risk to the buyer, these positions being reversed in the latter type. The full range of contract types is illustrated in Figure 6.2. Where the buyer or seller employs a third party as carrier, the risk between buyer and seller does not change.

The employer of the carrier will no doubt contract with the carrier on the basis that the risk is transferred to the carrier whilst the goods are in transit. However in, say, a CIF contract where the seller engages a carrier, the buyer will hold the seller responsible for loss or damage albeit that the seller may take action against the carrier.

Figure 6.1

	Manufacture	Delivery	Period of rejection	Period of warranty
Possession	Buyer	Buyer	Buyer until rejected	Buyer until defective goods returned to seller
Ownership	Seller (but buyer if interim payments made)	Buyer	Buyer (or seller if the contract permits)	Buyer – if goods are to be replaced ownership may revert to seller
Risk	Seller (even if prior payments made)	Depends on contract type (see Figure 6.2)	Buyer (or seller if the contract permits)	Buyer – if goods are to be replaced risk may revert to seller

Figure 6.2: Passing of risk

	Risk assumed by buyer at	Seller risk	Buyer risk
Ex-Words	Seller's premises	Minimum	Maximum
Free Carrier (named Port)	Carrier taking custody		
FOR/FOT (Free on Rail/Free on Truck)	Carrier taking custody		
FOB/Airport (Free on Board/Airport)	Carrier taking custody		
FAS (Free Along Side)	Goods placed on quay		
C&F (Cost and Freight)	Goods pass ship's rail		
CIF (Cost, Insurance and Freight)	Goods pass ship's rail		
Freight Carriage Paid to	Carrier taking custody		
Freight Carriage Insurance	Carrier taking custody		
Ex Ship	On board at destination		
Ex Quay	On quay at destination		
Delivered at Frontier	Frontier at country of destination		
Delivered Duty Paid	At ultimate destination	Maximum	Minimum

2.6. Documentation

One practical issue of the utmost importance is the paperwork associated with effecting delivery. Many deliveries are effected by a system of 'advice and inspection' notes. These may comprise a delivery note and certificate of conformance. The delivery note must be in strict accordance with the contract. If the delivery is 10 off Widget Mk 3 then the delivery note must not, for example, refer to Widget Mk 2 unless the customer has confirmed that MK2s are acceptable, in which event the contract should be amended accordingly. Similarly so with the certificate of conformance: whether this is a document to be signed solely by the seller or countersigned by the buyer the point remains that it is a certificate to the effect that the delivery being offered is strictly in accordance with the contract.

3 Defects after delivery

3.1. Introduction

At the point of delivery legal entitlement to the goods passes from the seller to the buyer. The seller ideally would like this to be the absolute end of responsibility. The contract has been performed, the goods are off his site and the customer has taken delivery. On delivery the supplier will usually 'take' his profit; this is an accounting convention that says the risk to the seller has disappeared and therefore it is safe to take the profit – into his books. Further work will simply erode the profit margin. Nevertheless the buyer is entitled to expect the goods will work satisfactorily for a reasonable period of time and that any defects found after delivery will be put right at the supplier's cost. The buyer's rights in this regard can be established in several ways, the principles of which are:

a) By including in the contract a specific condition relating to liability for defects found after delivery. This is known as express warranty.

b) By relying on the implied undertakings provided by the Sale of Goods Act.

3.2. Express warranty

In principle the buyer will want the supplier to carry unlimited, unbounded and unending liability to correct defects. The seller will naturally wish to limit his warranty obligation and to minimise the cost of corrective action. This he will pursue on five fronts:

a) A warranty period.

b) Limitation on what is covered by the warranty.

c) Limitation on the circumstances in which a defect counts as a warranty claim.

d) Actions the buyer must take on discovering the defect.

e) Limitations on the actions that the seller must take to correct the fault.

a) The warranty period. There are two key issues relating to the warranty period: one is the length of the warranty period and the other is the start point. The length of the period is highly variable and appears mostly to depend on custom and practice in the particular trade or sector of industry. The seller may offer his 'standard' warranty period or the buyer may wish to specify a period depending on his unique needs. It is nowadays common to have three-year warranties on household electrical goods and up to five years on motor vehicle bodywork where once 12 months would have been normal. The warranty period can be a powerful selling or marketing point as it not only gives protection to the customer but also gives him reassurance (and therefore encouragement to buy) that the product is safe and reliable. The start date for the warranty can be set at a number of points, eg:

    a) The time of physical delivery to the customer.

    b) The time of final acceptance by the customer.

    c) The time at which the customer takes the goods into use.

The time of physical delivery invites consideration of when and how that takes place. If the contract is for 50,000 widgets then most sensibly the warranty applies to each widget and the period for each starts on physical delivery of each. Thus a two-year warranty applying to 5,000 widgets to be delivered over three years will leave the seller with the cost of the warranty repairs potentially for five years. On the other hand, if the contract is for 3 mega widgets perhaps it is more relevant to commence the warranty on delivery of the final unit.

Physical delivery is one thing but there may be a delay before the customer takes the goods into use. Clearly the supplier would like the clock to start ticking on physical delivery, the buyer when he starts to use the equipment. A compromise here would be to agree that the warranty is two years commencing from delivery or 12 months from the date of taking into use, whichever period expires sooner. The final situation is one in which there are extensive contract acceptance or handover procedures. This may be where the nature of the goods – perhaps a power station or battlefield communications network – cannot be fully tested and stressed by the supplier before delivery. In that event the warranty should commence at the end of the acceptance or handover phase. This leaves the supplier with the problem of beginning his warranty period possibly well after the goods have actually been taken into use.

    b) Limitation of coverage. The limitation on what the warranty covers can be defined in several ways:

    a) By warranting the design.

    b) By warranting the product but only insofar as defective materials and/or workmanship are concerned.

The customer, of course, will not wish to see the warranty limited in these ways: he is only concerned as to whether the goods work or not. If not, the customer is not on the face of it interested in whether design or the materials or the workmanship was at fault. In practice this could be of paramount interest to the customer. Defective workmanship may mean only one unit is faulty, defective materials may mean that an entire batch is faulty and defective design may mean that all past production is faulty. Car manufacturers buying brake components from component suppliers will be keenly concerned as their warranty obligations to the end customer – the car buyer – may be to rectify the car, incurring labour and material costs, where perhaps only the liability for material costs can be passed back to the component supplier.

c) Limitation of circumstances. Limitation of the circumstances in which defects count as a warranty can be achieved by excluding defects such as the following:

a) Those caused by incorrect storage, operation or maintenance.

b) Those caused by fair wear and tear.

c) Those not notified promptly to the supplier.

d) The buyer's unauthorised modifications.

Earlier in the text the point of commencement of warranty was discussed. In some circumstances the customer may take delivery well before putting the article into use. If the goods are not stored properly during this period and defects are thereby induced then it would be unfair to expect the supplier to accept warranty liability for those defects, always provided that the supplier made available adequate storage instructions assuming that he knew that the customer would delay taking the goods into use. Incorrect operation could similarly excuse the seller from liability, again provided that the goods had been supplied with adequate operating instructions.

There is a grey area here insofar as reasonable behaviour is concerned. Even if the operating instructions for a domestic stereo system do not specifically say that the equipment should not be dropped onto concrete from a height of 6ft, a defect arising from being dropped could not reasonably be a warranty claim. On the other hand if switching the power on with the volume control set at maximum causes damage to the speakers, is it reasonable for the owner to call this a warranty defect if the instructions did not warn against this hazard? Possibly. The message really is that operating instructions must be as comprehensive as possible, although this may have some other disadvantage if, for example, customers do not find lengthy operating instructions attractive.

Similar concepts apply as regards maintenance. Some products (motor vehicles for example) carry warranties that are invalidated if maintenance is not carried out by an authorised agent in accordance with the service schedules. Some domestic electrical goods warranties are invalidated if the customer so much as takes the back off. Where the customer is permitted to carry out his own maintenance, instructions will need to be comprehensive and may need to go so far as to specify the qualifications or skills of the maintenance engineer and the equipment and facilities that need to be used for maintenance.

It may be necessary also to exclude fair wear and tear from warranty. This could include such things as components or modules where the technical performance is such that failures are predicted after certain running times ('Mean Time Between Failure'). Provided these are accepted by the customer as a limitation of the equipment's performance, then they could be deemed not to be within the scope of warranty.

As a matter of fairness the buyer ought to promptly bring to the attention of the supplier defects as they arise. Clearly it is unreasonable for a buyer to notify defects 12 months after they have occurred. What is a reasonable period of notice is somewhat difficult to decide. A major factor will be the nature of the goods. At the end of the day it will be a matter for negotiation. The supplier may want immediate notice; this may not be practicable or acceptable to the customer.

finally, the supplier will not usually accept any warranty liability if the buyer makes modifications to the goods. This means that the warranty condition becomes invalid whether or not the defect was caused by the unauthorised modification.

d) Obligations on the buyer. To minimise the seller's exposure he may wish to impose obligations on the buyer to mitigate the effect of any defects arising. This could be limited to the effect that the buyer must mitigate effects or comply with specific instructions set out in operating instructions or given by the supplier at the time he is notified of the defect.

The mitigating actions could range from undertaking some minor engineering process to ceasing operation of the equipment. In some cases – such as a television catching fire – the customer is not going to carry on using the equipment. However, a defect (not causing total failure) to a Tornado radar is most unlikely to cause the RAF to cease flying the aircraft or using its radar. The buyer may seek to negotiate with the supplier the acceptance of liability not only to remedy warranty defects but to reimburse the buyer for the extra costs that may arise from being deprived of the use of the goods.

To summarise: there may be limitations on the period of coverage of the warranty, the circumstances in which the warranty can apply and the obligations that can be placed on the buyer to mitigate the effect of defects.

e) Obligations on the seller. The question then arises as to any limitation on the actions that the supplier is obliged to take to correct the defect. The buyer will wish to have the option to decide whether:

a) The defective item should be repaired, modified or replaced.

b) The remedial action should be undertaken on site or by return to the supplier.

c) On-site remedial action should be undertaken by the buyer or seller.

These are undoubtedly the decisions to be made and not unnaturally the supplier will wish to reserve the decision-making responsibility to himself. If he can succeed in this then he may wish to go one step further and state that the nature of the remedial action will be his to determine. For example, a design defect on a printed circuit board may be capable of correction by a 'cut and strap' modification. The customer may prefer a new board with re-designed artwork.

Warranty of repaired/replaced items: the general rule is that repaired/replaced items benefit only from the unexpired period of the original warranty. It is open to the customer to negotiate something different but the supplier will do his best to avoid full warranty applying from the date of repair/replacement as this could be a completely unlimited obligation.

Recovery of the costs for warranty repair/replacements will be within the selling price of the goods. For a standard product sold with a standard warranty the supplier will monitor the type, frequency and cost of repair/replacement and build a suitable allowance into his selling price. Where the product is non-standard, ie developed or tailored to the customer's particular requirements, the selling price will still include an allowance for warranty.

In negotiating the warranty condition the customer will have regard to the direct link between the terms of the warranty and the

Figure 6.3: Express warranty

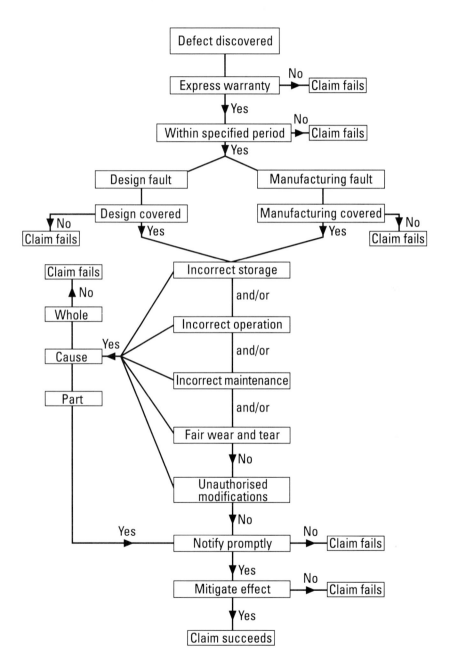

cost that will be built into the price. One way of describing this process by which the customer pays for his warranty benefits would be to say that it is a form of insurance policy. For a fixed sum of money (within the product price) the customer passes the risk of correcting failures for a period of time back to the supplier.

A possible flow diagram of an express warranty claim is shown in Figure 6.3.

3.3. Implied undertakings

Whether or not an express warranty is provided by the supplier and therefore allowed for in the price or paid for specifically as an 'extra' by a customer with particular requirements, the law nevertheless provides some protection as regards the quality of the goods. The 1979 Sale of Goods Act provides the buyer with the right to goods that are of merchantable quality and that are fit for the purpose. These rights only apply to the sale of goods within the meaning of the Act. Thus the Act may not apply to, for example:

a) Contracts of exchange.
b) Gifts.
c) Hire purchase.
d) Contracts for skill and labour.
e) Contracts for labour and materials.
f) Agencies.

Also the obligation relating to merchantable quality does not apply:

a) As regards defects specifically drawn to the buyer's attention before the contract is made.

b) If the buyer examines the goods before the contract is made, as regards defects which that examination ought to have revealed.

Certain aspects of the Sale of Goods Act were specifically drafted to protect the consumer. The consumer may – wittingly or unwittingly – rely on the Act as regards merchantability and fitness for purpose. However, as was seen in Chapter 3, in non-consumer contracts it is open to the parties to agree that these provisions of the Act do not apply to the particular transaction. Thus in a non-consumer contract where the buyer wishes to have an express warranty, the seller may offer this on the basis that it is in lieu of any and all implied warranties. In this buyer and seller are in opposed positions. The seller argues for clarity based on a precisely worded express warranty to the exclusion of all else. The buyer wants as many remedies as he can possibly get, comprising of both express provisions and implied undertakings.

4 Cancellation for convenience

In Chapter 3 some situations under which a contract is void or voidable were discussed. Repudiation, termination and recision were covered. These topics cover the situations in which a contract does not exist, could not be enforced or where a premature end comes about through the default of one of the parties (usually the seller). The one other scenario not mentioned so far is where the contract is valid, performance is proceeding but one side – almost always the buyer – wishes to discontinue the contract. Hence the idea of cancellation for convenience.

There is no common or statute law right to cancel for convenience: it can only be provided by a specific condition in the contract. As with cancellation for default the main interest lies in the buyer's potential desire to cancel. The seller's needs are to sell goods to make a profit and it is generally presumed that the seller would not wish to cancel for convenience. This is not impossible, of course, where, for example, the seller finds an alternative customer for the same goods but at a higher price. In these circumstances the seller might in practice try to negotiate a later delivery with the first buyer. In any event it is most unlikely that the buyer would give up his right to the goods for the convenience of the seller. Therefore it is far more likely that the buyer will require the right to cancel for convenience as his specific need may disappear.

Where the two parties agree to a cancellation for convenience clause a period of notice will usually be included. The seller may attempt to negotiate that only the balance (ie as at the time of notification of cancellation) may be cancelled and that payments must be made for work done. The seller will also be looking for recompense for loss of anticipated profits on the cancelled contract or part contract.

5 Customer-furnished equipment/data

Frequently the successful performance of the contract will require the customer to provide the seller with equipment and or information. Equipment may be required under three main arrangements:

a) Embodiment loan: As the name suggests this would be where the customer provides equipment for the seller to embody in the goods during manufacture. This could arise where the customer, for a variety of reasons, is able to buy component parts or subassemblies more cheaply than the seller, or where the seller is unable to buy the component parts.

b) Contract loan: The concept here is that items are loaned for whatever purpose is the actual subject of the contract. For example, in repair contract the customer's items for repair are known as contract loan items.

c) Ordinary loan: This would apply where, say, the customer loans the seller items of special test equipment or equipment into which the goods will ultimately interface so that the seller may test the interface before delivery.

These definitions are not universally used but they serve to illustrate the principles involved.

Whether the seller needs loan equipment or technical data from the buyer there are some common ground rules. In both cases:

a) The seller should advise the buyer as soon as possible of his needs.

b) The requirements should be specified as precisely as possible. Equipment should be defined in part number, specification, description or other unique identification. Data should be identified by description, format and medium (paper, tape, disc, etc).

c) The latest dates by which the equipment/data is required by the seller should be agreed.

d) Late, defective or incomplete provision of the equipment or data should be agreed as allowing the seller the right to a price change and/or change to the period of performance if these are consequent upon the late, defective, or incomplete provision.

It should be remembered that customer-furnished equipment will remain the property of the buyer whilst in the seller's possession albeit that risk of loss or damage will be the seller's liability until the equipment has been returned to the buyer. The other key aspect insofar as customer-furnished data is concerned is to ensure that the customer provides the seller with the right to copy and use the data for the purposes of the contract. If the data does not belong to the buyer he cannot give this right and in this event the seller will expect the buyer to indemnify him against third party claims of infringement of copyright or other intellectual property right.

Having specified the necessary customer-furnished equipment and data, having received it accordingly and checked it for damage or deficiencies, the supplier is then contractually bound to perform the contract. That is, if goods ultimately delivered to the customer fail, the fact that customer-furnished equipment or data was utilised will not be a permissible excuse.

As a matter of good practice, requirements for customer-furnished equipment or data will be drawn up into a schedule and included as part of the contract documents to facilitate change and control. The schedule will be accompanied by a contract condition placing the obligation on the buyer to supply the equipment and data.

Case study II in Appendix 3 shows the muddle that can arise if some of the foregoing issues are not covered clearly.

Payment

The four elements to payment are:
1) The customer's obligation to pay.
2) Establishing that payment is due.
3) The mechanism for invoicing.
4) Timing.

In this section some of the practical issues concerned with these four aspects are examined.

6.1. Obligation to pay

As a matter of law the customer is obliged to pay provided that the seller has performed his obligations under the contract. Given that the customer is obliged to pay, the question is what does he have to pay? Payment will be the price of the goods or an element of the price if the payment is interim, ie made before contract performance is complete. The contract will specify the currency or currencies of payment. Even in the UK payment may be in mixed currencies if a significant proportion of the work is subcontracted overseas. If the seller has to pay the overseas supplier in local currency then the seller will prefer the buyer to pay him in that currency for that part of the work.

This moves the exchange rate variation risk from the seller to the buyer. The buyer may be quite content to adopt this arrangement if he is able to buy the particular currency more cheaply than the seller or if to do otherwise is to accept a higher price from the seller as the seller builds into his price a contingency to cover the exchange variation risk.

The contract must also specify the applicable taxes and other charges that the buyer is obliged to pay. For example, payments may include VAT, import duty, carriage and insurance charges.

If the contract allows interim payments these will generally be on the basis of a regular reimbursement of costs actually incurred or payments of specified sums or specified percentages of the contract price. In the latter case the sums are payable on completion of predetermined stages of the work. The two approaches can be combined. For example, a contract of long duration in which it is not possible to define concrete stages for the early part of the work may permit regular cost reimbursement (progress payments) until the work becomes susceptible to stage definition.

The stage of milestones for a contract for development and supply of the Mark 200 Widget might, for example, comprise:

Stage	Milestone definition	% of price	Cumulative
1	Performance specifications	5%	5%
2	Final design review	5%	10%
3	Production drawings	10%	20%
4	Materials	5%	25%
5	10% Subassemblies	30%	55%
6	90% Final test	20%	75%
7	1st delivery	20%	95%
8	Final delivery	5%	100%

In practice the definition of these milestones must be spelt out in full so that there is certainty as to what the achievement of the milestone actually means. The seller will try to make the milestone definitions as soft as possible; the buyer as hard as possible. For example, the seller would propose that Milestone 1 is defined as issue of the performance specification; the buyer would argue for acceptance of the performance specification. Milestone 2 would be defined by the seller as the occurrence of the final design review. The buyer would look for something stronger such as acceptance by the buyer of the minutes of the final design review. The buyer would negotiate Milestone 8 as acceptance of the final delivery rather than just the physical event. In the extreme the buyer might wish to retain some payment until the expiry of any warranty period or the satisfactory repair of any warranty failures. As well as the respective aims of the buyer and seller it is as important to ensure that the definitions are sufficiently detailed. For example, Milestone 3 might be more fully defined as production drawings issued to the shop floor or approved by the quality manager.

The milestone scheme may also include a column to indicate the planned or forecast date for completion of each stage. It is important in these circumstances to refer to planned or forecast dates so as to avoid the possibility of a legitimate payment being withheld because, although the stage was achieved, the indicated date was not the date on which the event occurred.

Each stage may have more than one milestone associated with it and a separate payment. For example, a scheme might include the following stages:

Stage	Milestone	% of price
23	a) Drawing frozen	3%
	b) Tool setting completed	2%
	c) Components loaded	4%
24	a) Frames drilled	1%
	b) Corrosion treatment completed	2%
	c) Subassembly inspection completed	3%

The buyer ideally would like Stage 23 to describe drawings frozen, tool setting completed and components loaded before he is committed to pay anything for Stage 23. The seller will wish these to be and/or provisions so that even if one or more milestones in the stage are missed, there may nevertheless be some payment due. This is particularly so where there are constraints on the availability of payments, for example if payment under the contract will not be made more frequently than quarterly, or where it is not possible to plan in advance the exact timing or sequence of events. The more milestones and stages there are the better it is for the seller who can forecast receiving regular payments rather than risk all on one or two major milestones.

6.2. Payment due

The foregoing section has discussed the details that in practice describe the obligation to pay. From this the question of the point at which payment becomes due follows naturally. The four elements in this are:

1) What evidence is necessary to support a claim that payment is due?

2) Are there any time constraints on payment?

3) Are there other conditions of the contract that must first be satisfied in order for payment to be made?

4) Can the buyer withhold payments due?

The evidence necessary depends on the type of payment arrangements. If the contract provides for payment on delivery then the evidence is the appropriate delivery documentation signed by persons authorised in the contract. If progress payments are to be made, the evidence will be a certificate signed by the seller's accountant, finance manager or other authorised body to the effect that the costs claimed have actually been reasonably and properly incurred.

Where the contract is subject to stage payments then documentation must be produced as evidence that stages claimed have been completed. These stage completion certificates may be acceptable evidence if signed by an authorised officer of the seller or the buyer may wish himself to physically verify that the stage is complete. In the latter case the buyer may seek to avoid a stage scheme with too many milestones because of any inconvenience in verification.

There may be some time constraints on payment becoming due. If the buyer's own availability of funds is limited he will wish to include in the contract provisions to limit his actual expenditure to pre-set sums being available not earlier than pre-set dates, regardless of achievements under the stage payment scheme. He may include, for example, in the contract words to the effect that 'in any event payments shall not be made in advance of the following schedule:

£ 50,000 in Year 1
£150,000 in Year 2
£ 75,000 in Year 3'.

The second possible constraint on timing of payment is the

likelihood of the buyer reserving himself time in which to make payment even when a delivery or milestone stage is complete and an invoice submitted. This is quite legitimate insofar as the buyer must quite reasonably be permitted the time and opportunity to verify that all is in order prior to making payment. In practice the period can be quite long – 90 days is not unusual – and the length of the period is almost entirely a function of the respective bargaining positions and strengths of the two parties.

In practice the contract may also impose other preconditions for payment to the seller. For example, the buyer, if he is not the end-user, may say that he cannot pay until he has been paid by the customer. To the seller this is most unreasonable as he sees only the contract between himself and his buyer and the buyer's other affairs are of no concern to him. The buyer, on the other hand, has only placed the contract to help him satisfy his customer's requirements. The usual compromise is to line up the seller's claims for payment with the buyer's claims from his customer and to agree a long-stop whereby if the buyer does not receive payment from the customer through no fault of the seller, then the buyer will in any event pay the seller after the expiry of, say, 60 days.

The buyer may, in any event, have discretionary or prescribed powers to withhold payment, or indeed to recover payments already made. He may wish to possess the power to make interim payments at his sole discretion or to have the right to withhold or recover payments for any default or deficiency on the part of the seller or if, in his opinion, the seller is not making positive progress with the work. Unless he is in a superior bargaining position there is little the seller can do to resist the buyer's objectives in this regard although he may be able to secure agreement that there must be a period of notice before the buyer's powers to withhold or recover payments can be implemented and that he be given a reasonable opportunity to cure whatever is the problem.

6.3. Mechanism for invoicing

Having established that the buyer is obliged to pay and that payment is due it is equally important to ensure that there is a clear understanding of the mechanism for payment. Armed with what-ever evidence of payment due is necessary, the seller must be sure that his paperwork for invoicing is correct and in line with the contract. Errors in the customer's name and address or contract number or in the details of the stage or milestone or delivery for which payment is claimed can lead to the invoice being rejected. The bill must therefore be resubmitted which risks further delay in payment being made. The invoice must be correct in all its details; currency, VAT amount and VAT registration number are other potential areas for error.

6.4. Timing

From the foregoing and Figure 6.4 it can be seen that payments are subject to:

a) Making progress with the work according to any time plan.

b) Producing the right evidence of payment due.

c) Any funding availability restraints on the customer.

d) The customer's rights to delay payments for a period of time.

e) The customer's rights to withhold or recover payments.

f) Invoice rejection on the grounds of error or incompleteness.

Against this background the seller must make his predictions of cash intake so that he can make his arrangements accordingly in terms of his payments to employees and subcontractors and other disbursements.

If the seller has agreed quarterly stage payments with the customer, having the right to delay payment can cause great problems if employees are weekly or monthly paid and his own suppliers must be paid. Clearly he must negotiate the optimum payment terms with the customer and suppliers to ensure a stable and safe position.

⑦ Timeliness of performance

A general rule which the prudent businessperson – and certainly the contract administrator – should observe is that it should be taken that a contract which stipulates a time for delivery or performance is making timeliness a fundamental condition of the contract. Therefore failure to complete on time will allow the buyer to summarily terminate or rescind the contract.

If the contract is not clear or is ambiguous as to time then whether time is fundamental will depend upon the construction of

Figure 6.4: Payment

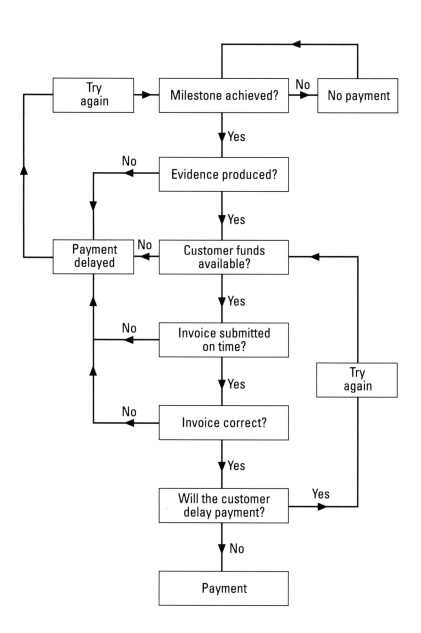

the contract and the apparent intention of the parties.

It is sometimes argued that unless the contract includes a 'time is of the essence' statement then it is not of the essence. This is an unreliable and dangerous assumption. It is safe to say that if 'of the essence' is included then time is a fundamental condition. If the statement is absent but the contract is clear as to when performance is required then it is also safe to say that it is fundamental. Vague expressions such as 'delivery to be as soon as possible', whilst conveying some feeling of urgency, could not be construed as declaring timeliness to be fundamental. After all it must be readily apparent from the contract at what point delivery is actually late otherwise how could timeliness be important?

A most important doctrine to bear in mind is that of 'waiver'. If the buyer does not act quickly to exercise his rights when his supplier is late then he is deemed to have waived his entitlement to timely delivery and hence his rights will expire. Even where the buyer immediately notifies the supplier of lateness and reserves his rights, this does not necessarily avoid the waiver rule.

Where timeliness of performance is a fundamental requirement there is an implication that lateness will cause the buyer damage. To save both sides the time and cost of legal action, rather than pursue rights to damages through the courts it is more constructive for the buyer and seller to agree in advance the likely level of damage that the buyer will suffer and make a contract provision for the monetary sum to be paid by the seller to the buyer in the event of lateness. This arrangement is known as liquidated damages. It is convenient to remember a handful of rules regarding liquidated damages:

a) The amount must be a genuine pre-estimate of the damages.

b) Any other sum would be construed as a penalty and not be enforceable.

c) If the same sum were to be payable against different events of obvious varying importance then again the arrangement would be seen as a penalty.

d) Entitling the contract provision 'liquidated damages' does not of itself suffice if the sum or construction appears to be of a penalty nature.

e) Once the contract is agreed the liquidated damages are

payable in the event of lateness whether or not the buyer is actually suffering any damage.

Despite the legal theory, many commercial contracts contain liquidated damages and they tend to be treated as a penalty for late performance or, to put it another way, as an incentive to early delivery. The legal theory is sound but often set aside in practice. Although the perception is therefore that liquidated damages are only used as a penalty, there is an advantage to the supplier in that he is limiting his liability for damages in the event of delay where otherwise he would be exposed to an unlimited claim for damages. Similarly the buyer should not always see imposing liquidated damages on his supplier as something of a victory as he is limiting his ability to claim against the supplier in the event that delay really did cause him substantial damages.

It is sometimes supposed that where the supplier is in breach the best remedy would be to apply to a court for a decree of specific performance. This simple concept is unlikely to be a helpful remedy in practice:

a) The supplier may simply not be able to perform so a decree of specific performance will get the buyer no closer to acquiring the goods.

b) Only a court can issue a decree.

c) The buyer cannot demand a decree as the courts will only issue one where damages would be inadequate.

d) A decree would not be issued if compliance were to necessitate constant court supervision.

So in many ways liquidated damages are a convenient and helpful device.

Typical liquidated damages would in essence provide for a sum of £X to be paid in respect of each day of delay up to a maximum of £Y or a certain percentage of the contract price. The points to bear in mind are:

a) Start date   – Be absolutely precise about the starting point for accrual of LDs.

b) Period of grace – It is usually reasonable to allow a period of grace between the due date for performance and the start date for LDs. Logically this is sensible in any event as it is unlikely that damage

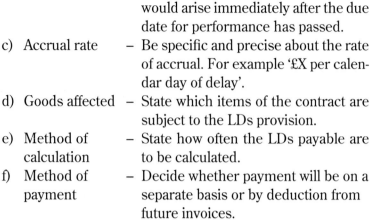

		would arise immediately after the due date for performance has passed.
c)	Accrual rate	– Be specific and precise about the rate of accrual. For example '£X per calendar day of delay'.
d)	Goods affected	– State which items of the contract are subject to the LDs provision.
e)	Method of calculation	– State how often the LDs payable are to be calculated.
f)	Method of payment	– Decide whether payment will be on a separate basis or by deduction from future invoices.
g)	Maximum liability	– Agree an overall limiting amount. The seller should aim to have this expressed as his sole and maximum liability for delay.
h)	Suspension of rights	– The seller should aim to have it expressly recorded that the buyer will not terminate for default during the period of operation of LDs.
i)	Force Majeure	– The seller should argue for an express provision for Force Majeure or Excusable Delays.
j)	Full and final settlement	– The seller should argue for payment of LDs to be in full and final settlement of all liability for delay.

In (h) – (j) the seller's position is made clear. The buyer conversely would aim to avoid undertakings so that the seller carries the greater risk and liability.

Going beyond the question of a simple delay in contract performance is the idea of the contract becoming impossible to perform. If it is genuinely the case that events occurred subsequent to the contract which rendered performance literally impossible then the contract can be dissolved on grounds of frustration. However, for this to apply the contract must not have made provision for the intervening event and the frustrating event must not be self-induced. A seller cannot look to frustration for relief if the work of the contract simply proved more difficult or costly than he had expected.

7

⬤ ⬤ ⬤ ⬤ ⬤ ⬤ ⬤ **C** **H** **A** **P** **T** **E** **R** ⬤ ⬤

Intellectual Property: an introduction

① Introduction

Intellectual Property (IP) and Intellectual Property Rights (IPR) are topics which cause people to feel uneasy. This is a complex subject area, especially when international dimensions are considered. Many larger companies have their own IP departments staffed by qualified patent attorneys and other legal staff. Other companies buy in specialist support.

Yet in business almost everything that a company employee touches has a connection with IP. Although IP is intangible (as compared with the tangible property a company has such as machinery), it is nevertheless one of the most important assets that a company possesses. Put simply:

> 'Today's ideas, know-how and skills are
> tomorrow's order, profit and security.'

Thus it could be said that it is almost a duty of every employee to grasp something of the basic principles of IP so that the company's future is held securely.

Intellectual Property, sometimes referred to as Industrial Property, could be defined as the intangible property created through the application of the intellect to technical or commercial matters. Since it is a form of property it has an owner or proprietor and has some value. The property is intangible since, although the documents representing the various forms of IP are tangible, the intellectual content is of an intangible nature.

More simply, IP could be described as the ideas, inventions, designs, know-how and reputation which belong to a particular company. IPR are the rights arising from contract, law or statute that entitle the owner of the property to protect and exploit it.

More and more the importance and value of IP and the need to protect and exploit it is being driven home to companies as they have to keep pace with advancements in technology and stay ahead of their competitors.

The commercial value of IP can be realised in basically four ways:

a) By selling a product which has been made by virtue of the IP – which may be a unique design or a unique manufacturing process or both.

b) By outright sale of the IP. In selling an idea, just as in selling a product, the seller has transferred all legal rights to the buyer who may do with the idea whatever he wishes.

c) By permitting use by others of the IP in return for some payment. This is known as licensing. Unlike a sale the licensor retains ownership and rights in the property and can exercise control over the use to which the licensee puts the property. Clearly the advantage to the licensee is that by acquiring IP he acquires the ability to enter new technology or geographic markets. This may be an extremely attractive alternative to carrying out his own research and development which may be prohibitively expensive and carries the risk of failure either to complete the development at all or to complete it in time to enter the particular market. On the other hand, the licensor has the opportunity to indirectly enter markets which hitherto had been closed to him, perhaps because of export or import restrictions. Alternatively the licensor may simply be seeking a continued income from designs which he may no longer wish to manufacture himself, for example where in his own territory the design is 'old technology' or where his own manufacturing facility has reached the end of its useful life.

The two parties to a licence might agree that the licensee will pay the licensor either a royalty based on the value of sales made or a fee not linked directly to the potential value of the licence, or both.

The advantage of a royalty is a potentially continuing source of income for the licensor but with the risk that no sales will be made. A simple fee only gives the licensee the risk of not achieving sufficient sales to recover the cost of the fee, but on the other hand once he has broken even he has no further payment to make to the licensor. A fee and royalties tend to be used where there is a transfer of technology.

d)   By the enhancement of a product selling price arising from reputation/goodwill. The current trend in 'designer' clothes is an example of this. It has always been the case that 'certain names' will sell better and at a higher price than others, but more and more designers and manufacturers are realising the importance of this aspect of IP.

The purpose in this chapter is to give:
a)   An introduction to the concepts.
b)   Advice on those aspects of IP which come within the ambit of contract administrators.

(2) The concepts

One way of grasping the significant aspects of IP is to imagine the creation of the device called the wheel. The IP in this device might be as follows:

Patent: The invention of the wheel being a circular device revolving on an axle as the basis for a means of moving things.

Copyrights: Any drawings of the wheel.

Design: Blue rim/yellow spokes.

Trade mark: The 'Ride easy'.

Trade secret/know-how: The technique for balancing the wheel.

Goodwill: The reputation gained by the reliability of the wheel.

(3) Intellectual Property law

The principal source of UK law is the Copyright, Designs and Patents Act 1988. The Act was a major piece of statutory reform and is divided into seven parts:

PART I: Copyright: Repeats the 1956 Copyright Act and provides a fresh statement of the law.

PART II: Rights in Performance: Revises the old provisions for performer's protection.

PART III: Design Right: Introduces a new concept of the

protection of designs.

PART IV: Registered Designs: Amends the Registered Designs Act 1949.

PART V: Patent Agents and Trade Mark Agents: Reforms the law relating to patent and trade mark agents, in particular removing the monopoly of patent agents.

PART VI: Patents: Revises existing patent law to remove anomalies and provide for County Court Jurisdiction.

PART VII: Miscellaneous and General: Relates to the fraudulent reception of broadcasts and cable programmes, fraudulent use of trade marks and provides for financial assistance to the Community Trade Marks Office.

It is not the intention to explore this Act or other sources of IP law in detail. It is a subject worthy of further study by the contract administrator and further reading is recommended at the end of this chapter. The aim here is to provide a basic understanding of the principles. For this purpose the following has been reproduced from the Patent Office booklet 'What is Intellectual Property'.

WHAT IS A PATENT?
It is a monopoly right to the exclusive use of an invention and can last for a maximum of 20 years. A patent is a property which, like any other business commodity, may be bought, sold, hired or licensed.

ARE ALL INVENTIONS PATENTABLE?
No, broadly speaking, to be patentable an invention must be concerned with the composition, construction or manufacture of a substance, article or apparatus, or with an industrial type of process, as distinct from artistic creations, mathematical methods, business schemes or other purely mental acts. In addition, a few categories of invention are specifically excluded from patentability.

DO ANY FURTHER CONDITIONS HAVE TO BE SATISFIED?
Yes. An invention has to be new and not obvious to a person of ordinary skill experienced in the particular technology.

WHAT RIGHTS DO PATENTS BRING?
The exclusive right to use the invention or let others use it under terms agreed with the owner of the patent. Also the right to take legal action against others who might be infringing the invention and to claim damages. The mere existence of a patent may be enough to

deter a potential infringer.

HOW IS A UK PATENT OBTAINED?

The first stage is the FILING of a full disclosure of the invention. This should include everything that is needed to carry out the invention since no additional matter can be added later. Next, the Patent Office carries out a SEARCH to ascertain whether the invention is new and non-obvious. Then follows PUBLICATION of the application in the state it was when first filed. Thirdly there is an in-depth EXAMINA-TION to determine whether the application meets legal and formal requirements and is technically sound. If objections are raised by the Office, the applicant must overcome these before GRANT of a patent.

HOW LONG DOES IT TAKE?

As a rough guide, the SEARCH REPORT would be issued within about 3 months after request, PUBLICATION would be about 18 months after filing and FIRST EXAMINATION about 18 months after publication. GRANT follows after official objectives are met. All stages up to grant must be completed within 4.5 years of the first filing date.

WHAT WILL THE PATENT OFFICE CHARGE?

The Patent Office charges fees for processing applications, the principal ones being for filing, search and examination. To maintain a patent in force, renewal fees have to be paid annually from the beginning of the fifth year after filing. A full list of current patent fees can be obtained from the Patent Office.

ARE THERE ANY OTHER COSTS?

Applicants are strongly advised to obtain professional help and if a Patent Agent is used their professional fees will generally cost several hundred pounds at least.

IS THE TIMING OF AN APPLICATION IMPORTANT?

Yes, but it is difficult to lay down any hard and fast rules. Whilst early filing of an application can be vital since it establishes a 'priority' for the applicant over anyone else who subsequently files an application for the same invention, there can often be important commercial reasons for delaying filing until absolutely necessary.

DOES A UK PATENT GIVE PROTECTION ABROAD?

No. It has effect ONLY in the United Kingdom and the Isle of Man.

However, the filing date of a UK national application can be used as a 'priority' date for the subject matter disclosed in the application when applying up to 12 months later for protection abroad. To obtain protection abroad, it is necessary to file applications for those countries – either individually or through the Patent Co-operation Treaty. Also, under the European Patent Convention, patents in up to 13 European States can be obtained by filing a single European application. However, to comply with certain national security provisions UK residents MUST obtain clearance from the UK Patent Office before applying for a patent abroad.

CAN THE PATENT OFFICE HELP DEVELOP THE INVENTION?
No. The Patent Office cannot provide any financial or other support since this would directly conflict with its role as an impartial regulatory body for the granting of patents. But there are both local and national organisations throughout the UK which will assist in developing inventions with commercial potential.

CAN ANYONE BE TOLD ABOUT THE INVENTION?
It is vital not to disclose the invention to anyone or to make commercial use of it before an application is made since this could prevent the grant of a patent or could invalidate a granted patent. If disclosure is necessary, care should be taken to ensure it is in the strictest confidence.

CAN AN INVENTION BE EXPLOITED WITHOUT A PATENT?
Yes – provided no-one else already has rights protecting the invention or a part of it. Such exploitation would prevent anyone subsequently getting a valid patent for it, but would not prevent others from copying it.

DO PATENTS HAVE OTHER USES?
Certainly! The technical disclosure contained in published patent specifications provides an enormous amount of information which constitutes an invaluable database for research – patents are often the earliest and/or only disclosure of technical matter. Moreover, companies are increasingly using patents for commercial information, eg in market research.

HOW NECESSARY IS IT TO GET PROFESSIONAL HELP?
It is not strictly essential but the strength of a patent is affected by how well it has been drafted and since it is both a technical and a legal

document its drafting is a job for an expert. So the greater the potential commercial value of an invention, the more advisable it is to obtain professional help, for example from a Registered Patent Agent.

COPYRIGHT

WHAT IS COPYRIGHT?

Copyright gives rights to the creators of certain kinds of material, so that they can control the various ways in which their material may be exploited. The rights broadly cover copying, adapting, issuing copies to the public, performing in public and broadcasting the material. In many cases, the author will also have the right to be identified on his work and to object to distortions and mutilations of his work. Moreover, a rental right is given to owners of copyright in sound recordings, films and computer programs and therefore the exploitation of such works by renting them to the public requires a licence from the copyright owner.

WHAT KIND OF MATERIAL DOES COPYRIGHT PROTECT?

Copyright protects original literary, dramatic, musical and artistic works, published editions of works, sound recordings, films (including videograms) and broadcasts (including cable and satellite broadcasts).

WHAT ABOUT COMPUTER PROGRAMS AND MATERIAL STORED IN COMPUTERS?

Computer programs are protected on the same basis as literary works. Conversion of a program into or between computer languages and codes corresponds to 'adapting' a work and storing any work in a computer amounts to 'copying' the work. Also running a computer program or displaying a work on a VDU will usually involve copying and thus require the consent of the copyright owner.

DOES MATERIAL HAVE TO HAVE NOVELTY OR AESTHETIC VALUE TO GET COPYRIGHT PROTECTION?

No, it simply has to be the result of independent intellectual effort. Technical descriptions, catalogues and engineering drawings are all examples of material which qualifies for copyright protection whatever the subject matter.

IS REGISTRATION NECESSARY?
No. Copyright protection in this country is automatic and there is no registration system – so there are no forms to fill in and no fees to pay.

HOW LONG DOES UK COPYRIGHT LAST?
Copyright in a literary, dramatic, musical or artistic work (including a photograph) lasts until 50 years after the death of the author. This is the case for both published and unpublished works. Films, sound recordings and broadcasts are protected for 50 years, published editions for 25 years.

CAN COPYRIGHT PROTECT INDUSTRIAL ARTICLES?
No. Copyright may protect the drawing from which an article is made but copyright cannot be used to prevent the manufacture of articles.

IS PERMISSION ALWAYS NEEDED TO COPY OR PUBLICLY EXPLOIT COPYRIGHT MATERIAL?
No, there are certain exceptions to the rights given to the creator of the material. For example, limited use of works is allowed for research and private study, criticism or review, reporting current events, judicial proceedings and teaching in schools.

HOW DO I GET PERMISSION TO EXPLOIT COPYRIGHT MATERIAL?
Normally by approaching the copyright owner, but there are several organisations which act collectively for groups of copyright owners in respect of particular rights; they may offer 'blanket' licence to users.

DOES THE WORK HAVE TO BE MARKED IN ANY WAY TO CLAIM COPYRIGHT?
Although some countries require that a work be marked with the international © mark followed by the name of the copyright owner and year of publication, this is not essential in the UK. However, marking in this way may assist in infringement proceedings within the UK and will be needed in certain foreign countries.

HOW CAN ORIGINALITY BE PROVEN?
Ultimately this is a matter for the courts to decide. However, it may help a copyright owner to deposit a copy of his work with a bank or solicitor or send a copy of his work to himself by registered post, leaving the envelope unopened on its return; this will establish that

the work existed at this time.

WHO OWNS COPYRIGHT?

The general rule is that the author is the first owner of copyright in a literary, dramatic, musical or artistic work. The main exception is where such work is made in the course of employment, in which case the employer owns the copyright. The copyright in films, sound recordings, broadcasts and published editions belongs to the film or record producer, broadcaster or publisher.

WHAT CAN BE DONE IF THE WORK IS USED WITHOUT PERMISSION?

Although there is no obligation to do so, it will usually be sensible to try to resolve the matter with the party who has infringed the copyright. Otherwise redress in the courts can be sought where injunctions and damages are available. Legal advice may be needed.

ARE NAMES PROTECTED BY COPYRIGHT?

No. There is no copyright in a name or title.

ARE IDEAS PROTECTED BY COPYRIGHT?

No. Although the work itself may be protected, the idea behind it is not.

WILL THE MATERIAL BE PROTECTED OVERSEAS?

Usually, but not invariably. The UK is a member of several international conventions in this field, notably the Berne Convention for the Protection of Literary and Artistic Works and the Universal Copyright Convention (UCC). Copyright material created by UK nationals or residents is protected in each member country of the conventions by the national law of that country. Most countries belong to at least one of the conventions including all of the Western European countries, the USA and USSR. A full list of the Conventions and their members may be obtained from the DTI.

REGISTERED DESIGNS

WHAT IS A REGISTERED DESIGN?

It is a monopoly right for the outward appearance of an article or a set of articles of manufacture to which the design is applied. It lasts for an initial period of 5 years and may be extended in four 5-year terms up to a maximum of 25 years. It is additional to any design right or copyright protection which may exist automatically in the design.

A registered design is a property which, like any other business commodity, may be bought, sold, hired or licensed.

ARE ALL DESIGNS REGISTRABLE?
No. Where the aesthetic appearance of an article is not significant or where there is no design freedom because the design of the part is determined by the shape of the whole, then the design is not registrable. Thus purely functional designs are not eligible for registration because their aesthetic appearance is not important, nor can designs such as car body panels be registered because their shape and configuration are determined by the overall design of the car. In other words, registered design protection will only be available for truly aesthetic, stand-alone designs where competitors do not need to be able to copy such designs in order to compete.

There are also other specific exclusions for certain types of designs and these include works of sculpture, medals and printed matter primarily of a literary or artistic character such as bookjackets and calendars. In general, copyright protection is afforded to these excluded designs.

DO ANY FURTHER CONDITIONS HAVE TO BE SATISFIED?
Yes. A design has to be 'new', ie it must not have been publicly disclosed in the United Kingdom before application for registration is made nor registered on an earlier design application, and it must be materially different from any other published design for the same or any other type of article.

WHAT IS THE DIFFERENCE BETWEEN A PATENT AND A REGISTERED DESIGN?
A registered design applies to the outward appearance of an article – its 'eye-appeal' – whereas a patent is concerned with the function, operation, manufacture or material of construction of an article.

WHAT RIGHTS DO REGISTERED DESIGNS BRING?
The exclusive right in the United Kingdom and the Isle of Man to make, import, sell or hire out any article to which the design has been applied or to let others use the design under terms agreed with the registered owner. The owner also has the right to take legal action against an infringer and claim damages and, of course, the fact that the design is registered may be sufficient to deter a would-be infringer.

HOW IS A DESIGN REGISTERED IN THE UK?

The owner of the design must apply to the Designs Registry at the Patent Office, providing representation of the design, an application form and a filing fee. The Registry make a search, mainly through previously registered designs, to determine if the particular design is 'new'. If it is and formal requirements are also met, a Certificate of Registration is issued. Otherwise registration is refused, against which there is right of appeal.

CAN MODIFICATIONS BE REGISTERED?

Yes. Further application may be made either to register a modified version of a previously registered design, or to obtain further registration of a previously registered design so as to apply it to a different type of article to that covered by the original registration.

HOW LONG DOES REGISTRATION TAKE?

Registration should normally be completed within six months, although a total of twelve months (extendable to fifteen) is allowed for an application to be put in order.

WHAT WILL THE PATENT OFFICE CHARGE?

The Patent Office charges fees for processing applications, and in most cases this need only be the filing fee. If it is wished to keep the registration in force after the initial 5-year registration period, fees have to be paid for each succeeding 5-year term. A full list of current design fees can be obtained from the Designs Registry at the Patent Office.

IS TIMING OF AN APPLICATION IMPORTANT?

Yes, but as with patents there are no hard and fast rules. Early filing of an application establishes 'priority' over others, but it may be commercially desirable to delay the application.

DOES A UK REGISTRATION GIVE PROTECTION ABROAD?

No. A UK registered design is effective only in the United Kingdom and Isle of Man. However, some countries accept registration of a design in the UK as equivalent to an independent registration in the countries concerned. Otherwise the UK application can be used to establish a 'priority' date for a separate application made in a foreign country.

CAN THE PATENT OFFICE HELP EXPLOIT A REGISTERED DESIGN?

No. The Patent Office cannot provide any financial or other support since this would conflict with the role of the Designs Registry as an impartial regulatory body for the registration of industrial designs. But there are organisations throughout the UK which will assist in exploiting designs with commercial potential.

CAN ANYONE BE TOLD ABOUT THE DESIGN?

Any time after the application has been filed. Before that date extreme care is needed to ensure that the design is not made available or disclosed to the public in any way whatsoever – otherwise, although registration might be obtainable, it may later be proved invalid. If disclosure to another party is necessary before filing of an application, then this clearly should be made in the strictest confidence.

ARE REGISTERED DESIGNS MADE PUBLIC?

Once registered, designs are laid open to public inspection at the Patent Office. In addition, registration details, but not the design itself, are recorded in the Register of Designs (which may be consulted by any member of the public) and published in the Official Journal (Patents).

HOW SOON CAN ARTICLES MADE TO A DESIGN BE MANUFACTURED AND SOLD?

Any time after the application has been filed. Before that date, extreme care is needed to ensure that the design is not made available or disclosed to the public in any way whatsoever – otherwise registration might not be obtainable. However, a design may be displayed at an exhibition certified by the Department of Trade and Industry before applying, as long as such application is made within six months of the opening of the exhibition.

DO REGISTERED DESIGNS HAVE OTHER USES?

Yes. Existing registered designs provide a large amount of technical and commercial information concerning the latest developments in product design.

DOES THE DESIGNS REGISTRY PROVIDE ANY OTHER SERVICES?

Yes. The Registry will conduct a search (on payment of a fee) to determine whether a design resembles a registered design. This is distinct from the search conducted as part of the processing of a registered design application.

DESIGN RIGHT

WHAT IS DESIGN RIGHT?

Design right is an intellectual property right which applies to original, non-commonplace designs of the shape or configuration of articles. Design right is not a monopoly right but a right to prevent copying, and lasts until 10 years after first marketing articles made to the design, subject to an overall limit of 15 years from creation of the design. A design right is a property which, like any other business commodity, may be bought, sold or licensed.

DO ALL DESIGNS QUALIFY FOR DESIGN RIGHT?

No. The design must be of the shape or configuration of an article; in other words 2-dimensional designs, such as textile or wallpaper designs, will not qualify, although these qualify for copyright and possible registered design protection. In addition, the design must not be commonplace; in other words, well-known, mundane, routine designs will not acquire design right.

WHO CAN OBTAIN PROTECTION THROUGH THE DESIGN RIGHT?

In general, design right protects designs created by nationals, residents or companies of the European Community, and designs created by nationals of New Zealand and the United Kingdom colonies.

IS REGISTRATION NECESSARY?

No. Design right is like copyright in that the protection arises automatically when the design is created. However, it may be wise to keep a note of when the design was first recorded in material for sale or hire. This information may be useful if someone challenges the owner's rights in the design or if it is believed that someone is infringing the owner's rights.

WHAT PROTECTION DOES DESIGN RIGHT GIVE?

Design right is an 'exclusive right' for 5 years after first marketing and then becomes subject to licences of right for the remaining 5 years of its term. This means that, in general, during the first 5 years if the design right is infringed by the unauthorised making of articles copying the design and by unauthorised trading in such articles, the design right owner has the right to take civil action in the courts seeking damages, an injunction or any other relief available to plaintiffs for infringement of a property right. During the final 5 years, anyone will be entitled to a licence to make and sell articles copying the design drawings or know-how available to the copier.

ARE THERE ANY EXCEPTIONS TO DESIGN RIGHT?
Yes. Design features enabling one article to be functionally fitted or aesthetically matched to another article get no protection. These so-called 'must fit' and 'must match' exceptions have been provided to ensure that competing designs for spare parts cannot be kept out of the market. These exceptions mean that competitors cannot be prevented from copying any features of a protected design which enable their own design to be connected to or matched with existing equipment designed by someone else. However, competitors will infringe design right if they copy features of a protected design where there is no need to do so.

WHAT ABOUT SEMICONDUCTOR CHIPS?
Designs of semiconductor chips will get design right protection. But in order to comply with a European Community Directive, the exclusive rights in semiconductor chip designs will last for the full 10 years in the market. In other words, licences to copy will not be available during the last 5 years of the term.

DOES THE DESIGN RIGHT GIVE PROTECTION ABROAD?
No. Design right is effective only in the United Kingdom. Protection may be available in other countries under, say, petty patent or registered design systems, but usually any protection will not be given automatically and must be applied for.

ARE THERE ANY OTHER FORMS OF PROTECTION FOR DESIGNS?
Yes. If the design is technically inventive it may well qualify for up to 20 years' monopoly protection under the patent system. Or if the design has 'eye-appeal' it may be eligible for up to 25 years' monopoly protection under the registered design system. Design drawings and graphic designs may get copyright protection.

HOW NECESSARY IS IT TO GET PROFESSIONAL HELP?
Because of the complexities surrounding protection of designs, both individuals and companies are recommended to seek professional advice, for example from a Chartered Patent Agent.

(4) Commonplace considerations

The foregoing serves as a very good introduction, but nevertheless an introduction only. It is not suggested that contract administrators should consider themselves equipped for patent filing or deciding between design registration or non-registration. Such things are strictly for the experts. However, very many commonplace contracts implicitly touch upon IP matters and to the extent that this is so there should be express terms in the contract. If the contract is for the supply of goods only the physical property transfers to the buyer who can do whatever he likes with them, to use them, modify them (which may invalidate any warranties) or sell them. Of course he only buys the physical property and thus has no right to manufacture or sell copies as no rights in the design have been sold.

In contracts which go beyond the pure and simple supply of goods there is the need to think about IPR issues, for example in the following instances:

a) If the contract calls for the provision of documents, handbooks or reports, whose is the copyright? Can the buyer make and distribute copies?

b) If the contract calls for design and development work, who owns the design? Can the seller and/or buyer exploit it commercially? Are there any licence arrangements to make?

c) If the seller is providing a design and the rights to exploit the design, what is the position regarding any proprietary features?

d) If, as a result of the contract, the IPR of a third party are infringed, is the buyer or seller or both or neither liable?

These are the situations that need to be thought through on a case by case basis. The point here is that the two parties to the contract can make any agreement they like as regards ownership of any rights in their respective IP. If there is a third party IP involved then their freedom will be limited by whatever is the contract or licence under which the third party IP is available to them.

Although all is open for negotiation and agreement, some general comments usually apply:

a) Ownership of proprietary information remains with the proprietor and the 'buyer' obtains rights under licence. The rights acquired are usually the minimum necessary to meet his needs. More rights – more cost.

b) Where the buyer or client is paying for the creation of a design and its associated documentation, IP may belong to the designer in which case the contract secures rights for the buyer as in (a) above. The IP may belong to the buyer in which event the designer may have rights under the contract to use the design for his purposes.

c) Use of somebody else's IPR usually involves a sum of money, either as a licence fee or royalty. In respect of his own IPR the seller may include the sum within the price for the work.

d) Where the contract is based upon IP to be provided by the seller it is usual for the seller to indemnify the buyer against third party action for infringement or alleged infringement. The converse also applies.

e) Where the buyer needs to acquire rights from the seller not only for his own internal purposes but also to pass on to his customers, these rights to 'sublicense' must also be secured under the contract.

Wherever IPR are involved, whether they belong to the parties (to the contract or to third parties) the ownership and terms (ie monetary sums and conditions) must be somewhere recorded in writing. This can be either within the express provisions of the contract or by a separate licence agreement.

A typical contract clause covering IPR is as follows:

Example A

Ownership and Use of Technical Data

1) Save as provided in this condition the Intellectual Property Rights in the Technical Data shall vest in the Subcontractor.

2) For the purpose of this condition 'Technical Data' shall mean all materials produced and delivered by the Subcontractor, its servants or agents for the Contractor pursuant to any development work performed under this Contract and shall include all specifications, production and working drawings, calculations, formulae, bills of material, technical information, computer software and firmware and other documents, models, mock-ups and all other data called for in and arising from such development work.

3) The Subcontractor hereby grants to the Contractor a royalty free non-exclusive, irrevocable licence to manufacture for the Contractor, for its own use in the event that the Sub-contractor is unable or unwilling to meet the reasonable requirements of the Contractor for price and delivery, those items necessary to maintain, modify or support existing equipments or to manufacture complete systems as required by the Contractor.

4) The Contractor is hereby granted the right to use, reproduce, adapt or otherwise modify software deliverables under this Contract for its own purposes. Such use, reproduction, adaptation or modification shall not be guaranteed by the Subcontractor unless such use, reproduction, adaptation, modification shall result from work contracted to it.

5) The Contractor is hereby granted the right to use, reproduce, adapt or otherwise modify Technical Data deliverables under this Contract for its own purposes. Such use, reproduction, adaptation or modification shall not be guaranteed by the Subcontractor unless such use, reproduction, adaptation or modification shall result from work contracted to it.

---

6) Before applying for Letters Patent or Registration of Design in respect of any invention or design first evolved, discovered or reduced to practice during work under this Contract, the Subcontractor shall consult with the Contractor with a view to determining whether an officer or employee of the Contractor is a part inventor of an invention or a part author of the design, and if so to agree the conditions under which the Contractor or its officer or employees shall be a party to the application.

7) Nothing contained herein shall derogate or purport to derogate in any way from the right of the Contractor, or a person authorised in writing by the Contractor, to use any invention or design pursuant to the Patents Act 1952 or such other as may for the time being be in force in relation to inventions and designs.

This example is extracted from a real contract. This was chosen rather than a hypothetical example to demonstrate how the wording (which is a little clumsy) ends up as a compromise of drafting between the two sides but also how pragmatic it is in its endeavours to address real issues rather than theoretical possibilities.

Clause 1 provides an unequivocal statement that the IPR belong to the subcontractor except to the extent that rights are conveyed to the contractor under later clauses.

Clause 2 provides a definition of the material captured by the IPR condition. It is important not only insofar as it lists the categories of material that are included but also because it specifies 'all materials produced and delivered'. This means that it is not limited to IP generated at the expense of the contractor but that it includes pre-existing IP which the subcontractor brings to the contract. It also embraces the idea of 'delivered by the subcontractor, its servants or agents'. This says that the subcontractor must be careful to secure similar rights with his suppliers so as to be free to perform his own obligations to the contractor. The definition is also interesting because it catches items such as working drawings and calculations which on the face of it are background information and not strictly essential.

Clause 3 includes a number of important concepts. In this the subcontractor grants a licence to the contractor to be operative only in the specified circumstances of the subcontractor's inability to meet the contractor's potential future needs. 'Royalty free' means that the contractor will not have to pay for such rights. 'Irrevocable' means the subcontractor cannot later change his mind and withdraw the licence grant. With this extensive right of the contractor the purpose of the catch-all definition in Clause 2 becomes clear. If the contractor could later find himself in the position of manufacturing spare or replacement units to the subcontractor's design then he needs as much background information as possible.

In Clauses 4 and 5 is found the basic grant of rights. This is quite extensive as the rights are only bounded by words 'for its own purposes'. As the purpose could be to compete against the subcontractor with his own product in his own markets this could expose the subcontractor to quite a risk. The final sentence in each case is quite reasonable as it relieves the subcontractor of any liability for work which he himself did not do.

Clause 6 is consistent with Clause 1 in that it recognises that the responsibilities for and the benefits deriving from patent application and design regulation lie with the subcontractor except to the extent that the contractor might have participated in creating the invention or design. The clause contemplates a separate agreement as to the terms relating to joint inventions. Although strictly speaking an agreement to agree is not legally enforceable the parties are saying that whilst conceptually joint inventions might arise, there is no point in establishing, nor indeed is there any basis for determining, the terms for that eventuality.

In Clause 7 reference is made to the Patents Act 1952 (which has subsequently been updated). Under this Act the Crown is empowered to authorise the use of patented inventions by persons other than the patent holder. The wording in Clause 7 is simply saying that the statutory law of the land has precedence over the contract condition. This is a general principle, that people cannot override national laws by making a provision in a contract – unless the law specifically allows it to be so excluded.

This particular condition does not include the conventional IPR indemnity clause mentioned earlier. This may be because it was covered elsewhere in the contract or maybe the contractor forgot or neglected to press for it. After all the subcontractor (in this case) is not likely to volunteer it. If the contractor's usage of the IP leads to a third party action for infringement, the action would be against the contractor and if there is no indemnity provision the contractor would be liable.

(5) Background and foreground material

One of the distinctions that must be considered is between so-called background and foreground material. In a contract where the buyer specifically commissions and agrees to pay for the development and design of a product there are fundamental questions to answer as to which of the parties will own the Intellectual Property in the design and whether or not the other party will nevertheless have any rights in the design.

At one extreme the buyer will own the IP in an outright sense and leave the designer with no rights whatsoever. This gives the buyer the complete freedom to sell or license the design to others, to have made and to sell goods to the design, to modify the design and to enjoy the benefits of the legal protection for his IP under copyright, patent and so on. The designer in these circumstances simply has no rights.

At the other extreme the designer owns the IP that he has created, is free to exploit it and enjoys the benefits of legal protection. The buyer's right would be limited to buying goods of the design from the designer and then to use those goods for his own purposes.

The former situation might arise where the buyer is in business to manufacture and sell goods of specialised design but chooses to commission designs from an outside specialist rather than possess intramural design and development skills. Thus the zero grant of rights to the designer is logically correct as the buyer would not wish his designer to become a manufacturing competitor. The latter case would arise where the buyer needs goods of a special design for a particular purpose but has no interest in exploiting the design by himself. A builder of power stations might need to commission the design of a special pump but has no intention of becoming a seller of pumps. Thus provided he has acquired the pump for his power station, he is content for the seller to own the pump design and to exploit it commercially (but perhaps not to other power station builders), perhaps in return for a levy of some sort.

Many compromise positions can be developed between these two extremes with joint ownership of IP, marketing agreements covering customers or territories that each would address, joint manufacturing, distributorship and agency deals.

However, once the fundamentals have been sorted out covering ownership and rights then it is necessary to consider in a little more detail the actual design material. In the first example where the IP and all associated rights are to belong to the buyer let us suppose that the buyer plans to manufacture goods to the design created by the supplier and let us suppose that the designer is also a manufacturer of goods of a similar nature. The buyer in this scenario wishes to acquire the detailed design and the know-how associated with manufacturing that design. The seller wishes to convey only details of the design – after all that is what the contract price ostensibly relates to – and not to reveal his know-how. If his know-how is divulged then he weakens his chance of getting future design work and puts his customer possibly in the position of being a stronger competitor to himself.

In this case the essence of foreground and background material can be seen. Foreground material is the IP created under the contract. Background material is the pre-existing knowledge that is brought to the contract without which the foreground IP cannot be created at all.

For example, an element of the design may be a metal plate with holes. The designer would say that he is being commissioned only to supply a drawing of the plate giving details only of dimensions, weight and composition. The buyer would say that he also needs to know how to make the plate with the minimum of scrap or rework, with the holes precisely drilled, whether the plate is to be cast or machined from solid, etc. The 'what' is foreground material. The 'how' is background material.

In practice arguments over the definition and delivery or availability of background information are sorted out. A number of possibilities arise:

a) If the price is high enough perhaps the designer will happily provide all background data.

b) The contract might specify that the work is to include the design of the product and the method of manufacture.

c) The designer might specify or supply special manufacturing equipment.

d) The designer might offer to provide technical assistance to the buyer's manufacturing process.

e) In return for background data the buyer may agree to order a certain number of units from the designer rather than manufacture them himself.

Items (d) and (e) are in any event a good idea because it is rarely the case that manufacturer A can build to designer B's design without some initial problem.

6 Summary

Although the topic of IPR is a complex matter a few simple *aide-mémoires* will assist the contracts administrator in practice:

a) Think about IPR. Do not gloss over them. Establish if they are applicable.

b) Define the IP. Be clear on background and foreground material.

c) State ownership, ie ours, theirs, or someone else's.

d) Define each party's rights:
Use.
Modify.
Adapt.
Exploit.

e) Establish the costs and terms of use.

f) Express relevant indemnities.

Further study is recommended and a visit to the UK Patent Office in Newport is worthwhile. A number of explanatory booklets and brochures are available from the Patent Office and these provide excellent background material. A more detailed appraisal can be found in Blackstone's *Guide to the Copyright, Designs and Patents Act 1988* published by Blackstone Press Limited.

8

CHAPTER

Efficient administration techniques

(1) Introduction

In Chapter 1 the aims of this book were given and included some specific techniques. This chapter examines the techniques associated with good contract administration.

Good contract administration relies upon data. For data to be useful they must be accessible; to be accessible they must be recorded. Whether recorded manually on paper or held in a computer store, the two most helpful methods of recording data or headings for data are on:

```
┌─────────────────────┐
│     Checklists      │
└─────────────────────┘
        ┌─────────┐
        │   and   │
        └─────────┘
┌─────────────────────┐
│     Registers       │
└─────────────────────┘
```

In earlier chapters – particularly Chapter 4 – the usefulness of checklists was demonstrated. This chapter introduces particular registers of information for specific functions which are the responsibility of the contract administrator.

Keeping the contract up-to-date

It is vital that there is always immediately to hand a complete and up-to-date copy of the contract. To say that it must be kept up-to-date implies that the contract as originally agreed and signed will have been subject to change. Changes fall into three categories:

a) Changes to the express conditions given effect by the formality of a numbered contract amendment and acceptance thereof.

b) Changes to an aspect of the contract (eg technical specifications) which take place under an 'enabling' condition of the contract but where no contract amendment per se is utilised.

c) Changes to the understanding or interpretation of the contract effected by a separate letter, report or meeting minutes.

Regarding (a), a register should be maintained to track the amendment status of the contract and to provide a rapidly accessible diary of the life of the contract and how the various amendments affect it. For example, it is useful to track the changing value of the contract. It is important to remember that contract amendments come into legal effect only once they have been accepted. The contract amendment register should therefore record not only the ostensible date of the amendment but also the date of the acceptance. An example of a contract amendment register is given in Figure 8.1.

Not only does the register provide a quick record of events but it also acts as a very useful *aide-mémoire* to the contract administrator who must ensure that all offered amendments receive a response, whether it be an acceptance, a rejection or a holding reply.

Regarding the type of changes referred to in (b), it is equally important that a proper record is kept of the changes. This is discussed in more detail elsewhere in this chapter but a useful technique to adopt is that the record of the changes is added formally to the contract from time to time using the contract amendment procedure. In this way there is a link between the contract amendment register and changes being authorised and recorded elsewhere.

It is more difficult to keep track of alterations to interpretation of the contract where these appear in separate correspondence or in the minutes of meetings. The best way is to make a note in the contract amendment register and annotate the working copy of the contract with a cross-reference to the relevant material.

Figure 8.1: Contract amendment register

Contract: 14C/130   **Description:** Supply of Type 14 trailers
Customer: Preston Engineering Ltd

Amend-ment No.	Date	Type	Accept-ance date	Old value	Change	New value	Description	Comment
–	4.1.90	Docs	6.1.90	£100K	–	£100K	Contract documents	
1	28.4.90	Telex	28.4.90	£100K	–	£100K	Consignee address	
2	6.6.90	Letter	10.6.90	£100K	–	£100K	New payment scheme	
3	8.8.90	Letter	10.8.90	£100K	£50K	£150K	Quantity increase	
4	5.10.90	Letter	Rejected	£150K			Type 14A requested	Too late to change – see letter 17.10.90

As far as a working copy of the contract is concerned, it is as well to be clear as to the following distinction:

MASTER COPY: Original document plus original amendments.

WORKING COPY: Photocopy of the original documents with amendments incorporated.

It is very convenient to maintain the working copy in an up-to-date state by word processor which enhances the readability of the document, especially where there have been many changes. If a word processor is used it is as well to make margin notes to show where amendments have been made.

A useful trick is to use a photocopier to produce a 'pocket' sized (maybe A5) version of the working copy. This is much easier to take to and use at meetings, rather than carry around large heavy documents.

It is most important that the original contract documents and the original amendments are kept separately and intact so that at any time – where for example there is doubt about the integrity or accuracy of the working copy – a check back may be made to discover what actually changed.

To avoid one of the pitfalls of using a working copy – particularly where copies are distributed – it is important that the document carries a note of any caveats or qualifications to the contract or its amendments that may have legal effect.

In addition to the master and working copies of the contract it is wise to keep an additional security or back-up copy with its amendments in a separate building as insurance against fire or other risks to the documents.

③ The contract file

As far as filing systems go, there are generally only two approaches that are followed:

THE HEAP SYSTEM
THE HIERARCHY SYSTEM

In the Heap System everything – including the contract and related correspondence, memoranda and minutes – is kept in the same file in one continuous heap. In the Hierarchy System the papers are broken down into discrete topics and each has its own file. This gives order to the papers whereas in the Heap System filing by date order is the only discipline.

The Heap System has the advantage that all the papers are together and a logical, chronological story can be followed. The disadvantage is that files can be bulky and the individual papers relevant to a particular topic will be dispersed amongst many others.

The Hierarchy System has the advantage of smaller files and easier access to specific topics but the disadvantage is that if particular material is required that does not obviously belong to a single topic or topics then a search will be necessary across several files. Copying papers across files may help to counteract this but it is wasteful and requires enormous discipline if it is to be thorough.

A Hierarchy System may comprise the following:

100: File series: 2 Stage heat shields – Williams Ltd
101: Pre-contract correspondence
102: Request for bids
103: Bid committee papers
104: Price and cost estimates
105: Quotation and proposal
106: Contract – master copy with amendments
107: Contract – working copy

108: Works order
109: Post-contract correspondence
110: Subcontract correspondence
    110/1 – Makeshift Components Ltd
    110/2 – Jerrybuilt Shelters Ltd
    110/3 – Tinpot Metal Bashers plc
111: Future licences
112: Committee papers
    112/1 – Health and safety
    112/2 – Quality control
    112/3 – Technical progress
113: Engineering change proposals

The aim is simply to divide the papers into sensible and manageable parts.

Figure 8.2: Contract file record sheet

Enclosure No.	Date	Description	Key document
1	1.2.90	Contract documents	Yes
2	4.2.90	Publicity notice	No
3	5.2.90	Acceptance letter with caveats	Yes
4	6.3.90	Acknowledgement of E3	No
5	10.4.90	Memo re: delivery dates	No
6	17.4.90	Response to E3	Yes
7	10.6.90	Quotation Item 6	Yes
8	14.8.90	Internal progress notes	No
9	21.9.90	Manuscript notes on negotiation of E7	Yes
10	6.10.90	Amendment No. 6	Yes
11	12.11.90	Amendment No. 7	Yes
12	14.11.90	Internal comment on E10/11	No
13	28.11.90	Response to E10/11	Yes
14	30.11.90	Progress report No. 1	Yes
15	16.12.90	Minutes progress meeting No. 1	Yes
16	17.12.90	Christmas invitations	No
17			
18			
19			
20			

Choice of the Heap or Hierarchy System is a matter of personal preference. Whichever is used, a useful technique is to mark each of the papers in the file with an 'enclosure' number and keep a list, either on the cover of the file or just inside, recording what the contents are. An example of this is given in Figure 8.2. Notice in particular the annotation as to whether the document is a key document or not. This will be useful later when the contract file is to be reviewed for closure purposes (see Chapter 11).

Quotations register

One of the key roles that the contract administrator usually performs is the processing of requests for quotations and the responses. This is another task where the use of a register is an invaluable aid in managing the activity and ensuring that things do not get forgotten.

Depending upon the volume and type of enquiries processed the register can be maintained as a:

Total list
List by contract
List by customer
List by territory
List by product/service

An example of a quotations register is given in Figure 8.3.

This is one example where establishing and maintaining the register on a computer database is very valuable so that repeats can be generated using any parameter or combinations of parameters, eg:

a)   By enquiry date and value.
b)   By quotation validity and customer.

As with all registers that record something dynamic it is important that the final column always gives the outcome. The purpose in providing quotations is not to provide quotations but to secure business.

Figure 8.3: Quotations register

Entry No.	Enquiry No.	Enquiry date	Type	Customer	Description No.	Contract date	Response date		Value	Validity	Out-come
							Target	Act			
1	28/14/A	1.8.90	Firm	Williams	Supply 100 Widgets	N/A	15.8.90	15.8.90	£150K	15.9.90	
2	ABC/14	5.8.90	Firm	Smith	MK 21 Lighters	N/A	16.8.90	15.8.90	£500K	16.9.90	
3	16/1/BAL	12.8.90	Budgetary	Grant Ltd	3 GR Systems	N/A		14.8.90	£2M	N/A	
4	–	–	Firm	Williams	Mini-Widgets	81A/14		16.9.90	£100K	16.10.90	
5	BT/4J	19.8.90	Firm	Jacksons	Mini-Widgets	N/A	25.8.90				
6											

⑤ Key contract details

Although it can seem a chore to keep it up-to-date, a register of key contract details (Figure 8.4) can lead not only to efficient contract administration but also to the speedy answering of requests for information that would otherwise take many hours of tedious re-search. For example, demands of the following nature are frequently made:

Example 1
List all contracts over 12 months' duration and £500K in value.

Example 2
List all contracts and their value in which liquidated damages apply.

Example 3
List all contracts in which issues of government property are made.

Example 4
List all contracts that include standard conditions 141, 153, 166 and 167.

The key contract details register is really one that must be developed on a customised basis but Figure 8.4 gives a good indication of the type of register to set up.

Figure 8.4: Key contract details register

1)	Customer name and address:			
2)	Contract number:			
3)	Contract description:			
4)	Contract price(s):	Item 1: Item 2: Item 3: Item 4	£ £ £ £	
5)	Contract delivery/ Duration:	– / – / –	to – / – / –	
6)	Key terms:	*Included* *Y or N*	*Relevant* *Period*	*Comment*
a)	Liquidated damages			
b)	Bonds/guarantees			
c)	Free issue property			
d)	Security provisions			
e)	Data retention			
f)	Government audit			
g)	Payment (i) On delivery (ii) Stage (iii) Progress			
h)	Cancellation			
i)	Standard Conditions No 1 No 2 No 3 No 4			

(6) Key contract dates

In a similar vein to the key contract details register is the key contract dates register (Figure 8.5). In this the aim is to summarise the chronological progress of the contract and its time-dependent or time-driven features.

Figure 8.5: Key contract dates register

1) Contract documents	*Date offered*	*Date accepted*	*Comment*
a) Initial document			
b) Amendment No 1			
c) Amendment No 2			
d) Amendment No 3			
e) Amendment No 4			
2) Deliverable documentation	*Date submitted*	*Date approved*	*Comment*
a) Quality plan			
b) Technical specification			
c) Quarterly financial report			
d) Implementation plan			
e) Certificate of type approval			
3) Meetings	*Date held*	*Date of minutes*	*Comment*
a) Monthly progress			
b) Quarterly review			
c) Steering committee			
d) Design review			
e) Production release			
4) Deliveries	*Start*	*Finish*	*Comment*
a) 1st Batch			
b) 2nd Batch			

Commercial issues

The final general register which can be well worthwhile keeping is the register of commercial issues (Figure 8.6). The idea behind this is to pick up the key issues that are commercially important and that are (or should be!) dynamic. The data so far described as the basis for the various registers are static. Certainly the contract amendment status changes from time to time but from that particular register it is difficult to see which items are more important than others.

In many ways this is the most useful register. For example, it is surprisingly simple in a big contract to forget what has been happening. Last month's problem has been overtaken in visibility by this month's crisis and yet last month's problem has not gone away: it remains there festering away to catch everybody out later.

Anything that affects:

Profit
Cashflow
Payment
Performance
Risk

should be drawn out and added to the register.

Figure 8.6: Commercial issues register

Contract No.: 418/23   **Description:** Plating Machinery
Customer: Wiggins Ltd

Entry No.	Date	Description	Risk	Outcome/Comment Residual action
1	28.10.90	Our letter advising supplier's industrial action.	LDs will accrue if no relief allowed.	
2	16.11.90	Wiggins's fax exercising quantity options.	Negative cash flow.	Get payment scheme updated.
3	14.12.90	Test Plan submitted.	Nugatory cost if plan not approved asap.	
4	15.1.91	Our letter querying wrong part numbers amendment 14.	Cannot deliver unless corrected by Wiggins.	

Payment

Once the contract is in place there are few things as important as getting paid. The principles behind payment are discussed in Chapter 6. In practice there are two essential ideas:

**The contract must precisely prescribe
payment and billing details.**

and

**Invoicing should be automatic – a matter
of routine.**

The checklist in Appendix 1, List K shows the details to be sorted out before billing can proceed. These details appear to be glimpses of the blindingly obvious but all too often it is error in the detail wherein lies the fault.

⑨ Quotations

One of the roles that the contract administrator has to perform is that of preparing quotations. Guidance is given in Chapter 4 on drafting quotations but sitting beneath the price and its associated statement of work, specification and conditions, is the basic cost estimate and the calculations that take an estimate of cost to a selling price.

No matter the type of industry, product or service all prices are comprised of the same fundamental building blocks:

Labour
Overheads
Materials/subcontract
Risk/contingency allowances
Special to contract allowances
Profit

These elements can all be seen in the following example.

Direct labour 100,000 hours at £15/hr =	1,500,000
Overhead recovery 20% of above	300,000
Materials	500,000
Subcontract work	200,000
Basic works cost =	2,500,000
Risk allowances:	
Design 10% of above	250,000
Manufacturing 5% of above	125,000
Sub-total	2,875,000
Special to contract allowances:	
Liquidated damages protection	25,000
Warranty	250,000
Cost of financing work in progress	100,000
Sub-total	3,250,000
Profit @ 10%	325,000
Selling price	3,575,000

In this classic price make up all the elements referred to earlier are included to the extent appropriate. The direct labour, subcontract and material estimated costs, all wholly attributable to the contract to which this price relates, are shown. The overhead recovery expressed as a percentage of the direct labour is there to recover this contract's proportionate share of the factory set up and running cost. The risk allowances are either standard percentage mark ups or calculated by reference to an estimate of what is reasonably likely to go wrong and the cost of putting it right. The base to which the risk allowances apply will vary according to circumstances.

In the above example the risk allowance has been applied to the subcontract element because some of the design work is to be done by subcontractors. On other occasions the design risk allowance may be applied to the direct design labour only. Similarly for the manufacturing risk. The other categories mentioned earlier in this chapter could each be estimated and a specific allowance made. The practice is to make a specific allowance for major risk areas only, although quite commonly an overall contingency factor may be applied to cover risk in general.

The special to contract allowances are in respect of those features unique to the particular contract which imply cost or risk. Special warranty requirements – perhaps a warranty period of twice the usual time – imply both cost and risk. If the contract includes a liquidated damages clause then the supplier is wise to include in his price an allowance for having to pay the customer for his lateness. These are only examples, of course. It is vital that the contract is thoroughly scrutinised for any features that imply cost or risk.

The final element in the price build up is profit. Many companies have different standard profit mark ups depending on the product, market and customer.

In a fiercely competitive environment it is necessary to match the ideal price build up – with all its allowances and contingencies – to whatever intelligence there is as to the likely winning price. It is no good having a safe price in terms of full coverage of all costs, risk and profit if it is not a winning price. It should be remembered that the difference between the basic works cost and the selling price is the buffer or margin between profit and loss. It is assumed that the basic works cost is the minimum figure for which the work can actually be done. The selling price is the maximum which the customer will pay. The sum included for profit is notional only. Efficient performance with elimination of the perceived risks will convert the whole margin to profit. Inefficient performance and ineffective risk management can erode the margin to zero and plunge the contract into loss. In the example the profit opportunity between the basic works cost and selling price is £1,075,000 which is much higher than the notional £325,000.

Different companies have different cost accounting systems and thus each will have differing treatments of categories of cost and handling of risk, but the foregoing example serves to illustrate the principles involved.

The only other factor not mentioned in the foregoing, but which sometimes is applied, is that of a negotiating margin. This is an additional sum included in the price which can in whole or in part be eliminated in negotiation. The building in of something to give away – so that the real allowances and margins are protected and preserved – is a feature to which the customer will be alert.

Converting a cost estimate to a price is something that readily reduces to a standard routine, the essence of which is to take the cost estimates for each element of the quotation and then apply company prescribed allowances together with any special to contract allowances all in a standard format to arrive at the final selling price. In practice the format may (Figure 8.7) have to be more voluminous to accommodate individual estimates for each item of the Statement of Work. Commonly a formal structure for these elements is established. Frequently it is called the Work Breakdown Structure (WBS). An example of a top level WBS is given in Figure 8.8. The WBS may be broken down into many smaller elements called work packages which provide the basis both for cost estimating and for financial monitoring once the work of the contract is underway.

Figure 8.7: Price formulation

			Year 1		Year 2		Year 3		Year 4		Total	
		Rate	Hours	Cost	Hours	Cost	Hours	Cost	Hours	Cost	Hours	Cost
LABOUR	DESIGN	£60/Hr										
	PROD	£50/Hr										
MATS	DESIGN	N/A										
	PROD	N/A										
RISK	DESIGN	5%										
	PROD	3%										
INFLATION		6% p/a										
FINANCING COST		8%										
INSURANCE		2%										
WARRANTY		5%										
LDs		7.5%										
LEVY		N/A										
PROFIT		20%										
PRICE												

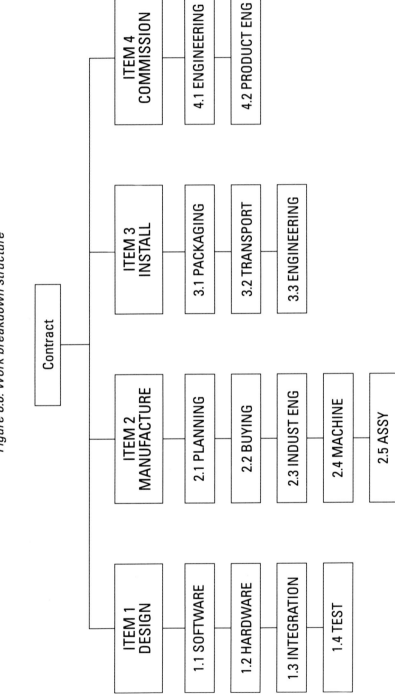

Figure 8.8: Work breakdown structure

(10) Contract changes

Many types of contract are subject to changes to the scope of the work, its nature or to quantity. In business transactions it is open to the parties to agree to vary the requirements of the contract together with a variation in the consideration. It is also open to the parties to legislate within the contract conditions for changes which are conceptually contemplated at the outset but which may or may not arise, or where the precise description of the change can only emerge at some later time. This may perhaps be where the contract includes some initial development activity at the conclusion of which there will be a review of the balance of the requirement and an adjustment made where necessary.

Changes of this type can be proposed by the seller or the buyer.

The convention is that if either side proposes a change which the buyer takes up then the buyer will also pay for the seller's cost of preparing a detailed change proposal. If the seller initiates a proposal which the buyer does not take up then the preparation costs are usually ascribed to the seller's account.

If the contract is to legislate for potential changes then it must prescribe the form or format in which the change will be proposed and authorised. This is usually structured in the following manner:

Effect on cost/price
Effect on time
Effect on anything else

This allows the buyer to quickly focus on three key questions:

Can I afford it?
How long will it take?
What else will change?

The format of the change proposal form will vary between industries and types of contract but an illustrative sample is given in Figure 8.9.

Figure 8.9: Contract change proposal

1) *Contract No:*   A98/63
2) *Description:*   Widget redesign
3) *CCP serial number:*   43
4) *CCP date:*   1.12.90
5) *CCP validity:*   2 months
6) *CCP description:*   To replace the P14 interface link with fibre optic cable. See attached detailed explanation.

7) *Effect on price:*

Item affected	*From*	*By*	*To*
1	£100,000	£20,000	£120,000
2	£400 each	£50 each	£450 each
3	£16,000	No change	£16,000

8) *Effect on time:*
   Item 1: Completion delayed 2 months.
   Item 2: Deliveries delayed 6 weeks.
   Item 3: No change.

9) *Effect on anything else:*
   a)   The following documents will be updated if the CCP is approved:
     – Design plan
     – Technical specification
     – Production drawings
   b)   600 Units delivered under contract A98/25 will require modification to ensure commonality of spares – budgetary estimate £20,000

10) *Signatures*

   Proposed:......................Authorised: ....

The important things to observe are:

a) Make sure the change description is comprehensive.

b) State the validity of the CCP – the ability to provide one or more features may lapse after a period of time.

c) Wherever practicable (especially where financial data are given) specify not only the change but also the old and new positions.

d) Wherever possible specify what is staying the same as well as what is being changed.

e) Specify what effects there may be outside of the particular contract.

f) Be clear (on the form or within the contract) that the status of the CCP is equivalent to that of a formal quotation, ie capable of being accepted.

g) Be clear what the authorising signature means, eg agreement to the entirety of the proposal or just to commence work.

In a contract which is subject to many CCPs it is as well to maintain a register.

(11) Summary

In these paragraphs much has been said of checklists and registers and it is helpful to make two final comments.

Firstly, many of the data are common to several of the lists and there is a temptation to set up one enormous database covering all lists and registers for all contracts. With modern computer systems this is certainly feasible from a technical point of view; however, experience shows that the up-to-dateness of the database is inversely proportional to the volume of data held. In practice it can be more 'person friendly' to use individual lists/registers, some of which are maintained manually.

Secondly, it is not the intention that people should slavishly follow all the lists/registers illustrated. It is a matter of choosing the most appropriate ones and adapting them as necessary.

All the principles apply equally to subcontracts and to contracts and it is not difficult to see how the list of registers might quickly be lengthened by additional items where the job responsibilities demand it. For example, there may be registers for:

Subcontracts
Confidentiality agreements
Teaming agreements
Licences
Bonds/guarantees
Deliveries made
Goods delivered but not invoiced
Debtors

but the secret is to invent a suitable register, maintain it and develop it to improve its usefulness.

Other administration techniques

Once this way of thinking has become second nature and the discipline of checklists/registers has been adopted, good contract administration will begin to flow naturally. Nevertheless there are a few hints which may help along the way:

12.1. Bring forward systems

One of the important aspects of the contract administrator's job is to ensure that things do not get forgotten. Once a letter has been sent it is all too easy to assume that the recipient will reply or act promptly. It is only safe to assume that this will not happen. Thus a bring forward system is a useful back-up technique. It can be in the form of a diary or in the form of physically returning the file (or papers) to the desk or top of the in-tray for review.

12.2. Day file

Here the idea is simply to keep a running file in date order holding a copy of all outgoing external and internal correspondence. A once or twice weekly flick through this file provides an excellent *aide-mémoire* as to what has been happening and what needs chasing. It also provides invaluable information for those 'sod's law' occasions when the file is urgently needed but has gone missing!

12.3. Time management

There are many good courses and a great deal of literature on time management and these include good training techniques for those who are not naturally well organised. However, one general tip not usually passed on is this. A lot of the job involves dealing with 'post' which is used generically to include:

Mail
Internal paperwork
Minutes of meetings
Reports
Action requests
Instructions (written or oral)
Procedures
Notices.

'Post' arrives once or twice or maybe throughout the day and time should be set aside to deal with it. It should be sorted and dealt with strictly in the following order of priority:

FIRST: Anything the boss wants done.
SECOND: Correspondence from customers.
LAST: Everything else.

This proven order of action does everything to promote career progression, promote the interests of the company and last and definitely least get rid of the dross!

9

○ ○ ○ ○ ○ ○ ○ ○ ○ C H A P T E R ○ ○ ○

Effective communication and personal skills

① Introduction

In earlier chapters the benefits of good contract administration were described in terms of their necessity to optimise commercial performance. Nowhere so far has there been a definition of what contract administration is. This has been left until this point because it is hoped that the earlier material will have pointed the way. Contract administration may be described thus:

> 'An understanding of the contract and of the environment within which it is to be performed. Progressing that performance and the related issues that arise. Collecting, assimilating and disseminating data connected with the contract. Providing effective liaison with all parties concerned with the contract to promote understanding and successful commercial performance.'

This is something of a mouthful but it proved impossible to find a more succinct definition because of the several separate and distinct elements. If this definition is dissected the distinct elements can be drawn out.

1.1. The contract and its environment

Somebody has to be familiar with the whole of the contract, its structure and contents as well as its purpose and intent. In particular the role of the contract administrator is to know his way around the so-called 'terms and conditions' bit. Even if he is not an expert on every single condition, clause and paragraph, even if he is not an expert on LDs, IPR or indemnities, he should nevertheless know what express provisions the contract does and does not contain. He should be able to say in broad terms what each of the provisions mean and where to look for more detail.

The classic example of where the contract administrator can bring 'expert' knowledge (and expert knowledge is required where the contract is silent on an important point) to the game is in answering the following proposition:

> 'The contract doesn't mention payments
> so we're unfunded and can't get paid.'

The answer, of course, is that the contract does not have to mention payment because payment of the agreed price becomes due on contract performance. It is a part of basic contract law. The contract need only make specific mention if there are to be payments made in advance of contract performance or if payment is to be made at some time significantly after performance.

Similarly:

> 'The contract has no Limit of Liability
> so we have no money.'

If there is no limit of the customer's liability stated, his liability is open ended which is good news not bad.

In most instances, of equal importance to what has been said above is the environment within which the contract was negotiated and within which it is to be performed. Continuing good relationships with regular customers and suppliers is very important. Thus the way in which issues surrounding the contract are to be dealt with must take cognisance of that relationship not only from the point of view of amicability but also in the strict sense of setting precedents and the like. The contract administrator must have sufficient overall grasp of the picture to be able to offer such advice as:

> 'Yes we could stop work on Contract XX
> until they pay us; on the other hand we are
> extremely late on Contract YY and they have
> waived the LDs.'

1.2. Progressing performance

With any contract, whether it is a routine order or a major project, there is a danger that everybody will think somebody else is responsible and inevitably things will be missed. The contract administrator must see it as part of his responsibility to chivvy everybody:

a) Are deliveries up-to-date?
b) Are we invoicing *and* being paid?
c) Are warranty returns being actioned?
d) Are purchase orders up-to-date?
   etc.

Even where there exists an overall project, programme or contract plan, he must make sure that it is consistent with the contract. Too often people work to internal planning documents which bear no resemblance to the contract and hence to the customer's expectations.

When issues arise over the contract or amendments thereto or over prices or almost any contractual or contract-related query, the administrator is the person to progress matters to a conclusion. Whatever is the issue it will not (usually) go away by itself and it is risky to simply assume that somebody else will deal with it. In this the register of commercial issues mentioned in Chapter 8 is invaluable.

1.3. Collecting, assimilating, disseminating data

One of the greatest talents that the contract administrator can possess is a tidy, systematic and factual approach. Some questions warrant and are susceptible to a yes/no or simple factual answer:

Has amendment 55 been accepted?
What is the price for item 4?
Do we have force majeure?
What was the date of contract?

Without facts and data to hand, people rely on unreliable memory or guess the answer. The contract administrator can eliminate the risk of memory and guesswork by knowing the right answer and having it readily available to feed into meetings, discussions and paperwork.

1.4. Communication

This ought to be a statement of the obvious, but sometimes the obvious is not quite so apparent as it should be. In most organisations no single person is entirely responsible either for winning the contract or for performing it. It may seem that only one person is responsible but this is not so. Many people are involved and they must talk. The thing they have in common is the contract and so it is logical that the contract administrator is a principal focal point and communications channel. The contract administrator must want to 'own' his contract as shown in Figure 9.1.

Figure 9.1

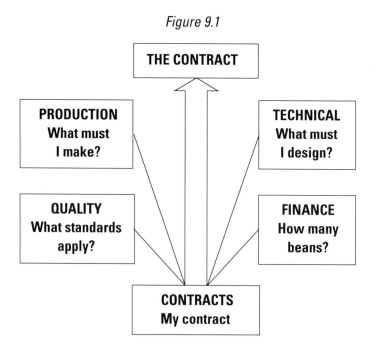

② Methods of communication

To liaise effectively with anyone you must know what you are talking about. If the registers suggested in Chapter 8 are summarised:

Contract amendments
Quotations
Key contract details
Key contract dates

Commercial issues
Change proposal
Subcontracts
Confidentiality/teaming
Licences
Bonds/guarantees
Delivery
Not invoiced/debtors

it is quickly realised that the contract administrator has to hand an enormous volume of information which, when combined with his knowledge of contract and commercial principles and their implications, means that he surely does know what he is talking about.

Communication happens in three principal ways:

Telephone
Written material
Meetings/discussions

The subject of meetings and discussions is covered in the next section.

2.1. Telephone

Telephone discussions must encapsulate the following principles:

a) Identification of caller and callee.
b) Statement of purpose.
c) Discussion.
d) Summary and conclusion.

There cannot be many people who can claim that they never had a phone call in which they have not been sure to whom they were speaking or one in which they felt that the callee probably was not sure who was calling him. The purpose in liaising is to communicate a message. The sense and the purpose of the message is all but lost if the sender and the receiver are not properly identified the one to the other.

Whenever a telephone call is made, make sure that both people know (and write down) the:

Name
Function
Telephone number

of the other person. This is the minimum information to gather. Just as when people meet pleasantries are exchanged, it is as important to do this on the telephone. In professional life almost all phone calls are something akin to a negotiation. Whether with customers, suppliers, internal colleagues, bosses or subordinates, it is likely that the callee will have an opposing view or aim or set of priorities to the caller. Even information-gathering calls can be adversarial if the callee is not disposed towards helping the caller. Thus, whoever the callee and whatever the purpose, it is worthwhile trying to calibrate and gauge their mood.

Once the mood of the callee is measured, the purpose and tone of the call can be refined or modified accordingly. At worst, perhaps it might be as well to truncate the call and try another day.

> 'Hi Bill, how are you? Did the golf
> go well?'
> 'No. Ten over par. Sheila's not
> forgiven me for missing the kid's
> party.'
> 'Sorry to hear that Bill – I'll
> give you a call tomorrow.'

If the preliminaries go well, the call can proceed. The purpose must be stated clearly if the call is not to degenerate into waffle or chat. For example, do not say:

> 'Hi Bill, it's John. I was wondering how
> you felt about the cost over-run.'

When it is much clearer to say:

> 'Hi Bill, it's John. I have just had a call from
> Finance complaining about the cost over-run
> on Contract AB/123. I have to respond by
> close of play and plan to say that it's
> too late to recover the situation. Do you
> agree and have you any comments to add?'

In this the caller has made clear:
   a) The background.
   b) The precise contract in question.

c) The purpose of the call.

d) The deadline.

e) The response expected from the callee.

The discussion can be as wide or as narrow, shallow or deep, long or brief as the topic demands. The onus is on the caller to guide the conversation to a summary and conclusion such that the purpose has been achieved.

> 'So there it is John, that's how
> the over-run has happened. OK?'

To leave the conversation here would leave John with no positive conclusion and his purpose would not be achieved.

> 'So in summary Bill, you believe that there
> are some extenuating circumstances and that one
> further letter to the customer may do the
> trick. Fine, that's what I'll tell Finance
> and that you will have the letter done by
> Friday.'

This objective approach to telephone calls is a method that has to be practised. Often people are given the task:

> 'Ted, can you phone Eric and ask
> him about the new machinery.'

Yet if the purpose in the call is not clear then no one will be the wiser and time will have been wasted. If in doubt ask:

> 'OK, I'll call Eric and ask if the machinery will
> be installed by Friday and if so when will
> production start. Is there anything else you
> want to know?'

So remember:

PURPOSE
DISCUSSION
SUMMARY AND CONCLUSION

The summary is as important as the conclusion. The conclusion may be a one-line statement of the agreed course of action.

However, if the callee is to relay the conclusion to others he may be expected to explain it and this he can only do by summarising the discussion on the phone. For this reason it is as well for the caller and callee to summarise what has been said. After all, it is not impossible for them to have arrived at an agreed conclusion without having been on the same wavelength throughout the discussion!

2.2. Written material

Written material comes in broadly three categories:
a) Correspondence – internal and external.
b) Meeting minutes.
c) Reports.

a) Correspondence: The question of external correspondence is discussed in detail in Chapter 4. There is no reason at all for internal correspondence to observe the Hexagon Principle to any lesser extent than for external correspondence. Certainly the draughtsman of internal correspondence must always have the Pentagon Objective in mind.

When people look to the contracts department for advice, what they want is usable, relevant help and not academic advice. People can read the contract and they are not interested in the legal theory behind it. What they need is:

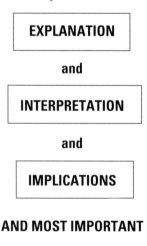

EXPLANATION

and

INTERPRETATION

and

IMPLICATIONS

AND MOST IMPORTANT

A POSITIVE COURSE OF ACTION

Compare these two internal memoranda.

Example A

From: J Williams   To: F Jenkins
Date: 3 July 1992   Project Manager

CONTRACT A123/687

Thank you for your memorandum querying the pricing conditions. I can advise as follows:

Clause 28 of the contract says:

'The price shall be agreed under the two tier system with a target date of 30 June.'

As it is already past that date it is too late.

Example B

From: J Williams – Contracts   To: F Jenkins –
Date: 3 July 1992   Project Manager

CONTRACT A123/687

Thank you for your memorandum querying the pricing conditions.

The contract contains a so-called two tier pricing clause. The effect of this is that if *we* delay pricing beyond the target date (30 June) the work earns a lower rate of profit.

What we must do, since the date has passed, is to write formulating reasons for the delay being excusable. If this succeeds there will be a short term cash flow problem while the debate is concluded.

In the second memorandum, the contract has been explained, the implications given in terms of profit and cash flow and a course of action laid down – and it was not difficult!

b) Meeting minutes: In the subject of writing the minutes of a meeting the first question to consider is whether the minutes are to record the discussion in full or whether summary notes and a list of actions will suffice. In general, the latter will usually suffice. In particular, internal meetings rarely require a full record of the debate. Meetings with customers or suppliers can demand a greater degree of detail but it should be remembered that the greater the detail the greater the chance of inaccuracy, the minutes take longer to produce, are excessively lengthy and are guaranteed not to be read!

In the business environment the purpose of many meetings is to arrive at decisions and in the majority of cases it is the decision that is important and, after the event, the discussion that leads up to the decision is of far lesser interest.

So the two approaches may be summarised:

a) Detailed minutes   –   are a record of full debate;
                           –   take longer to produce;
                           –   may be less accurate;
                           –   may not be read.

b) Summary notes/actions are –   quick to produce;
                           –   more accurate;
                           –   easier to read;
                           –   more punchy.

From a practical point of view detailed minutes also take longer to review and agree for accuracy at the next meeting. People are notorious for forgetting what they actually said, or for wanting to re-write history by retrospectively 'changing' what was said!

The most important aspects of noting actions are:

a) Specify a *person* who is responsible.
b) Specify a date for the action to be cleared.

Naturally for a deadline to be meaningful the minutes and actions must be issued promptly. Human nature and pressure of work being what it is, at the end of the meeting people dash off to do other things and forget about their actions until they receive the minutes or until the next meeting, whichever is the earlier! So the secretary must see it as essential that the minutes are issued promptly and ideally within one working day.

For larger meetings where there may be unfamiliar faces two small ideas may help:

1) Send a piece of paper around the table for people to fill in their name and job.

2) Use a diagram of the people to take notes.

For example, draw a quick sketch of the table and letter the people:

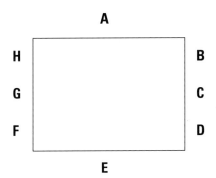

It is easier to make short notes:

'A said to B.'
'D felt this was wrong.'

But make sure you have the picture orientated with the list of names so that the minutes ascribe comments to the person who made them!

If you are not sure of some of the notes you made, show the minutes to another attendee in advance of issue for advice/comment. Two heads are always better than one.

As always, the Hexagon Principle should be followed, and it is advisable to adopt a stylised format for the minutes which you can use automatically time and time again.

As you are in the process of taking notes, put a star against actions. There can be nothing worse than the poor secretary suddenly being asked to summarise the actions so far and having to wade through mountains of tatty manuscript hoping to spot them!

An example of a set of minutes is given in Figure 9.2.

Figure 9.2

CONTRACTS REVIEW MEETING
14.12.90

NOTES AND ACTIONS

Present: J J Smith – Contracts
P D Brown – Finance
K A Black – Projects

Action

1. *Minutes of 14.11.90 Meeting*
Agreed to be accurate. No actions arising.

2. *Mk 24 Deliveries*
2.1 Delivery of 100 units delayed by one month due to late supplier.
2.2 By 16.12.90 advise customer of force majeure   JJS
2.3 By 20.12.90 re-assess cash flow   PDB

3. *Purchase of Vax Computers*
3.1 KAB investment appraisal was reviewed.
A final decision is needed by 31.1.91.
3.2 Cost analysis to be updated by 15.1.91.   PDB
3.3 Presentation to be given to Capital Expenditure Committee on 8.1.91.   KAB

4. *Next Meeting*
18.1.91 in JJS's office 09.00.
Distribution: Those present plus J A Green.

---

c) **Reports:** Report writing is another medium of communication which requires careful practice. The Hexagon Principle and Pentagon Objective must be followed, of course, but as with most longer forms of written material the key is to have a formalised structure in mind. This will depend upon the nature of the report but, for example, a report covering a particular problem might have the following structure:
a) Introduction.
b) Background.

c) The problem.
d) Possible solutions.
e) Recommendations.
f) Summary and conclusion.

The report does not have to have specific headings of this kind provided that it does follow a logical start–middle–finish path and not ramble. Most of all it is important that in most cases the report gives:

THE PROBLEM

and

THE SOLUTION

In business the old adage could not be more true:

'If you come to my office with a
problem and no solution you are
part of the problem.'

A report made orally should be as structured as one put in writing.

Another type of report is the SITREP or situation report. This simply reports progress and the status of a particular topic. If the types of register referred to earlier are being maintained the contract administrator will have to hand a sizeable databank from which to readily extract data for a sitrep. Nevertheless, no report – not even a sitrep – should be seen simply as a static statement of facts and information. What is looked for is emphasis on what is important. So even a simple report on the amendment status of the contract amendments should include a section such as 'Risks and Vulnerabilities'. For example, a report that says:

'Amendment 27 was issued on 3.11.90.'

tells nobody anything. The report should say:

'Amendment 27 was issued on 3.1.90.
However, it is unacceptable because
the current prices were not authorised
for the additional quantity. The consequent

delay will impact the Mk22 implementation
programme. Customer has been advised
and a meeting arranged for 28.11.90.'

③ Meetings

Everybody goes to meetings – *Meetings Bloody Meetings* as the title
of one of the video films has it. What are these meetings?

Review meetings
Progress meetings
Liaison meetings
Control meetings
Monthly meetings
Quarterly meetings
Management meetings
Steering committee meetings
Tender review meetings
Budget meetings
Production meetings
etc.

It is easy to become trapped or sucked into meetings and treat
them as part of the humdrum and yet they are in some ways the most
important vehicles for liaison. What is needed is an understanding
of how meetings work in a mechanical sense. If it is possible to look
behind the ostensible purpose and see what is going on it is possible
to improve the effectiveness of the meeting and one's contribution
to it. The chart in Figure 9.3 enables just this.

Of course there are variations on these themes: for example,
if there is a meeting to convey information of a decision then this
broadly falls into the 'inform people' group. However, whilst the
emphasis, procedure and leadership style indicated in Figure 9.3 are
appropriate, it is probable that the number of people who may join
the meeting should be less.

The one type of meeting that is strictly outside this general
framework is the negotiation meeting. This is discussed separately
in Chapter 10.

Figure 9.3: A framework for meetings

1) The purpose of a meeting can be:	To inform people.	To get people's ideas.	To let people participate in a decision.
2) The meeting should go through stages:	Information and orientation only.	Information, judgement and finding of criteria for a solution.	Information, judgement and finding of criteria for a solution, plus arriving at a final decision.
3) How many people can join the meeting:	Any amount.	Not more than 12 splitting up in sub-groups of 4–6.	Not more than 12, 7 or 4 even better.
4) Who should attend the meeting:	Those who must know.	Those who can contribute.	Those who are responsible.
5) The emphasis in the meeting is on:	The content: – clear; – logical; – sensible.	The content and effective interaction: – listening; – understanding; – evaluating.	The content, interaction and procedure: – information; – judgement; – decision; – who does what and when.
6) What procedure should be followed:	A talk, lecture or introduction with the possibility of asking questions.	Group discussion where one tries to arrive at the main criteria for the decision through the information stage and process of judgement.	Group discussion where one tries to arrive at the main criteria for the decision through the information stage and process of judgement. Then select the best decision to fit the criteria.
7) Style of leadership:	Formal and rather structured.	Less formal exchange of opinions and judging of the information. Functional leadership where possible.	Becoming more formal in the last part of the meeting in order to arrive at the final decision which meets the agreed criteria.

 Communication

So far general principles of liaison have been discussed but these must be considered in the context of the person with whom the liaison process is to take place. These commonly are:

    a) External: Customers.

                     Suppliers.

                     Advisers.

                     Consultants.

b) Internal: Technical.
               Financial.
               Marketing.
               Production.
               Sales.

The one thing they have in common is that they all speak a different language. For example, to the marketing man 'IPR' means the Institute of Public Relations and not Intellectual Property Rights. The accountant sees profit as earnings before interest and tax; the project manager sees it only as the difference between the cost of the job and what he was paid. To the engineer 'output' is the power coming from an amplifier; to the production manager it is the number of widgets delivered in the month.

So if the communication with these strange beings is to be effective their language must be understood and they must understand the language of the contracts administrator. It is well worth the time and trouble to go and see the people and find out what they do, how they do it and what their terminology means. Experts and specialists like to talk about their pet topics and will be only too happy to explain.

Ideally all company employees, and in particular those in the contracts/commercial function, should know in broad terms at least:

What we sell
Where we sell it
How we designed it
How we make it
What profit we make
How the cash flows

Nobody can know this without talking to other functions or departments.

In the external environment it is even more important to understand and visit customers and suppliers. It is important to appreciate their culture, character, procedures and policies. This cannot be done by correspondence or by telephone.

5 The role of personality

In the real world everybody is different and it is undeniable that the contribution each person can make – and, as importantly, the way in which the contribution is made – is linked not just to intelligence, education, training and experience, but also to personality. If little thought was given, personality types might be categorised as:

Strong versus **weak**
Aggressive versus **submissive**
Reactive versus **proactive**

These obvious antonyms serve little use. In his book *Management Teams – Why They Succeed or Fail* Dr R Meredith Belbin describes eight personality types based on several years of practical research. He calls these types the Chairman, Shaper, Plant, Monitor/Evaluator, Company Worker, Team Worker, Resource Investigator and Finisher. Their principal characteristics are given in Figure 9.4 and a more detailed picture in Figure 9.5.

Appendix 4 gives the Belbin Self-Perception Inventory – a questionnaire and analysis that enables a self-assessment to be done to analyse one's own character type.

The title of Dr Belbin's book reveals its primary purpose. The objective was to establish why some teams perform better than others in the context of work-place tasks. The conclusion was that success or failure depends upon the mix of character types.

A key difference from other analyses and a fundamental principle of the Belbin work is that people do not come in variations that are either good or bad but that the personality types *all* have valuable characteristics and whilst these are balanced by weaknesses, the correct combination of types will cancel out the weaknesses and produce a successful team.

A team might be two people or it might be 20. Simplistically at least eight would be needed to ensure a presence of all types, but this is not necessarily so. The majority of people exhibit a primary and a secondary Belbin personality type, so a good blend can be achieved with fewer than eight.

Figure 9.4: Belbin Personality Types

Key role	Typical contributions to the team
Chairman	1) Clarifying the goals and objectives of the group. 2) Selecting the problems on which decisions have to be made, and establishing their priorities. 3) Helping establish roles, responsibilities, and work boundaries within the group. 4) Summing up the feelings and achievements of the group, and articulating group verdicts.
Shaper	1) Shaping roles, boundaries, responsibilities, tasks and objectives. 2) Finding or seeking to find pattern in group discussion. 3) Pushing the group towards agreement in policy and action and towards making decisions.
Plant	1) Advancing proposals. 2) Making criticisms that lead up to counter-suggestions. 3) Offering new insights on lines of action already agreed.
Monitor/ Evaluator	1) Analysing problems and situations. 2) Interpreting complex written material and clarifying obscurities. 3) Assessing the judgements and contributions of others.
Company Worker	1) Transforming talk and ideas into practical steps. 2) Considering what is feasible. 3) Trimming suggestions to make them fit into agreed plans and established systems.
Team Worker	1) Giving personal support and help to others. 2) Building onto or seconding a member's ideas and suggestions. 3) Drawing the reticent into discussion. 4) Taking steps to avert or overcome disruption of the team.
Resource Investigator	1) Introducing ideas and developments of external origin. 2) Contacting other individuals or groups of own volition.
Finisher	1) Checking detail. 2) Self-control. 3) Sense of urgency.

Figure 9.5: Belbin Personality Types – Detailed characteristics

Chairman
1) Clarifies group's objectives and sets its agenda.
2) Stable, dominant, extrovert.
3) Presides over and co-ordinates; not necessarily brilliant and rare for many of the good ideas to emanate from him.
4) Self-discipline and 'character'.
5) Is dominant but in a relaxed non-aggressive way.
6) Trusts people unless there is evidence that he shouldn't.
7) Not jealous.
8) Focuses people on what they can do best.
9) Good communication.
10) Sets criteria but does not domineer.
11) Social leader.

Shaper
1) Anxious, dominant, extrovert.
2) Task leader.
3) Impulsive, impatient – easily frustrated.
4) Full of nervous energy.
5) Quick to challenge and quick to respond to challenges.
6) Does not harbour grudges.
7) Most prone to paranoia.
8) Principal function is to give shape to the application of the team's efforts.
9) Tries to unite ideas and produce patterns.
10) Exudes self-confidence which often belies self-doubts: his drive has a compulsive quality.
11) Sees team as an extension of his ego.
12) Intolerant of woolliness and vagueness – can make team uncomfortable but makes things happen.

Plant or Creator – Vital Spark
1) Dominant, very high IQ: got his name by helping an ineffective team. Planting a high IQ individual can make a weak team effective.
2) Scatters seeds which others nourish.
3) Ideas person – originality and radical timing.
4) Most imaginative as well as most intelligent.
5) Most likely to start searching for original approaches.
6) More concerned with fundamentals – large issues than detail – but can make careless mistakes.
7) Thrustful and uninhibited in a way that is uncharacteristic of an extrovert.
8) Can be prickly, especially when criticised.
9) Danger that spends too much time on own ideas rather than what group is there for.
10) May be bad at taking criticism of his ideas and may be offended and sulk – may withdraw.

11)   It can take a lot from the Chairman, eg flattery etc., to get ideas out of him.

Monitor/Evaluator

1)   High IQ, stable introvert; in a balanced team it is only the Plant and Evaluator who need a high IQ.
2)   A cold fish: serious not exciting. Measured dispassionate analysis.
3)   Not original ideas but most likely to stop team from committing itself to a misguided project.
4)   Least motivated member – ego involvement does not cloud his judgement.
5)   Best skills: assimilating and interpreting and evaluating large volumes of complex written material.
6)   Can lower group's morale by being a damper at the wrong time.
7)   Can be competitive with those who overlap with him, ie Chairman or the Plant.
8)   Lacks warmth and imagination.
9)   But judgement rarely wrong.

Company Worker

1)   Stable and controlled – a practical organiser.
2)   Turns ideas into manageable tasks.
3)   Sorts out what is feasible and actionable.
4)   Strength of character and a disciplined approach.
5)   Sincerity, integrity and trust. Not easily deflated or discouraged.
6)   Sudden change of plan may throw him.
7)   Needs stable structures and tries to create them.
8)   Doesn't like airy-fairy ideas.
9)   Can be overcompetitive for status and can unbalance the team.
10) But more often near the balance of the team: other team members can go to him to find out what is happening.

Team Worker

1)   Stable extrovert; low in dominance.
2)   Most sensitive of team. Most aware of individual needs and worries.
3)   Knows about private lives and families.
4)   Likeable, popular, smoother – cement of team.
5)   Loyal to team, builds on ideas.
6)   Good listener, communicates freely and encourages others.
7)   Counter-balances friction of Shaper and Plant.
8)   Does not like confrontation.
9)   When team is in difficulty, he is particularly valued.
10) Certainly missed if not there.

Resource Investigator – Fixer

1)   Stable, dominant, extrovert.
2)   Most immediately likeable – relaxed, sociable.
3)   Tends to be positive and enthusiastic, but puts things down as quickly as picks them up.
4)   Masses of outside contacts.

5)   Salesman, diplomat, liaison officer. Can be mistaken for ideas person but lacks originality that distinguishes the Plant.
6)   Needs pressure.
7)   Preserves team from stagnation and losing touch.

Finisher
1)   Anxious introvert – worries about what might go wrong.
2)   Only at ease when has personally checked every detail.
3)   Maintains permanent sense of urgency.
4)   Self-control, character – impatient and intolerant of more casual members of team.
5)   Compulsive about order.
6)   Can get bogged down in detail and might worry the group.

What relevance has all this to communication? The point is that if individuals are able to see their own strengths and weaknesses *and* the strengths and weaknesses of others analysed from a business effectiveness viewpoint, then a number of opportunities naturally emerge:

a)   To focus and capitalise on one's own strengths.

b)   To find means of compensating for one's own weaknesses.

c)   To get the best from others by concentrating on their strengths.

d)   To compensate for the weaknesses of others.

These things are easier to do, once the Belbin analysis has been absorbed, than might seem to be the case. For example, as circumstances dictate it is possible to roleplay a missing character type. In a meeting full of Plants and Shapers there will be a mass of ideas but nobody evaluating the advantages and risks. Thus if one person is prepared to step out of his normal role and force himself to adopt the Monitor/Evaluator role then the meeting will become more effective.

With a little practice, this is a very powerful technique to employ in maximising personal and hence company performance.

10

⬤ ⬤ ⬤ ⬤ ⬤ ⬤ ⬤ Ⓒ Ⓗ Ⓐ Ⓟ Ⓣ Ⓔ Ⓡ ⬤ ⬤

Negotiation

① Introduction

In doing business the parties to any transaction normally and naturally have opposing aims, for example:

A buyer wants to buy at the lowest price.
The seller wants to sell at the highest price.

Therefore a perfectly normal process within business life is the reconciliation of opposing views so that a deal can be made.

In many transactions the opposing views are reconciled almost by routine with hardly anybody noticing what has happened: the deal may be closed by the seller offering a standard discount for prompt payment. Yet even in this simple example the two sides have moved from their initial positions – the seller in offering a lower price and the buyer making arrangements to settle invoices quickly – to effect a compromise.

The *Oxford English Dictionary* defines the word 'negotiate' as 'confer with a view to compromise'. Compromise has sometimes been said to be the British disease: 'the good old British compromise'. There is some truth in this as undoubtedly the objective is to secure everything that your side wants whilst yielding nothing. In practice, though, unless the arguments are overwhelmingly in your favour it is unlikely that you can secure all in return for nothing. Indeed, even where the power of your arguments logically defeats everything the other side has to say you can still be faced with a simple but highly effective 'No'.

So perhaps in the everyday real world something of a combination of the British disease and the Attila the Hun approach is needed:

Aim to win everything but be prepared to yield something.

After all, if the deal is worth something to you – and the fact that you are at the negotiating table at all usually means that it is – then aiming to win everything but not being prepared to yield anything is a recipe for no agreement unless the other side simply gives in.

So what role does the contract administrator have to play in negotiation? Surely negotiation is left to the experts? The police train specially selected personnel to negotiate with kidnappers or terrorists. Nationalised industries appoint chairmen more for their skills in negotiating with unions than for their knowledge of the industry. Key negotiations are conducted by directors, not by administrators.

All this is true but remember two vital things:

a)   As the opening paragraphs explained, virtually every transaction effects some reconciliation of opposing positions. Even the most mundane decision potentially implies cost or risk and thus the contract administrator has a vital role to play in protecting the company's interests.

b)   Where difficulties blow up into an issue requiring negotiation at a higher level, very frequently the administrator must support those negotiations, and the actions that he has taken in the preceding weeks or months may be crucial to a successful outcome.

It can almost be said, therefore, that the contract administrator should not see himself merely as an administrator but as a full-time negotiator looking after the company's interests, either on his own account in matters of apparent routine or in making a key and real contribution to higher level negotiations.

In many ways the most important features of negotiation can be summarised into four principles:

1)   Know what is important.
2)   Say the right thing.
3)   Don't say the wrong thing.
4)   Avoid the traps and pitfalls that the other side
       may lay.

These are only motherhood statements but each is a truism in itself.

Countless books and manuals have been written on the art and skills of negotiation. The reader is commended to these invaluable works as they provide instruction in many aspects such as:

a) Venue, timing, etc.
b) Positional versus principled argument.
c) Role-playing.
d) Hard man/soft man.
e) Humour.
f) Stonewalling.
g) The 'walkout'.
h) Individual techniques.
i) Aggression.
j) Listening skills.

As well as illustrating the approach that one's own side may adopt, background material such as this may provide an insight into the opposition's plans and tactics.

The purpose of this chapter, however, is not to repeat what can be read elsewhere in specialist volumes but to draw out key points which experience shows are fundamental in contract negotiation.

② Purpose

Before describing these points, it is pertinent to focus on the purpose and importance of the commercial negotiation. The negotiation itself might be related to:

a) A pre-contract issue.
b) The process of agreeing the contract.
c) A difference of interpretation during contract performance.
d) A failure by the other party affecting contract performance.
e) A third party act affecting contract performance.
f) An event affecting the contract, but not previously contemplated and therefore not legislated for within the contract.
g) A dispute over completion or acceptance of the work.
h) A post-contract claim.

Whatever the issue generating the need for negotiation, then the seller has potentially at stake:

a) Profit.
b) Cash.
c) Reputation.
d) Nugatory work.
e) Diversion of effort.
f) Delay.

and the buyer has potentially at stake:

a) Profit.
b) Cash.
c) Reputation.
d) Nugatory work.
e) Diversion of effort.
f) Delay.

Thus, and not surprisingly, each of the two parties may have as much to lose or win as the other. Cynically put, one side's profit is the other's loss – although this will be seen as an over-simplistic view of what transpires in negotiation. Nevertheless the point is well made that each party is faced in the extreme with success or disaster. That is to say that when all the normal processes by which progress is achieved and agreements made have been exhausted, the parties must meet face-to-face to negotiate. Letters, routine meetings, minutes and phone calls have all failed and it is down to the negotiators to thrash out an agreement. Indeed, it is a well-established rule of thumb and good practice to follow that if a single round of correspondence has failed to resolve a problem once it has become an issue, then negotiation should be the next step. Further rounds of formal correspondence are likely only to cause entrenchment of the respective positions and thus inhibit a satisfactory agreement as both sides feel bound not to yield principles that the written correspondence may record as being immutable.

③ Prior events

Almost invariably negotiations are preceded by events that are recorded or by propositions that are argued in writing. Care should always be taken about what is put in writing and in other than routine matters advice should be sought on what to say and how to say it. Frequently you can be caught out by unintentionally or unconsciously giving a commitment or yielding a principle that subsequently proves to be vital.

④ Serious matters

Whilst care must be taken, these comments are not intended to caution that things should not be put in writing to the other party. Indeed in any commercial negotiation – and in the extreme, in front of a court of law – the volume and accuracy of documentary material is important and may be crucial. In general, factual information is most important (for example dates of meetings, events, records of phone calls) and opinion and speculation should be avoided. In particular, the following should not be discussed, without considered prior thought:

a) Costs/price.
b) Cash flow/payment arrangements.
c) Programme/delivery.
d) Liability for delay, mistakes, accidents.
e) Liability for poor technical performance, reliability.
f) Ownership of design rights.

These, after all, are matters for the contract and are not to be treated lightly.

In summary, it can be said that:

a) The negotiation stage is a crucial milestone and one in which the company may stand to win or lose its shirt.

b) Most negotiations are preceded by some degree of correspondence or documentary material which is, or becomes, germane to the negotiation.

The good administrator will continuously bear in mind the sensitivity required in written material and will practise the skills in his support to the actual negotiation.

And so to the key points…

⑤ Preparation

Almost all successful negotiations are based upon thorough preparation. Too often the date for the negotiation is fixed as the first available date in people's diaries. If it is the first available date then impliedly the days leading up to the agreed date are already planned to be occupied by other events – holidays, meetings, etc. In those circumstances preparation for the negotiation has to be squeezed in amongst many other things. Similarly, if the preparatory meeting is left to the last minute then it may be too late to gather information or to consult other people when the need for further information or consultation is only identified in the pre-meeting discussions.

Rule: Allow sufficient time.

It is the responsibility of the intended leader of the negotiation to arrange the pre-meeting. It is the responsibility of those in support to make the time available to support and attend the pre-meeting.

The pre-meeting must be seen by all participants as absolutely crucial. It is the meeting at which the plan for the negotiation will be thrashed out and clearly it is madness for participants to the negotiation not to meet beforehand. It is wrong to think that the participants have all necessary information in their heads, can simply meet on the day and that a successful negotiation will ensue.

Rule: The preparatory meeting is crucial.

The primary objective of the pre-meeting is to establish the negotiation plan; however, equally vital is the gathering and assimilation of information. It is in this area that the administrator can make his greatest contribution to the preparation stage. The lead negotiator must have to hand all related information so that he can analyse what is useful to him, what is useful to the other side and what can be discarded. Notice that for this purpose he needs *related* information rather than just *relevant* information. (Although irrelevant information may have its place in the negotiation by way of red herrings, diversionary tactics and time-wasting tangents.) Although it sounds senseless, the hardest part of the process is in thinking what is related to the issue in question. At the pre-meeting, the lead negotiator will already have a number of questions for the other participants to answer or investigate and report upon. However, the administrator may have been involved with the other side for a considerable period of time and has been involved in many meetings, reports, discussions, presentations and demonstrations.

Amongst the enormous mass of information that this represents the administrator must recollect and volunteer almost everything that comes to mind. He should never conceal anything that he or the company has said or done or anything that the other side has said or done which weakens his own side's position. If weaknesses are identified the negotiation plan can accommodate counter-measures to be deployed if and when the other side attacks the weaknesses. The pre-meeting is also the opportune time to identify the people and personalities on the opposition team.

Rule: Maximise information.

In conceptual terms, the objective of the pre-meeting is to create the negotiation plan but if we return to the definition 'confer with a view to compromise' then the essence of the plan must be a clear view of the other side's likely objectives and in *both* cases a view of how the objectives might be compromised in order that agreement can be reached.

Rule: Identify both sides' objectives.

In considering the opposition's objectives there is a subtle distinction to be drawn between his objectives and what is actually important to him. For example, if he feels considerably aggrieved one objective may be to extract a price reduction, ie some financial retribution for his hurt. However, what may be of far greater importance is improved delivery or different bells and whistles. Again, background intelligence on the opposition's real needs may very well be something that the administrator may have and this key information must be fed to the lead negotiator.

Rule: Identify the opposition's real needs.

A further facet of the opposition's likely situation is that there may be many areas on which he really cannot compromise. On occasions these may appear to be trivial and on the face of it represent points to be easily won. However, there may be valid reasons for the other side being unable to give in and it is most helpful to know what these issues are. Once known, then depending upon the progress of the negotiation and upon the negotiation plan, these points may be yielded to help-him-so-he-will-help-you, or, at the other extreme, they may be used as a means to contrive a breakdown in negotiations – all through the other side's intransigence.

Rule: Identify what is difficult for the opposition to yield.

These last few points could more generally be described as 'identify strengths and weaknesses'. However, the aim has been to go beyond such a simple statement and indicate the type of information which will help in the development of the negotiation plan.

The negotiation plan

Montgomery – or it may have been Rommel, but perhaps both of them! – said 'planning is everything but nothing ever goes according to plan'. This wonderful statement encapsulates the principle that no matter how thorough the preparation, how good the rehearsal and how comprehensive the plan, there will inevitably be unexpected and unpredictable events, questions, issues and difficulties to deal with. Nevertheless, the existence of a plan with its goals and objectives gives a stable framework from which to diverge and also a framework to aim to return to once the unexpected has been dealt with.

Rule: There must be a plan.

The plan itself must enshrine some of the work done in the preparation phase. Clearly the plan must centre on the objectives of the negotiation and it can be useful to develop a matrix in the following manner:

		Opposition's position		
		Impossible	Difficult	Easy
Our	Must have			
aims	Nice to have			
Bonuses				

If there are objectives in the 'must have' but 'impossible to attain' segment then the purpose of the negotiation must be re-examined and, if necessary, redefined. Possibly the purpose devolves on the one hand to simply maintaining (or opening) dialogue to on the other hand commencing a series of negotiations.

Rule: Categorise your objectives.

Similarly, it is essential that if the opposition's objectives and real needs have been identified, then a matrix can also be drawn.

		Our position		
		Must not agree	Yield under pressure	Throwaways
Opposition's	Must have			
aims	Nice to have			
Bonuses				

Once again, topics in the opposition 'must have' but we 'must not agree' must cause a reassessment of the purpose of the negotiation.

Rule: Categorise the opposition's objectives.

It is the task of all concerned to ensure that technical objectives – yours and his – are viable. It helps no one to go in with impossible objectives.

Rule: Be realistic.

On the question of advice to the lead negotiator, it is the responsibility of the individuals involved in the preparation or to be involved in the negotiation to thoroughly and honestly brief the lead negotiator. Even if people believe errors have been made it is unforgivable not to brief the leader. The lead negotiator must know the complete and real picture if he is to successfully prosecute the deal.

Rule: Thoroughly brief the lead negotiator.

Having covered the objective, the plan must have an intended structure for the negotiation. If the discussions proceed to plan then the chances of success are improved. The structure should include the following topics:
  a) Opening position.
  b) Order of play.
  c) Manner of tabling issues.
  d) Timing of offers/counter-offers.
  e) Information to be tabled.
and, where appropriate, the timing and mechanics for breaking for

lunch, time-outs, etc.

Rule: Structure the negotiation.

Most importantly, the negotiating team must have clearly defined roles and contributions to make. Each member must be fully briefed on his own specialist subject and on the generality of the negotiation plan.

Rule: Allocate specific functions to each member of the negotiation team.

It should be a taken-as-read rule of all negotiations that the team will follow the leader.

Follow the leader

Experience shows that in the vast majority of negotiations the actual process of negotiation occurs between just two people – one on each side – regardless of the respective team sizes. This is hardly surprising since negotiation may be likened to a game of chess. It would be ludicrous to think of a chess game being played equally well by a team as by a single person. The single person controls the tactics within an overall strategy, sacrifices pieces or positions and captures pieces or territory as part of an overall game plan. The golden rule must be that the negotiation is the responsibility of the leader and all other participants are there to support him.

Rule: The leader is responsible.

To effectively support the leader the administrator must develop listening skills so that he is sensitive to the line being pursued by the leader and to its probable purpose, and so that he is alert and prepared to put forward supporting arguments if invited to do so by the leader.

Rule: Listen well and be sensitive.

One of the worst things that can happen to the leader is for one of his team accidentally – or even worse intentionally – in the heat of the moment to usurp the leader's role. If that problem is bad then the seriousness is increased tenfold if the usurper – or indeed a supporter – deviates from the agreed negotiation plan. At best this will cause confusion and at worst is a recipe for disaster.

Rule: Stick to the plan.

However, as Montgomery said, nothing ever goes according to plan. Diversions from the plan must be orchestrated by the leader and the team, if they have been listening well and have been sensitive to the general trend in the negotiation, will see how and to what extent the plan is being abandoned. The leader will be conscious of the need to let the team know his thinking and will find a way of letting everyone know even if it means calling a time-out.

Rule: Recognise when the leader is deviating from the plan.

A further action to be avoided is the tabling openly at the meeting of 'new' information. As the discussion proceeds it is not unnatural for people to recall additional data, to see a new slant on certain things or indeed to have been given further information after the pre-meeting but before the negotiation. Whatever the reason, the worst thing a team member can do is to table it, leaving the leader with the awful prospect of trying to recover from a self-inflicted shotgun wound to the foot. If there is new information to consider, it should be communicated to the leader. Again, it is preferable to have a time-out rather than potentially destroy the painstakingly achieved progress through an ill-timed presentation of extra information.

Rule: Don't throw in new information.

Regardless of the leader/supporter functionality, the team is nevertheless there as a team representing the company. It should be seen by the opposition as being united and of a common view. It destroys the credibility of the entire enterprise if the team appears to be divided, or not equally briefed or, in the very worst extreme, antagonistic to one another. For example, if a participant should say to the leader 'actually I disagree with you there' then the negotiation will almost certainly plummet. It is an unforgivable mistake which the opposition should ruthlessly exploit. There may well be disagreement but it should not be made public and if the person believes the leader has got it seriously wrong he must find a discreet (but rapid) means of letting the leader know.

Rule: Don't drop the team in it.

Having got to the point where the negotiation is in progress, everybody is supporting the leader and generally sticking to the plan, there are nevertheless a variety of other fundamentals which need to be taken on board if the administrator is to maximise his contribution.

8 Other fundamentals

In many cases the commercial negotiator shows a certain reluctance to take specialists to the negotiation for support. This reluctance flows from a great fear that the specialist will hinder, not help, through his not unnatural wish to answer questions. If there are technical issues to resolve then the presence of a specialist may be unavoidable. From the point of view of the lead negotiator there is a great danger that in his eagerness to display his deep understanding and knowledge of the subject the specialist will rush to answer all the wrong questions from the other side. All of us have a basic intellectual desire to demonstrate that we can answer the question. In a negotiation the other side will be seeking to put questions on areas in which they perceive your position to be weak. To answer such questions fully and frankly is to pull the proverbial rug from beneath one's feet. It is far better, within reason, to feign ignorance, promise to check later or find some other way to avoid giving a direct answer.

Rule: Avoid answering awkward questions.

Even worse than answering awkward questions is answering questions in areas where you have no expert knowledge. The leader has enough to deal with without having to interrupt his own people to prevent them going off into the wrong subject.

Rule: Don't stray into areas in which you are not the expert.

Another potentially dangerous facet of the answering of questions – where, of course, it is in your interest to do so – is to be economical with the truth. From a legal viewpoint there are significant risks in lying as you and the company may be guilty of fraud, attempted fraud, or misrepresentation. Economy with the truth is not free of these risks, but the general objective must be to answer questions with the minimum of information.

Rule: Be economical in answering questions.

There is good information and bad information when it comes to the actual negotiation. Beforehand, all information is good, even if in itself it is bad news, but once at the meeting one of the worst statements anybody can make is one that begins with the words 'I don't know if this helps or not', for as sure as anything, if he does not know, the chances are that whatever he is going to say will help the other side. In any event he is giving his own side no more time than the opposition to consider the information and its implications.

Rule: Don't volunteer information.

One of the golden rules in any negotiation is not to lose sight of the objectives. It can be all too easy to get carried away and perhaps submerged in vast volumes of information, intellectual debates, slanging matches or whatever, but the light at the end of the tunnel is the objective of having the meeting in the first place and once in sight it should be pursued relentlessly.

Rule: Don't lose sight of the objective (s).

A feature of the negotiation that often comes as something of a surprise is the apparent attitude of the opposition and the atmosphere in which it is conducted. Whatever the subject of the negotiation it is likely to have cropped up as an issue following a considerable period of friendly relations. For example, where a contract has been running smoothly for some time, the interface between the two parties will have been amicable. Routine progress meetings and reviews will have passed off with the two sides congratulating themselves on their close co-operation and the friendly manner in which the business is conducted. Suddenly there is an issue to resolve which normal activities and correspondence have failed to settle. A negotiation is necessary and the other side appears in a far more aggressive, difficult and formal manner than previously. This, of course, is not really surprising and indeed one's own side will be in a similar mode. It should therefore be seen as a normal part of negotiation and, whilst excessive aggression or rigidity is rarely a recipe for success, it should not be found off-putting.

Rule: Don't forget it's tough.

Even though the negotiation should be expected to be tough it is a very stimulating and potentially rewarding activity. By and large the best negotiators are those who not only have the technical and personal skills to carry it off successfully but also enjoy it for its own sake. Similarly, the administrator should see his participation in the same light and hopefully expect not only to make his contribution but also to take some degree of personal satisfaction from it.

Rule: Don't forget to have fun.

The final fundamental is the concept of the good deal, ie a deal which both sides find satisfactory. It is unusual to be negotiating with another party where there has been no previous business with them nor any likelihood of further transactions in the future. Thus, if an overall balance of good relations is to be maintained, both sides must leave the table content, more or less, with their half of the bargain. The negotiation should not be seen as a pitched battle from which a clear victor and a clear loser must emerge.

As the negotiation draws to a conclusion it is the job of the lead negotiator to decide if he is being offered an acceptable deal overall. Amongst many other things, in making his decision he will take into account the consequences of not making an agreement on the day. These may include delayed payment, late delivery, lost profit and indeed the chances of improving upon the offer if the leader decides to wait for a further negotiation at some later date. The team should be aware that these deliberations are running through the lead negotiator's mind and they should support his decision, whatever it may be. These considerations apply equally to both sides.

Rule: Observe the 'good deal' principle.

Finally it should not be forgotten that the other side will have good points and, in an extreme case, the opposition may actually be in the right and you in the wrong. This is no reason, though, to agree with them. Similarly, the temptation must be resisted to support the opposition's case.

Rule: Don't argue the other side's case for them.

Summary of the rules

The various issues and practicalities that should be borne in mind are summarised as follows:

PREPARATION	:	Allow sufficient time.
	:	The preparatory meeting is crucial.
	:	Maximise information.

	:	Identify both sides' objectives.
	:	Identify the opposition's real needs.
	:	Identify what is difficult for the opposition to yield.
NEGOTIATION PLAN	:	There must be a plan.
	:	Categorise your objectives.
	:	Categorise the opposition's objectives.
	:	Be realistic.
	:	Brief the lead negotiator.
	:	Structure the negotiation.
	:	Allocate specific functions.
FOLLOW THE LEADER	:	The leader is responsible.
	:	Listen well.
	:	Stick to the plan.
	:	Recognise deviations.
	:	Don't throw in new information.
	:	Don't drop the team in it.
OTHER FUNDAMENTALS	:	Avoid answering awkward questions.
	:	Don't stray.
	:	Be economical in answers.
	:	Don't volunteer information.
	:	Don't lose sight of the objectives.
	:	Don't forget it's tough.
	:	Have fun.
	:	Remember the 'good deal'.
	:	Don't argue the other side's case.

10 Examples

To illustrate the operation of some of these principles, there follow some actual examples where the commercial negotiation was scuppered, jeopardised or hindered by well-intentioned participants in the negotiation failing to observe the self-preservation rules.

Example 1

The customer wished to place a contract for the supply,

installation and commissioning of electronic equipment. The scope of work was not fully defined and some development work would also be necessary. The key features of the customer's needs were that the requirement could only be satisfied by a single supplier and that delivery on time was absolutely crucial.

The supplier was in a very good position to negotiate a favourable contract. He decided that in the particular circumstances his optimum method for exploiting the opportunity in terms of increased profitability was to negotiate a bonus scheme for timely delivery rather than, for example, attempting to charge high prices. The negotiation plan was thrashed out and centred on two key principles:

1) The supplier would formally table a programme of work and delivery dates which clearly showed that under a conventional contract the customer's vital date would be missed.

2) Outline details would be proposed for a cash bonus scheme that would indicate a high probability of meeting the vital date.

The supplier's negotiation team was led by the commercial manager with the project manager in support. A preparatory meeting was held and the role of the project manager was defined as being to provide technical arguments and reasons why delivery could not be brought forward under a conventional contract and the special measures that could be taken if a bonus scheme were to apply. Crucial to the success of the strategy would be resistance to pressure from the customer to improve delivery with no bonus scheme.

The negotiation meeting commenced and, exactly as predicted in the pre-meeting, the customer's angle was:

a) The importance of timely delivery.

b) His wish to place a contract quickly.

c) His difficulty in acquiring authority to include a bonus scheme.

The supplier stuck to his line until in desperation the customer said, 'Look, if we place a conventional contract with you, can you advance the delivery plan you've offered?' The supplier's project manager leapt in with words to the effect 'of course'. The supplier's team had thereby pulled the rug from beneath its own feet and its position, so carefully developed, collapsed.

It is not difficult to see the mistakes of the supplier's project manager. These were:

a) He did not stick to the plan.

b) He did not follow the leader.

c) He gave a straight answer to an awkward question.

In addition he yielded to the emotional 'cry-for-help' pressure forgetting the 'it's tough' rule.

Example 2

The company had arranged a meeting with three other companies to negotiate the essential features of a teaming agreement. The features were the scope of work, volume of effort and applicable prices – these three variables being interdependent. The nature of the overall job was such that each of the four companies would wish to secure a wide scope of work, a sizeable volume of effort and, not surprisingly, high price. The lead company needed to settle a compromise of these 12 variables between the four organisations within an overall ceiling value.

A preparatory meeting was held but the lead company's project manager became unavailable and the agreed tactic was to concentrate on the arguments which would be put forward by the other three companies in defining their own position and to leave the lead company's own contribution til last in the probability that it would go through almost on the nod.

The negotiation started well with close adherence to the plan. However, the lead company could not escape having its own contribution interrogated. Choosing his words carefully the lead negotiator asked his project manager to describe the technical nature of the work (as opposed to asking him to defend the level of effort proposed). The project manager replied by saying that the leader was probably not yet aware of some paper in the system that conveyed a large reduction in the company's planned amount of effort. Whilst this may have been true, it nevertheless undermined the company's position at a stroke. In this example the mistakes made were:

a) The project manager did not attend the pre-meeting.

b) Therefore there was no chance at all of everybody sticking to the plan.

c) The project manager did not listen properly.

d) The project manager threw in new information.

Example 3

The supplier and customer had been involved in a long-running argument over whether the supplier's proposed design met the requirements of the contract. The customer had steadfastly maintained that the design was not adequate and that the supplier must change it at his own cost. The supplier was in a diametrically opposed position. It had proved impossible to resolve the issue on purely technical grounds as these aspects were extremely complex and the issue hinged on differing interpretation and differing expert opinion on the two sides. Whilst arbitration was open to the two sides, it was in neither's interest to follow such a course of action. To do so would have meant the customer tolerating unacceptable delays in delivery – there being no practicable alternative method available to him. The supplier would have been starved of cash flow for an extensive period of time.

In an attempt to move forward, the supplier and the customer had agreed without prejudice to each's position that the supplier should put forward a change to the design and a price quotation for the additional work. It was quickly agreed that the change was desirable and that it would correct the perceived weakness in the design. This, of course, did not settle the question of who should pay.

The customer called the supplier to a meeting at the customer's premises which were geographically considerably distant from those of the supplier. The commercial manager and project manager had a pre-meeting at which it was agreed that if the customer was not preparing to alter his stance he would have communicated the fact by telephone or in writing. Thus it was a good sign that the customer sought a face-to-face meeting, particularly in view of the distance involved, as at the very least the customer was known not to capriciously waste people's time. The plan for the meeting was that a compromise on sharing the costs would be acceptable, albeit that it would be a hard slog fought for inch by inch.

The predictions about the meeting proved to be accurate and the customer repeatedly came down heavily with his much-stated view that he carried no liability whatsoever for additional costs. Nevertheless, slowly but surely progress was made towards a compromise settlement until in nothing short of exasperation the supplier's project manager blurted out the question 'If you're not liable, then you won't pay and why have you called us to this meeting?' Although not catastrophic, this put at risk the progress so far made and almost invited the customer to bring the shutters down

and entertain no further discussion. The rules ignored were:
   a) Stick to the plan.
   b) Follow the leader.
   c) Don't forget it's tough.

Example 4

The supplier had arranged a meeting with the customer to discuss a potential order for a range of products which the customer had bought previously from the supplier. The nature of the work was relatively involved and included elements to be supplied by several major subcontractors. There were many issues to be discussed, including the question of where certain risks were to be carried. The supplier's aim was to establish the principle that as between himself and the customer, he, the supplier, carried the risk. This was an important point as the price to be agreed would be linked to, amongst other things, the level of risk inherent in the job.

At the pre-meeting it was agreed that the project engineer would support the commercial manager and answer only those questions which the commercial manager put directly to him.

At the meeting with the customer, the supplier put forward the various relevant arguments to sustain the principle that he was proposing. As a natural part of the process the commercial manager gave examples of how in practice a real problem would fall to his account since he carried the risk. At the worst possible moment the project engineer interrupted to say that in the examples given, that was not how the problem had been dealt with in previous contracts. The interruption was in part made in frustration through his not understanding the significance of the apparently irrelevant principles. This statement caused the negotiation to take five steps backwards from the point of view of the supplier. Once again some basic rules had been overlooked in the heat of the moment:
   a) Stick to the plan.
   b) Don't drop the team in it.
   c) Don't stray.
   d) Follow the leader.
and, of course, the project engineer had completely lost sight of the objectives.

These examples are based upon actual events and are not exaggerated for effect. Apparently trivial or helpful comments, no matter how well-intentioned, can destroy a carefully constructed negotiation. From the lead negotiator's point of view these major or even minor disasters present immediate problems:

    a) To recover the ground lost with the other side.
    b) To explain away his own side's comments.
    c) To avoid an argument developing on his own side.
    d) To maintain his side's professionalism.

(11) Chain of events

To return to a theme from the opening paragraphs of this chapter, it is usually the case that a negotiation is preceded by a chain of events, meetings and correspondence most of which at the time may seem to be routine. However, since earlier events are bound to feature in the negotiation, everybody having contact with the other side must keep at the front of his mind the potential benefit or potential damage that specific statements, promises and actions may have in the future. In particular, it is as well to remember the following:

> If the other side has said or done something of value to me, I must get him to confirm it in writing, failing which I will write to him to confirm.

> If I have said or done something of value to me, I will write to the other side to confirm it and seek his written acknowledgement.

The value of documentary evidence – formal correspondence, minutes of meetings, notes of telephone calls, etc – cannot be underestimated.

Events leading up to the negotiation can have a material impact on success or otherwise. For example, within a proposal that had been sent to the customer was a particular assumption forming a key part of the offer, albeit described in fairly innocuous terms. The customer picked it up and queried it on the engineering interface with the supplier. The engineer formed his own view that it was trivial and led the customer to believe that it was of no consequence at all. As a deliberate, well-thought-out tactic, this possibly could have been a legitimate ploy. In the actual circumstances the engineer allowed the customer to believe that the point was not seriously made. When the negotiation meeting commenced the supplier then had an uphill struggle to convince the customer that he was indeed serious. The moral of this story is to be found in the final general rule describing the administrator's role in the commercial negotiation:

> All players must work in close contact with the commercial negotiator in preparing the ground with the opposition.

(12) Event planning

Using the analogy of the chess game, the negotiation itself may be likened to the 'end game'. Extending the analogy to the levels at which chess is played, two distinct variations can be seen:

Beginner's Level: In which the two players move their pieces almost at random until by chance an opportunity for checkmate arises and the end game is only then conceived.

Advanced Level: In which the end game is planned from the outset and each move by the opponent is countered by moves that aim to restore progress towards the end game.

In business the equivalent to the 'beginner's level' is a situation in which events are following a normal and natural course, a crisis or problem then emerges and a negotiation then takes place to effect resolution. The equivalent to the 'advanced level' is a situation in which it is estimated from the outset that a negotiation will be necessary before an agreement is reached and thus all events over which control can be exercised must be pre-planned to achieve progress towards the desired end. Just as in advanced chess, the side which can see the greatest number of moves ahead and predict the opposition's counter moves is the more likely to succeed.

Where the company is involved in an 'advanced game' the importance of the liaison between departments cannot be over-stressed.

(13) A final rule

The final rule is one which applies to all participants in the negotiation. Put very simply, the rule is:

THINK BEFORE YOU SPEAK.

or put more bluntly – engage brain before mouth.

The knack, of course, is to follow the politicians' habit of talking without really saying anything. Whilst many people would say that politicians take this to the extreme, the principle is nevertheless sound. To sit in silence whilst thinking about the answer is almost as bad as giving an ill-considered reply. Therefore to talk around the subject or off it entirely allows the prospect of, at best, taking the discussion along some alternative route which the better suits your purpose or at worst allows thinking time before giving a substantive response.

11

◉ ◉ ◉ ◉ ◉ ◉ ◉ ◉ C H A P T E R ◉ ◉

Contract closure

① Introduction

'Can you tell me if this contract is closed?' is a question that is often put to the contract administrator by the accountant or quality manager or project manager or indeed any of the managers or other people who have an interest in the contract. Sometimes even the customer may enquire if the contract is finished or closed.

Although not meant as an irritant, the proper answer to the question is 'please define what you mean by "closed"'. People have very different ideas of what they mean. For example, is a contract closed when:

All the goods have been delivered.

Almost certainly not. If payment is due on delivery there is invariably a time lag between physical delivery and the raising of an invoice. Indeed is it certain that there is an automatic mechanism to ensure that an invoice is being raised at all? Quite naturally most companies concentrate attention on big contracts or major clients and it can be that invoicing smaller jobs gets forgotten or overlooked even though delivery is completed.

So can it be said that a contract is closed when:

All the goods have been delivered and an invoice raised.

Fairly obviously even this is deficient as an invoice must not only be raised but paid as well. Most customers avoid paying supplier invoices until the last possible minute and thus it cannot be assumed that once an invoice is raised it will automatically be paid;

at best the payment is unlikely to be promptly made.

So can it be said that the contract is closed when:

All the goods have been delivered and all invoices raised and paid.

This is a step in the right direction as we get closer to the original definition of the contract in the first place – an exchange of promises. When the promises have been fulfilled the contract is completed. The seller promised to supply the goods and the buyer promised to pay. Both promises must have been discharged for the contract to have been completed. So here we have a better definition of when the contract is closed:

Both sides have discharged their respective promises.

Here we have enshrined a key principle. The contract represents promises made by both parties. Too often an organisation concentrates on its plans and programmes for completing its obligations rather than looking at both sides of the agreement.

Nevertheless the definition is a good one. What we must look at is what comprises the promises. For example, if the goods have been physically delivered but not yet formally accepted in accordance with any prescribed arrangements the promise to supply the goods (ie to supply goods which conform with the requirements of the contract) has *not* yet been discharged. Until the goods are accepted they may be rejected (if they do not conform) and if they are rejected clearly the contract has not been completed.

Further, we must be clear as to what comprises the total promise. For example, are there documents or data to be supplied as well as the goods? Was there an obligation to demonstrate the goods or to provide training facilities? Any number of things may exist within the contract as parallel or secondary requirements to the key purpose of the contract. Thus we have the complete definition of when the contract is closed:

Both sides have fully *discharged their respective obligations.*

Or is it?

Supposing there are residual obligations that survive the ostensible finish of the contract. For example, there may be obligations to retain records or to retain and maintain data or expertise.

Perhaps the contract contains guarantees about the goods such that if in some way they prove to be defective the supplier would have to remedy the problem. If such is the case perhaps the contract is never finished. To resolve this we need to think back to one of the fundamental bases of the contract, that is, the contract comprises:

a) Conditions: fundamental requirements.

b) Warranties: subsidiary requirements.

When the conditions of the contract have been satisfied the contract is completed in the sense that if there are other things left undone they must be of the nature of warranties and failure to do them would not allow the contract to be terminated. Nevertheless they remain as liabilities. Here then we have the final definition of when the contract is closed:

Both sides have fully discharged their respective obligations and liabilities.

Thus we start to see the importance of properly thinking through day-to-day definitions that help us to understand when the contract is closed. For example:

'When the goods are delivered':   is not good enough.
'When the goods are delivered,
accepted and guarantees have
expired or have been discharged':   is better.

But why is all this so important?

If we do not know how to define when the contract is complete, we do not know when the work is complete or that no further cost will arise. Thus we leave the company exposed to unidentified and unquantified risk and cost!

So far we have considered the definition of a closed contract in the context of looking outwards to a customer. It is equally important to look in two other directions:

a) Outward to subcontractors or suppliers to ensure that those contracts are also completed.

b) Inward to ensure that in-house procedures, regulations and the like have all been satisfied.

Thus in practice the definition of a closed contract and the processes involved in closing a contract can be far more complex than appearances would suggest at first sight.

② Important features

Set out below is a full list of the matters that should be addressed in closing a contract. These will vary according to the nature of the work and individual companies will have variations on the general theme according to the differing accounting systems. A summary of these items is included as Checklist L in Appendix 1.

2.1. Prices

In certain types of contract the prices are not necessarily agreed at the outset. Contracts based upon the following fall in this category:

a) Where the prices will be based upon reimbursement of cost – clearly the final costs are not known until the work is finished and thus the prices for the contract can only be agreed after the event.

b) Where the payments have been made based upon provisional, pegged or interim prices.

c) Where the prices are to be adjusted in line with performance, ie where incentive or bonus arrangements apply.

d) Where the prices are to be adjusted in line with changes in economic conditions under a VOP or CPA arrangements.

e) Where the price is to be in line with currency fluctuations under an exchange rate variation mechanism.

f) Where the price is to be renegotiated or amended as a result of additional work being required or where the contract is agreed to have been completed with some work left undone.

In some of these categories the delay in finalising prices can be considerable. In (a), if there is a requirement for costs to be audited before final agreement then the delay may take months. In (b) and (c) if the adjustments are to be made on the basis of published indices or other data there is always a delay in the information becoming available.

The objective is to make sure that the final price is the maximum entitlement, that it is agreed and that there is a written record or confirmation of its agreement.

2.2. Delivery

Whether the contract is for the supply of goods or services or both, it is fundamental that all the goods and services have been delivered or completed and that proof of acceptance by the customer has been received in a form specified in the contract. In particular if the customer has required additional work or has been content to agree the contract as finished albeit that some work has been left undone, it is important that the proof of acceptance is embracing of such variations.

2.3. Options

Some contracts include the customer's right to buy additional quantities or further services under the contract and the right can be utilised at any time after the contract is placed but before the expiry of a period that should be specified in the contract. These rights are known as options.

Before the contract is closed it must be checked that the contract:

      a) Did not include any options.

or   b) Included options but none was taken up within the permitted period.

or   c) Included options that have been exercised and that all the contract closure processes here described are applied to the options as well as the original contract.

2.4. Payments

The contract simply cannot be deemed completed until all payments have been made. It is important to check this thoroughly. It is not adequate to simply confirm that there are no unpaid invoices outstanding. A check must be made to ensure that the monies actually received equate to the full contract price and that there are no outstanding retentions of any kind.

2.5. Purchase orders

The term 'purchase order' is used as a generic heading to cover all of the elements of the contract which are extra-mural rather than from within the company's own resources. These may include:

      a) Major subcontracts.

      b) Purchased items.

      c) Items rented.

      d) Items leased.

e) Items acquired under licence.

f) Hire charges.

g) Storage costs.

Major subcontracts should be closed following the same principles described here for contracts. Indeed all contractual agreements of this nature should be examined to ensure that all the obligations have been fulfilled and that no further costs will arise.

Final costs and billings from third parties under the general heading of purchase orders can take quite a while to flow through. Invoices might not have been raised or prices with suppliers may have yet to be finalised for the same reasons that the contract price may not have been finalised. Once all costs have come through, a check should be made to ensure that they have been allocated properly and charged to the contract as appropriate.

2.6. Internal orders

In the majority of contracts, the price comprises a number of different elements but essentially split between overhead costs and costs charged directly to the particular contract. Within the company there will be an accounting system that permits direct charges to be collected against the individual contract. If the work of the contract is considered finished, then the booking arrangements must be closed so that no further costs can accidentally find their way onto the contract or that if additional costs legitimately arise, the company is conscious of the need to cover them. If the contract is thought closed, the company's accountants will have taken its full value and its earned profit through the books of account and thus it is a cardinal sin to later disturb the financial aspects of the contract.

Ensuring that booking points are shut off is central to the purpose of closing the contract.

2.7. Residual materials

Closely related to the closing of the booking points is the issue of residual or redundant materials or excess work in progress that has been procured against the contract but is after the event surplus to the requirement. Such items should be:

a) Transferred to stock.

or b) Disposed of.

or c) Delivered to the customer if the contract terms require it.

The aim is to leave the contract 'clean' not only in terms of paperwork but also of bricks and mortar, nuts and bolts, or whatever.

2.8. Disputes

It is feasible that any contract, whether of low value or high value, short or long duration, may give rise to disputes between customer and company, company and suppliers or between the company and another party with whom there is no direct contractual relationship.

The dispute may be over something relatively simple:

Have all the goods been delivered?

or something more complicated:

Has the customer delayed the company and
hence caused costs to rise?

The former should be simple to resolve – provided the contract was clear and the contract administration sound – but the latter would take longer. Disputes over who is to blame for delays are always difficult to resolve as inevitably past events will be contradictory or confusing and hard, irrefutable evidence will probably not exist.

There may be a dispute with an injured third party under product liability. Whatever the nature of the dispute, it may be settled through negotiation or by arbitration or by litigation. One way or the other the contract cannot be safely considered closed until any and all of these have been put to bed.

2.9. Customer owned property

Many contracts involve the company holding the customer's property during the course of the contract. The reasons for this can be quite varied including:

a) The work of the contract may be to embody articles which the customer has elsewhere procured into higher level assemblies or installations.

b) The work of the contract may involve the customer returning or sending his property to the company, for example if the work is repair, restoration or refurbishment.

c) The nature of the work may be so specialised or customised that the customer issues special-to-type jigs, tools, dies or test equipment.

In these circumstances the terms of the contract will specify that the customer's property remains his property even whilst it is in the possession of the company. Thus at the end of the contract the property must be accounted for and properly disposed of, for example:

a) Returned to the customer.
b) Retained but allocated to a further contract.
c) Sold off and the proceeds credited to the customer.

In the case of doing anything other than returning the items to the customer the method of disposal must be agreed with him before implementation.

2.10. Documents

UK government contracts and subcontracts invariably contain provisions regarding national security. Contracts and subcontracts emanating from overseas governments may include requirements as regards security. Contracts between commercial bodies may also contain requirements for the protection of commercially sensitive information.

Whether of national security or commercial security the contract provisions or requirements naturally focus on documentary material. The material may subsist in paper form, on disc, on tape, on photographic medium including microfilm, or in the memory store of a computer. Whatever the media, the contract will include requirements for the disposal of the material at the end of the contract.

Indeed national or commercial security sensitivities may surround not only documentary material but also physical articles in themselves. For example, the very appearance of the item, whether a stealth bomber or a designer dress, may be sensitive in this way.

All requirements for the treatment of or disposal of sensitive documents and other material must be discharged before the contract is complete.

2.11. Warranty

Where there is included in the contract an express warranty two fundamental checks need to be made:

a) Has the warranty period expired?

b) Have all obligations under the warranty provisions been discharged?

These appear to be blindingly obvious points. However, the real purpose behind the first question is that if the period has expired then there must be in place a mechanism to prevent further returns being accepted as free-of-charge work against the contract – or against overheads if warranty work is not a direct charge. This seems simple enough in principle but in practice it is easier to make something happen than to stop something from happening.

If warranty claims have been made a check should be undertaken that any work accepted as a valid warranty charge has been satisfactorily completed. After all, warranty work is not usually given much priority as it does not generate cash or profit – in fact the opposite. So it is easy for warranty returns to languish until the customer chases them.

Even if warranty costs are not charged against the contract directly, the obligation in law giving rise to those costs does flow directly from the contract and thus the contract cannot be considered closed until the obligations have been discharged.

2.12. Bank guarantee and bonds

In some contracts there is a high risk of non-performance because of one or more of a number of factors, for example:

a) Political instability.

b) High technical risk.

c) Lowly financial standing of the supplier.

In these and similar circumstances the cautious customer will require a promise from a third party, perhaps a national bank or a government department, that in the event of non-performance of the contract by the supplier the customer will be paid a specified sum of money in lieu of performance. Such a guarantee or bond represents a liability as far as the supplier is concerned and needs to be cancelled once the work of the contract is performed.

2.13. Letters of credit

The letter of credit represents the inverse of the bank guarantee, or bond. Where payment to the supplier is at risk because of political uncertainty, poor track record of payment or similar, then the supplier can be paid by an independent third party such as a bank. That is, the customer must arrange credit with his bank and the supplier then draws on that credit as he performs his contract with the customer.

At the end of the contract it is important to ensure that the credit facility has been utilised to the full value of the contract.

2.14. Third parties

In addition to the contracts with suppliers, hirers and subcontractors mentioned earlier, there can also be contractual relationships with third parties where their contribution is in some ways peripheral to the contract itself. These may include:

a) Agents.
b) Consultants.
c) Licensors.

In any event these relationships only exist because of the contract and the values of payments to those third parties may be derived from the contract value by way of a percentage or scale of fees.

2.15. Offset and countertrade

An increasing number of contracts are international and an increasing proportion of those contracts include offset or countertrade arrangements whereby – in essence – part of the consideration of the contract is that the exporter agrees to import from the customer's country goods of specified value. This agreement may be discharged as part of the contract or by separate contract and may be based upon similar commodities on the one hand or on dissimilar commodities on the other. Any such agreements must be closed as part of the process of closing the contract.

2.16. Teaming, collaboration and similar agreements

The winning of some contracts is through more than one company working together under a signed teaming agreement or collaboration agreement. Frequently these agreements self-terminate once the objective – securing the contract – is achieved. Occasionally such agreements survive the achievement of the objective and remain extant through to the end of the contract and perhaps beyond. This will certainly be the case where the scope of the agreement is broader than the immediate contract in question.

Once the contract is finished the agreement should be reviewed to ensure that it too is completed or that it legitimately remains in force or that it is amended to reflect the completion of the contract.

2.17. Data retention

The contract may require that certain data generated under the contract or associated with it be retained after completion for a certain period of time. Typically a contract for research, design or development will include such requirements. The two key questions are:

    a) Have arrangements been put in place to retain the data?

    b) Has it been established how any costs associated with the retention will be recovered?

Something apparently as simple as (a) is often overlooked and as ever the cost implications must not be ignored. Possibly the cost can be covered in the initial contract price or perhaps charged to overheads.

2.18. Patent applications, etc

If the nature of the contract is one of research, design or development, then the contract will produce intellectual property. The contract should specify whether the buyer or seller owns that property and the rights each has in it. As well as ownership and rights there is the question of protection. Inventions are protected by patent. Other forms of property – for example, trademarks and designs – may be protected by registration. Both patent and registration processes can be lengthy and complicated but at the very least the intellectual property must be identified and the processes commenced before the contract can be considered closed.

③ Contract amendment(s)

As part of the process of closing the contract things forgotten, things left undone, and things unresolved will crawl from the proverbial woodwork. This is the time to clear such issues up and to agree with the other party a final amendment to ensure all is neat and tidy.

Indeed on major contracts where many amendments have arisen over the years it is not uncommon for the two sides to have their respective copies of the contract not correlate exactly the one to the other. Again, this is the time to rationalise the paperwork to ensure that both sides agree that the contract is closed.

④ Contract file

Once the contract is closed the contract file should be reviewed, tidied and checked for completeness. Duplicate and unnecessary papers should be removed and destroyed. It is difficult to define what papers are unnecessary but the following should be kept:

    a) The contract and its amendments.

    b) Pre- and post-contract correspondence.

    c) Minutes of external meetings.

    d) Internal memoranda and minutes only to the extent that they impact directly on (a), (b), or (c).

It is suggested that the final enclosure in the file is a copy of the closure checklist carrying the signatures of the relevant department managers who carry responsibility for the various aspects of the work.

Once this documentary review has taken place and a general tidy up done, then files should be archived in a company-approved manner. Archived files should generally be retained for a minimum period of six years.

⑤ Summary

The checklist described is intended to be exhaustive and so the contract administrator should not be put off by the apparently grand headings. Items such as bonds and collaboration agreements are not really as daunting as they may seem.

In practice it may be sensible to use the checklist exactly as provided or to use variations of it, eliminating the topics that never arise. Although the checklist is exhaustive it is, of course, only exhaustive in a general sense. Contracts in a particular industry will have requirements that are unique to that industry. Therefore the checklist that is provided here should be used as a basis for drawing up a checklist or series of checklists that are tailored to the specific industry and company.

As a final note of importance it should be remembered that the contract closure procedure is intended to be initiated once the work is at an end. The presumption is made that this will be following completion of deliveries or supply of all services or as appropriate. Occasionally a contract may come to a premature end through termination for default or for convenience. It is important that the contract closure procedure should be completed for all contracts, even those which come to an end earlier than anticipated.

1

● ● ● ● ● ● Ⓐ Ⓟ Ⓟ Ⓔ Ⓝ Ⓓ Ⓘ Ⓧ ● ●

Checklists

List	Description	See Chapter
A	Letter drafting	4
B	Drafting contract documents	4
C	Drafting contract conditions	4
D	Preparing tenders	4
E	Summary quotations	4
F	Budgetary estimates	4
G	Requests for quotation	4
H	Shortform RFQ	4
I	Budgetary request	4
J	Contract amendments	4
K	Payment routine	8
L	Contract closure	11

Checklist A
Letter drafting

BASICS

1) Addressee's full name and address
2) Addressor's full name and address including telephone/fax number
3) Date
4) Correct form of address, eg 'Dear Sirs'
5) Unique reference number
6) The other party's reference number
7) The contract, order or enquiry number
8) Correct close, eg 'For' and 'on behalf of'
9) Correct close, eg 'Yours faithfully'
10) Job title beneath signature

HEXAGON PRINCIPLE

11) Clarity
12) Concision
13) Accuracy
14) Precision
15) Completeness
16) Relevance

PENTAGON OBJECTIVE

17) Maximise profit
18) Optimise cash
19) Minimise risk
20) Protect ideas
21) Secure orders

FINAL CHECKS

22) Does the letter harm me?
23) Is anything said that later might work against me?
24) Will the other side react satisfactorily and have appropriate counters been included?

Checklist B
Drafting contract documents

THE MANNER
1) Clear
2) Concise
3) Accurate
4) Precise
5) Complete
6) Relevant

THE MESSAGE
7) The What – definition and specification
8) The When – timescale and timing
9) The Where – destination
10) The How – method of delivery
11) The What Else – dependencies
12) The How Much – price and payment

THE MEANING
13) Risk, liabilities and responsibilities
14) Intellectual Property Rights

THE STRUCTURE
15) Schedule of requirements – summary of the message
16) Contract conditions:
    a) Capture the message
       - The What
       - The When
       - The Where
       - The How
       - The How Much
    b) Include relevant standard conditions
    c) Capture the meaning
       - late delivery
       - loss/damage to goods
       - transit risks
       - injury or death
       - loss or damage to property
       - third parties
       - acceptance and rejection

- warranties
- Intellectual Property Rights
- bonds/guarantees

17) Statement of work
   a) Link the schedule to detailed definitions (eg specifications)
   b) Meetings
   c) Reports
   d) Data
   e) Documentation
   f) Demonstrations

18) Specifications
   a) List or include all relevant specifications
   b) Ensure linkage with the message and the meaning
   c) Include order of precedence

19) Payment plan

20) Deliverable items
   a) List items actually deliverable
   b) Provide full description and part numbers

21) Deliverable data
   a) List deliverable data – CDRL
   b) Define format   – DID

22) Programme plan
   a) Dates and programme for deliverable articles
   b) Dates and programme for deliverable data/documentation
   c) Dates and programme for customer provided material
   d) Dates of meetings

23) Other plans, etc (as appropriate)
   a) Quality plan
   b) Purchasing plan
   c) Manufacturing plan
   d) Development plan
   e) Test plan
   f) Acceptance plan

24) Other basics
    a) Contract number
    b) Correct, legal form of the parties' names
    c) Correct addresses
    d) Effective date of contract
    e) A contents list
    f) A list of definitions

Checklist C
Drafting contract conditions

The list of the topics to be covered and their possible structure is covered in List B which provides a checklist to aid the drafting of contract documents. Some such topics need no further explanation within the necessarily general confines of this book. This list aims to emphasise additional considerations of more detail than is provided in List B only to the extent that this is possible in general terms. This list should therefore be read in conjunction with List B.

1) Price
   a) Specify currency or currencies
   b) State *and define* status, eg
      – firm
      – fixed
      – provisional
      – interim
      – lump sum
      – incentive
   c) State position on taxes/duties, eg
      – VAT
      – import duty
      – overseas local
      – taxes/duties
   d) If variable, state by what device, eg
      – exchange variation
      – variation of price
      – cost escalation
   e) State inclusions and exclusions
   f) Cross refer to payment arrangements
   g) If variable (see (d) above) state
      – when adjustments are to be made
      – what the adjustment is, eg by mathematical formula, including any fixed elements
      – if based upon published indices, where they are to be found
      – what arrangements will apply if the indices are provisional/delayed/not available

h) State any
   – discounts
   – offsets
   – retentions

2) Payment
   a) State the basis, eg
      – on delivery
      – in advance
      – in stages
      – based on milestones
      – based on progress
      – retentions, eg
         – on completion
         – on acceptance
         – on warranty
   b) State method of payment
      – invoice
      – against letter of credit
      – against bank guarantee
   c) Identify supporting paperwork, eg
      – certificate of conformity
      – advice and inspection note
      – milestone completion certificate
      – end user certificate
   d) Define credit period, eg
      – 30 days from receipt of valid invoice
   e) Specify procedures for, eg rejected invoice
      – obligation to notify
      – payment arrangement if rejection invalid
   f) State precise location and addresses to which invoices should be sent
   g) If stage/milestones apply
      – define each stage/milestone
      – specify target date of achievement
      – state if achievement can be out of sequence
      – specify any evidential paperwork, eg test results
      – early passing of property

3) Delivery
   a) Start date

  b) Finish date
  c) Delivery rate
  d) Place/terms of delivery, eg – Ex-works
                                  – FOB
                                  – FAS, etc
  e) If other than ex-works state destination and carriage arrangements
  f) Packaging details

4) Specifications
  a) Accurate document reference numbers
  b) State issue status or issue date

5) Meetings
  a) How often
  b) Where held
  c) Terms of reference
  d) Status and number of representatives

6) Reports
  a) How often
  b) What volume
  c) Number of copies

7) Documentation
  a) How approved
  b) Approval timeframe
  c) Implications of non-approval

8) Demonstration, tests, etc
  a) Mandatory witnessing?
  b) Period of notice
  c) Implications of failure
  d) Implications of failure to attend

9) Acceptance/rejection
  a) Event(s) or procedures that convey acceptance
  b) Period for rejection
  c) Method of rejection
  d) Rejection consequences
     – appeal, period of cure, property and risk reversion
  e) Required remedies following rejection

10) Warranties
  a) Express warranty
  b) Period

      c) Start date
      d) Definition of defect
      e) Scope of warranty, eg design or materials, etc
      f) Exclusions
      g) Actions on buyer
      h) Actions on seller
      i) Remedies
      j) Residual warranty
      k) Sole liability
      l) Exclusion of implied undertakings

11) Timeliness of delivery
      a) Early delivery allowable?
      b) Delivery out of sequence allowable?
      c) Implications of late delivery
         – penalties
         – liquidated damages

12) Indemnities
      a) Loss/damage to goods
      b) Personal injury/death
      c) Public liability

13) Intellectual Property Rights
      a) IP and ownership
      b) Buyer's rights
      c) Seller's rights
      d) Customer's needs
      e) Third party rights
      f) Indemnities
      g) Fees and royalties
      h) Payment arrangements

Checklist D
Preparing tenders

A tender is an offer of contract and hence this checklist is primarily the same as for drafting contract conditions with the addition of some features unique to the tender phase. Therefore the majority of this list is identical to List C.

1) Price
   a) Specify currency or currencies
   b) State *and define* status, eg
      - firm
      - fixed
      - provisional
      - interim
      - lump sum
      - incentive
   c) State position on taxes/duties, eg
      - VAT
      - import duty
      - overseas local
      - taxes/duties
   d) If variable, state by what device, eg
      - exchange variation
      - variation of price
      - cost escalation
   e) State inclusions and exclusions
   f) Cross refer to payment arrangements
   g) If variable (see (d) above) state
      - when adjustments are to be made
      - what the adjustment is, eg by mathematical formula, including any fixed elements
      - if based upon published indices, where they are to be found
      - what arrangements will apply if the indices are provisional/delayed/not available
   h) State any
      - discounts
      - offsets
      - retentions

2) Payment
  a) State the basis, eg
    – on delivery
    – in advance
    – in stages
    – based on milestones
    – based on progress
    – retentions, eg
      – on completion
      – on acceptance
      – on warranty
  b) State method of payment
    – invoice
    – against letter of credit
    – against bank guarantee
  c) Identify supporting paperwork, eg
    – certificate of conformity
    – advice and inspection note
    – milestone completion certificate
    – end user certificate
  d) Define credit period, eg
    – 30 days from receipt of valid invoice
  e) Specify procedures for, eg rejected invoice
    – obligation to notify
    – payment arrangement if rejection invalid
  f) State precise location and addresses to which invoices should be sent
  g) If stage/milestones apply
    – define each stage/milestone
    – specify target date of achievement
    – state if achievement can be out of sequence
    – specify any evidential paperwork, eg test results
    – early passing of property
3) Delivery
  a) Start date
  b) Finish date
  c) Delivery rate

   d) Place/terms of delivery, eg   –   Ex-works
                                      –   FOB
                                      –   FAS, etc
   e) If other than ex-works state destination and carriage
       arrangements
   f) Packaging details
4) Specifications
   a) Accurate document reference numbers
   b) State issue status or issue date
5) Meetings
   a) How often
   b) Where held
   c) Terms of reference
   d) Status and number of representatives
6) Reports
   a) How often
   b) What volume
   c) Number of copies
7) Documentation
   a) How approved
   b) Approval timeframe
   c) Implications of non-approval
8) Demonstration, tests, etc
   a) Mandatory witnessing?
   b) Period of notice
   c) Implications of failure
   d) Implications of failure to attend
9) Acceptance/rejection
   a) Event(s) or procedures that convey acceptance
   b) Period for rejection
   c) Method of rejection
   d) Rejection consequences
       – appeal, period of cure, property and risk reversion
   e) Required remedies following rejection
10) Warranties
   a) Express warranty
   b) Period
   c) Start date
   d) Definition of defect

      e) Scope of warranty, eg design or materials, etc

      f) Exclusions

      g) Actions on buyer

      h) Actions on seller

      i) Remedies

      j) Residual warranty

      k) Sole liability

      l) Exclusion of implied undertakings

11) Timeliness of delivery

      a) Early delivery allowable?

      b) Delivery out of sequence allowable?

      c) Implications of late delivery

         – penalties

         – liquidated damages

12) Indemnities

      a) Loss/damage to goods

      b) Personal injury/death

      c) Public liability

13) Intellectual Property Rights

      a) IP and ownership

      b) Buyer's rights

      c) Seller's rights

      d) Customer's needs

      e) Third party rights

      f) Indemnities

      g) Fees and royalties

      h) Payment arrangements

14) Items unique to the tender phase

      a) Date and unique reference number

      b) Reference to customer enquiry

      c) Statement of what comprises the entire tender

      d) Response to any special notices or instructions to tenderers

      e) Name and telephone number/fax of contact point for queries

      f) Validity

Checklist E
Summary quotations

1) Customer's full name and address
2) Customer's reference number
3) Date of enquiry
4) Date of quotation
5) The word **QUOTATION** emboldened/emphasised to draw attention
6) Descriptions with relevant part nos or specification nos
7) Quantity
8) Delivery
    - start
    - rate
    - finish
9) Price
    - unit or lot
    - type, eg firm, VOP, CPA, etc
    - VAT ex or VAT inc
10) Payment
    - against delivery, stages or progress
    - invoice terms
11) Packaging
    - standard
    - consignment address
12) Terms
    - standard terms
    - specific terms
    - model terms
    - previous terms
13) Validity
    - date or period
14) Assumptions/exclusions
15) Contact point
    - undersigned or some other named person

Checklist F
Budgetary estimates

1) Customer's full name and address
2) Customer's reference number
3) Date of enquiry
4) Date of estimate
5) The words **BUDGETARY ESTIMATE** emboldened
6) Description
    - as full as possible
7) Estimate
    - value with statement of economics base and VAT position
8) Likely timeframe
    - duration
    - linked to date of contract
9) Terms
    - outline likely terms
10) Assumptions/ exclusions
    - identify key issues
11) Reiterate budgetary status
12) Contact point(s)
13) Intellectual Property Rights
    a) IP and ownership
    b) Buyer's rights
    c) Seller's rights
    d) Customer's needs
    e) Third party rights
    f) Indemnities
    g) Fees and royalties
    h) Payment arrangements
14) Special notices or instructions to tenderers
    a) Specify details for return of tenders
        - name
        - address
        - due date
        - due time
    b) Number of copies
        - technical

- commercial
- priced/unpriced

c) Acceptance of portion
- state whether the right is reserved to accept all or part of the tender

d) Part tenders
- state whether tenderers may tender for a part only

e) Return of data, etc
- state arrangements for return of any data issued as the basis upon which tenders were to be prepared

f) Options
- state if options are required and/or if unsolicited options will be considered

g) Delivery
- state whether delivery offers different from that specified will be considered

Checklist G
Requests for quotation

A request for quotation or invitation to tender is a request for an offer of contract or it is the basis from which a contract may be offered. Hence the checklist is largely identical to List C.

1) Price
   a) Specify currency or currencies
   b) State *and define* status, eg
      - firm
      - fixed
      - provisional
      - interim
      - lump sum
      - incentive
   c) State position on taxes/duties, eg
      - VAT
      - import duty
      - overseas local
      - taxes/duties
   d) If variable, state by what device, eg
      - exchange variation
      - variation of price
      - cost escalation
   e) State inclusions and exclusions
   f) Cross refer to payment arrangements
   g) If variable (see (d) above) state
      - when adjustments are to be made
      - what the adjustment is, eg by mathematical formula, including any fixed elements
      - if based upon published indices, where they are to be found
      - what arrangements will apply if the indices are provisional/delayed/not available
   h) State any
      - discounts
      - offsets
      - retentions

2) Payment
   a) State the basis, eg
      - on delivery
      - in advance
      - in stages
      - based on milestones
      - based on progress
      - retentions, eg
        - on completion
        - on acceptance
        - on warranty
   b) State method of payment
      - invoice
      - against letter of credit
      - against bank guarantee
   c) Identify supporting paperwork, eg
      - certificate of conformity
      - advice and inspection note
      - milestone completion certificate
      - end user certificate
   d) Define credit period, eg
      - 30 days from receipt of valid invoice
   e) Specify procedures for, eg rejected invoice
      - obligation to notify
      - payment arrangement if rejection invalid
   f) State precise location and addresses to which invoices should be sent
   g) If stage/milestones apply
      - define each stage/milestone
      - specify target date of achievement
      - state if achievement can be out of sequence
      - specify any evidential paperwork, eg test results
      - early passing of property
3) Delivery
   a) Start date
   b) Finish date
   c) Delivery rate

        d) Place/terms of delivery, eg   – Ex-works
                                   – FOB
                                   – FAS, etc
        e) If other than ex-works state destination and carriage arrangements
        f) Packaging details

4) Specifications
        a) Accurate document reference numbers
        b) State issue status or issue date

5) Meetings
        a) How often
        b) Where held
        c) Terms of reference
        d) Status and number of representatives

6) Reports
        a) How often
        b) What volume
        c) Number of copies

7) Documentation
        a) How approved
        b) Approval timeframe
        c) Implications of non-approval

8) Demonstration, tests, etc
        a) Mandatory witnessing?
        b) Period of notice
        c) Implications of failure
        d) Implications of failure to attend

9) Acceptance/rejection
        a) Event(s) or procedures that convey acceptance
        b) Period for rejection
        c) Method of rejection
        d) Rejection consequences
           – appeal, period of cure, property and risk reversion
        e) Required remedies following rejection

10) Warranties
        a) Express warranty
        b) Period
        c) Start date
        d) Definition of defect

        e) Scope of warranty, eg design or materials, etc
        f) Exclusions
        g) Actions on buyer
        h) Actions on seller
        i) Remedies
        j) Residual warranty
        k) Sole liability
        l) Exclusion of implied undertakings

11) Timeliness of delivery
        a) Early delivery allowable?
        b) Delivery out of sequence allowable?
        c) Implications of late delivery
           – penalties
           – liquidated damages

12) Indemnities
        a) Loss/damage to goods
        b) Personal injury/death
        c) Public liability

13) Intellectual Property Rights
        a) IP and ownership
        b) Buyer's rights
        c) Seller's rights
        d) Customer's needs
        e) Third party rights
        f) Indemnities
        g) Fees and royalties
        h) Payment arrangements

14) Special notices or instructions to tenderers
        a) Specify details for return of tenders
           – name
           – address
           – due date
           – due time
        b) Number of copies
           – technical
           – commercial
           – priced/unpriced

c) Acceptance of portion
   - state whether the right is reserved to accept all or part of the tender
d) Part tenders
   - state whether tenderers may tender for a part only
e) Return of data, etc
   - state arrangements for return of any data issued as the basis upon which tenders were to be prepared
f) Options
   - state if options are required and/or if unsolicited options will be considered
g) Delivery
   - state whether delivery offers different from that specified will be considered
h) Tender activities
   - specify details for
     - bidder's conference
     - procedures for questions and answers
i) Tender validity
   - specify period of validity required
j) Bonds
   - specify any bonds required:
     - bid bond
     - performance bond
k) Form of response
   - specify
     - structure
     - number of volumes
     - maximum size (eg number of words)
     - compliancy statement
l) Adjudication process
   - specify
     - timing
     - presentations
       - place
       - date
       - content
     - demonstrations
       - place

           – date
           – content
        – who pays for presentations or demonstrations
        – pre-contract clarifications/negotiations

m) Decision basis
    – cheapest compliant
    – published adjudication criteria/scheme

Checklist H
Shortform RFQ

1) Supplier's full name and address
2) Reference number and date
3) Description with relevant part nos, etc
4) Quantity
5) Delivery
   - start
   - date
   - finish
   - best delivery
6) Price
   - unit or lot
   - type, eg firm, VOP, CPA, etc
   - VAT ex or inc
7) Payment
   - delivery, stage or progress
8) Packaging
9) Terms
   - standard
   - specific
   - model
   - previous
10) Validity
   - date or period
11) Reply by date
12) Assumptions/exclusions
13) Contact point
14) Emphasis enquiry only

Checklist I
Budgetary request

1) Supplier's full name and address
2) Reference number and date
3) Description – as full as possible
4) Timeframe – specify or ask for outline proposal
5) Terms – outline terms
6) Assumptions/exclusions
7) Contact points

Checklist J
Contract amendments

1) Names and addresses
2) Date
3) Contract number
4) Contract title
5) Amendment number
6) Relevant preamble
7) Details of amendment
8) All other terms and conditions remain unchanged
9) Confirmation of acceptance

Checklist K
Payment routine

1) Paperwork
   a) Prescribed invoice proforma
      – buyer's
      – seller's
   b) Supporting documents
      – delivery notes
      – advice notes
      – inspection certificate of conformance
      – insurance certificate
      – receipt notes
      – milestone completion certificate
2) Signatures
   a) Seller
   b) Buyer
   c) Invoice approval process
3) Timing
   a) Within any prescribed time limit
   b) Allow time for checking
   c) Credit period
4) Details
   a) Seller's name and address
   b) Buyer's name and address
   c) Invoice address (if different from (b))
   d) Payment address (if different from (a))
   e) Correct amount
   f) Correct currency
   g) VOP adjustments if applicable
   h) Addition of VAT at correct rate
   i) Description accurate
      – description
      – part number
      – quantity
   j) Packaging/post instructions

Checklist L
Contract closure

1) Prices
All prices agreed and written confirmation.

2) Delivery
All deliveries complete and services supplied and proof of acceptance to hand.

3) Options
Option period expired and any options taken up fully delivered.

4) Payments
All payments received including retentions.

5) Purchase orders
All purchase orders and/or subcontracts chargeable to the contract, including rental agreements, licences, lease, storage, etc, completed, closed and costs transferred to the contract.

6) Internal orders
All internal order numbers closed.

7) Residual materials
All residual materials transferred to stock or disposed of/ delivered to customer.

8) Disputes
Disputes, investigations, appeals, arbitrations, litigation, etc and any actions therefrom are complete.

9) Customer owned property
Customer owned property, including tools and test equipment, returned, disposed of or transferred to another contract with prior approval of the customer – if sold the proceeds have been credited to the customer's account.

10) Documents, etc
Documents and material have been disposed of in accordance with the contract procedures.

11) Warranty
The warranty period has expired and all warranty obligations have been completed.

12) Bank guarantees/bonds
Bank guarantees/bonds have been cancelled and returned.

13) Letters of credit
    Letters of credit have been fully drawn down and credit agreements and associated liabilities are closed/cancelled and documents returned as appropriate.

14) Third party payments
    Third party payments have been made and all obligations discharged including agents, consultants, licensors (including levy payments).

15) Offset and countertrade
    Offset, countertrade and similar obligations complete (where separate related contracts exist these must be closed).

16) Teaming agreements, etc
    Agreement in writing obtained from the parties that all obligations and liabilities relating to the agreement have been discharged.

17) Data retention
    Arrangements have been put in place to retain and maintain data, eg design/manufacturing as required by the contract.

18) Patent applications
    All actions regarding patent applications, etc have been completed.

19) Contract amendments
    Contract amendment necessary to formalise the closure activities has been received and accepted.

20) Contract file
    The contract document has been checked and the files are tidy and complete (duplicate and unnecessary papers destroyed). No activities remain to be undertaken by either party.

Closure activities complete

NAME ....

SIGNATURE ....

COMMERCIAL DEPARTMENT

DATE ....

2

A P P E N D I X

Case study I: Blue Horizon

① The participants

Macho Enterprises Plc: Prime Contractor

Middleman Products Ltd: Subcontractor

Tiddler Components Ltd: Supplier

	Macho	*Middleman*	*Tiddler*
Contracts manager	Colin Macho	Chris Middleman	Clive Tiddler
Projects manager	Penelope Macho	Paul Middleman	Peter Tiddler
Purchasing manager	Brian Macho	Brenda Middleman	Bill Tiddler
Sales manager	Simon Macho	Steve Middleman	Sarah Tiddler

② The correspondence

MIDDLEMAN
PRODUCTS LTD

Tiddler Components Ltd

For the attention of Sarah Tiddler

28 August

Dear Sarah

Blue Horizon – New Technology Widgets

You may know that we are expecting to receive an order from Macho Enterprises for the supply of NTW MK VII for their Blue Horizon project.

We have indicated that we would plan to include TCL LSI/3000/6F units in the NTW MK VII.

Please confirm that TCL could supply the items and if so let me know what the cost would be for 5000 off. Please reply by 3 September.

Yours sincerely

Paul Middleman
Project Manager

TELEX

Middleman Products Ltd

For the attention of Paul Middleman – Project Manager

NEW TECHNOLOGY WIDGETS

Thank you for your letter.

Cost for 5000 off LSI/3000/6 units is £100 each. Delivery 4 weeks f.r.o. subject to standard conditions.

Are we still OK for golf Saturday week?

Regards

Sarah Tiddler
Sales Manager

2 September

TELEX

Tiddler Components Ltd

For the attention of Clive Tiddler – Contracts Manager

BLUE HORIZON

Macho have secured the order and given us an intention to proceed.

Delivery of TCL LSI units must start 1 November if we are to meet Macho programme.

Purchase order in preparation.

Regards

Paul Middleman
Project Manager

2 October

TELEX

Middleman Products Ltd

For the attention of Paul Middleman – Project Manager

BLUE HORIZON

Congratulations and thank you for your telex 2 October.

Work is in hand and we look forward to receipt of formal purchase order.

Regards

Clive Tiddler
Contracts Manager

3 October

TIDDLER COMPONENTS LTD

Middleman Products Ltd

For the attention of Brenda Middleman

3 October

QUOTATION

Dear Brenda

BLUE HORIZON

Further to Paul Middleman's 2 October ITP we are proposing to deliver 5000 off LSI/3000/6 units on 15 November.

Price each of £120 plus VAT invoicable following delivery.

Yours sincerely

Clive Tiddler
Contracts Manager

TIDDLER COMPONENTS LTD

Middleman Products Ltd

For the attention of Paul Middleman – Project Manager

3 October

Dear Paul

BLUE HORIZON

I am glad we're straight on the Blue Horizon job. The 5000 off should be with you on 3 November providing you can let me have the electrical interface data by 5 October.

Yours sincerely

Peter Tiddler
Project Manager

MIDDLEMAN PRODUCTS LTD

PURCHASE ORDER

To: Tiddler Components Ltd

Order No: A123/4

Please supply:

Qty	Spec	Description	Price
5000	LSI/3000/6E	LSI FOR NTW MK VII	£100 EACH

Delivery: 500/Week commencing 1 November

Packaging: Retail trade

Terms: Standard

Acceptance: Please confirm acceptance

Signed: ....

Brenda Middleman
Purchasing Manager
6 October

TIDDLER COMPONENTS LTD

Middleman Products Ltd

For the attention of Brenda Middleman – Purchasing Manager

10 October

Dear Brenda

ORDER NO A123/4

Thank you for your purchase order dated 6 October which is acceptable although the price and delivery require revision in line with our 3 October quote.

Yours sincerely

Clive Tiddler
Contracts Manager

MACHO ENTERPRISES PLC

Middleman Products Ltd

For the attention of Steve Middleman – Sales Manager

20 November

Dear Steve

BLUE HORIZON

Unfortunately Blue Horizon has been cancelled and we cannot go ahead with the New Technology Widget Order.

Yours sincerely

Penelope Macho
Project Manager

③ Summary of events

Date	From	To	
28 Aug.	Middleman Project	Tiddler Sales	Request cost of 5000 off LSI/3000/6F.
2 Sept.	Tiddler Sales	Middleman Project	Cost £100 each 5000 off LSI/3000/6 Delivery 4 weeks f.r.o. standard conditions.
2 Oct.	Middleman Project	Tiddler Contracts	Advises Middleman have intention to proceed, says LSI delivery must start 1 Nov.
3 Oct.	Tiddler Contracts	Middleman Project	Work is in hand. Looking forward to formal purchase order.
3 Oct.	Tiddler Contracts	Middleman Purchasing	Quotes £120 each for LSI/3000/6. 5000 off to be delivered on 15 Nov.
3 Oct.	Tiddler Project	Middleman Project	Promises 5000 off on 3 Nov. if electrical interface data provided by 5 Oct.
6 Oct.	Middleman Purchasing	Tiddler	Purchase order 5000 off LSI/3000/6E. £100 each 500/week commencing 1 Nov.
10 Oct.	Tiddler Contracts	Middleman Purchasing	Accepts purchase order subject to price and delivery revisions.

④ Questions

1. Does a contract exist between Middleman and Tiddler?

2. When did the contract come into being?

3. What is to be supplied and when?

4. What status does Peter Tiddler's letter about electrical interface data have?

5. What is the price?

6. What are the terms and conditions of the contract?

7. Does cancellation of Blue Horizon give Middleman an opportunity to cancel the order with Tiddler?

⑤ **Analysis**

1. The primary criteria for the existence of a contract are:
   1. Legal capacity of the parties.
   2. The contract must be legal and possible.
   3. Intention to create legal relations.
   4. Consideration.
   5. Offer and acceptance.

In this instance it is safe to assume that Middleman and Tiddler have the legal capacity to enter into contracts. Their limited company status indicates incorporation within the Companies Act and clearly they intend to carry on the business of trading. Criterion 1 is satisfied.

The contract – if it is such – is legal and possible. The sale of the LSI units is not illegal either in the criminal sense or in the civil sense. That is to say it can be assumed that the goods in themselves are not illegal (as prohibited substances may be), that the act of selling them is not illegal (as sale of firearms may be) and that Tiddler actually has the right to sell them, ie that they do not belong to somebody else. The contract is also possible in the sense that a 'contract' for a perpetual motion machine would not be possible, for example. Thus the contract is legal and possible and criterion 2 is satisfied.

The question of an intention to create legal relations is slightly more difficult. In principle there is no doubt that Middleman intended to buy LSI units from Tiddler to satisfy the Macho order. Clearly Tiddler were keen to sell. However, the early correspondence could not be construed as conveying a specific intention at that time. For the time being it is assumed that the intention did exist on both sides although the timing of events as will be seen later is important. Criterion 3 is satisfied.

Consideration: in this case the obligation to pay money for the goods is clear. Each side may have a different view of the price but it is certain in principle that Middleman intended to pay. Which is the correct price is discussed later. If the lower price stands and if that would mean Tiddler selling at a loss the consideration is still sufficient. Criterion 4 is satisfied.

It may be void for mistake. However, in contracts which are wholly or partly executed as can be assumed here the courts are loath to set aside a contract if it is reasonably clear that the parties intended there to be contract. In these circumstances the courts would attempt to deduce the intentions and hence impute an offer and acceptance.

Offer and acceptance is far more clear. At no time is there a clear offer met with an unqualified acceptance. On top of that it is not entirely certain what the subject of the contract is. LSI/3000/6, LSI/3000/6E, LSI/3000/6F are all mentioned. As has been said, there is no agreed price and delivery is also uncertain. In the extreme a court may decide that the contract is void in the face of all this uncertainty.

2. It could be said that Tiddler's 3 October letter saying work is in hand in reply to Middleman's 2 October letter stressing the importance of starting delivery on 1 November created a contract, especially as Middleman did nothing afterwards to disabuse Tiddler from the belief that they had been asked to start.

The later issue of the purchase order and subsequently its qualified acceptance are formalities only, unless it is clear – and provable – that Tiddler should have known that only a properly authorised purchase order could commit Middleman to contract.

3. Assuming then that, whether or not a contract existed in the strict legal sense during the early part of the events, and that both parties proceeded in the belief that a contract existed, the question arises as to what should be supplied and when.

If in practice there was no significant difference between the LSI/3000/6, LSI/3000/6E and LSI/3000/6F it may not matter what was delivered. If E and F are versions of a 6-series family having no form, fit or function difference insofar as Middleman's New Technology Widget was concerned, there should be no cause for complaint from Middleman. If there are differences then both sides have a good argument. Tiddler were consistent between 2 September and 3 October in offering to supply the LSI/3000/6. Although the initial request for quote had mentioned the 6F, Middleman did not query the two Tiddler letters. However, Tiddler failed to query the number in their response to the purchase order which referred to the 6E. This misunderstanding is potentially the most serious of the defects in this chain of events. If Middleman genuinely needed the 6F as per their enquiry or the 6E as per the purchase order and Tiddler tried to deliver the 6 version then the delivery would be rejected – causing

Tiddler severe problems – and Middleman could fail to perform their contract (assuming Blue Horizon had not been cancelled) with Macho.

The question of time of delivery is equally fraught. This time both parties were consistent. Middleman twice said that delivery must start on 1 November and Tiddler mentioned only 3 and 15 November (this in itself is very poor, two Tiddler representatives independently giving different dates). Tiddler also referred to this in response to the purchase order and indeed their initial offer mentioned 4 weeks from receipt of order and at that time there was sufficient time for Middleman to place the order. Tiddler's later letter on 3 October is also consistent with this.

One problem is that if Tiddler agreed that the 2 October letter was the go ahead, then the wording of that letter suggests that 'time was of the essence' to Middleman. In that case Tiddler would be in fundamental breach of contract if they did not deliver on 1 November, entitling Middleman to cancel the contract.

A further complication is the mention on the purchase order of delivery in batches. Although Tiddler queried the delivery it is not absolutely clear if they were querying the batch requirement or the start date or both. For Tiddler to plan for single delivery but in practice to send batches could give them cash flow and storage problems. For Middleman to plan batches but receive single delivery would give cash flow and storage problems to Middleman.

The balance of weight appears to be on Tiddler's side and thus a single delivery on 3 November would have been correct, but what of the electrical interface data problem?

4.   The letter is certainly consistent with the offer of delivery 4 weeks from receipt of order if it is assumed – as Tiddler did – that the 2 October letter from Middleman was the instruction to proceed. It clashes with the 3 October letter from Clive Tiddler which mentioned the 15th and did not refer to the interface data. Perhaps the contracts man was assuming that the data would not arrive by 5 October or perhaps he just did not want to commit his company to such a tight delivery obligation given the risk mentioned above that the contract could be interpreted as 'time is of the essence'. In any event the dependency on receiving the interface data was not mentioned by Tiddler in either quotation or specifically in the

response to the purchase order.

If delivery by Tiddler was delayed beyond 15 November and Middleman did not provide the electrical interface data on time it is unlikely that Tiddler could successfully argue that the delay was the fault of Middleman.

5.   Assuming that there is no price difference between the LSI/3000/6, LSI/3000/6E and LSI/3000/6F then is the price £100 each or £120 each?

The initial enquiry from Paul Middleman asks for the cost. It is not clear whether he meant to ask for an estimate (for guidance purposes) or a quotation (capable of acceptance). In this context, asking for a cost does not help. A price from Tiddler may be a cost to Middleman. Sarah Tiddler's reply is no more helpful although when Clive Tiddler did quote formally on 3 October nobody from Middleman queried the discrepancy.

The difficulty may be resolved if Middleman knew either that Sarah Tiddler did not have authority to quote or that Tiddler quotations are only official if communicated on formal 'quotation' paperwork. Tiddler did comment on the price shown on the purchase order and so the £120 price probably stands although perhaps Middleman might push Tiddler for a reduction if in good faith they had already used £100 in quoting to Macho.

6.   This is almost impossible to say. Tiddler's standard conditions were referred to in Sarah Tiddler's letter but for the financial reasons discussed above Tiddler would prefer that letter not to be formal. However, Clive Tiddler's quotation – which Tiddler would prefer to be the formal quotation – did not mention terms. The purchase order referred to Middleman's standard terms. Tiddler did not comment on this in responding to the purchase order. The balance is slightly in Middleman's favour.

In practice if neither set of conditions contained anything that gave rise to dispute the parties would probably ignore each other's conditions and thus it would never be known as to which applied. Many business transactions are carried on in this way and hence occasionally it is wondered why time is devoted to the terms and conditions. The answer can be seen in the parallel with insurance – it is there as a safeguard against the small chance of something going wrong and when something does go wrong the safeguard must be sufficient and appropriate.

7.   On the basis that a contract between Middleman and Tiddler exists then the Blue Horizon cancellation notified by Macho has no effect on the Middleman/Tiddler relationship. If Middleman could establish that it is their standard conditions that apply then it is likely that those (ie the conditions favourable to the buyer) would include a right for Middleman to cancel the contract for their own convenience. If not, Tiddler would be entitled to insist that Middleman negotiate a settlement relating to the cost or value of work done, cancellation charges and lost profits if the contract is to be prematurely terminated.

6 Summary

The sketchy example used may appear to be exaggerated but such events do happen, particularly where matters are complicated – as they are in practice – by the involvement of more people, more correspondence, telephone and other discussions, interdepartmental communication and other problems, etc. The main points illustrated are:

a) The need for certainty, clarity and consistency in all communication.

b) The need for clear co-ordination between different departments.

c) The need for clear understanding on all sides of who is authorised to do and say what.

3

○ ○ ○ ○ ○ ○ Ⓐ Ⓟ Ⓟ Ⓔ Ⓝ Ⓓ Ⓘ Ⓧ ○ ○

Case study II: Widgets

① **Scenario**

② **Contract clauses**

③ **Questions**

④ **Analysis**

Scenario

1. Spiffo Controls Ltd has accepted a contract from Windup Rotary Ltd to supply 300 mini widgets. The contract was accepted on 1 April with delivery to be complete by 30 October.

2. The contract provides for payment to be made in three stages: 25% in May, 50% in September and 25% in November.

3. The contract contains clauses on delivery, acceptance, risk, property and warranty.

The following sequence of events takes place:

a) Work is put in hand by Spiffo.

b) Windup computer on the blink and first payment to Spiffo is delayed to 1 July.

c) 24 June Spiffo advise first batch complete.

d) Windup collect first batch, all of which fail acceptance test on 3 July.

e) Windup return first batch, 10% of which are damaged in transit.

f) Spiffo deliver second batch on 28 August. Windup reject the delivery as no prior notice was given.

g) Windup withhold September stage-payment.

h) 28 September Spiffo advise that 90% of the first batch and 100% of the second batch are ready.

i) Windup agree to take delivery of 90% first batch and 100% second batch on 30 September although they are not happy about a claim from Spiffo that Windup are responsible for the 10% damaged in transit. Spiffo deliver and the goods pass acceptance test on 18 October.

j) In October Windup make the second stage-payment.

k) 28 October Spiffo advises that third batch is ready. Windup refuses to take delivery until the 10% of first batch is delivered. Spiffo advised by Windup that final payment will be withheld.

l) 14 November Windup rejects 5% of the first batch under warranty.

② Contract clauses

Delivery

The seller shall deliver the articles to the buyer's works at Stockton-over-Puddle. Delivery shall be made in three equal batches according to the following schedule:

Batch 1: Friday 26 June
Batch 2: Friday 28 August
Batch 3: Friday 30 September

Delivery is required in the week leading up to the above-mentioned dates and seller is required to give the buyer 24 hours' notice of consignment. The buyer shall be under no obligation to accept articles outside of the required delivery or if no notice of consignment is received.

Acceptance

The articles shall be deemed accepted following testing by the buyer in accordance with the agreed acceptance test plan.

Risk

Risk in the goods shall pass to the buyer following acceptance.

Property

Property in the goods shall pass to the buyer on delivery unless the contract provides for interim payments in which event property shall pass to the buyer during the course of manufacture.

Warranty

The seller shall warrant the goods against defective materials or workmanship for 30 days. Property and risk in goods rejected under warranty shall revert to the seller who shall replace the defective goods at his own cost with conforming goods within 15 days.

(3) Questions

1. Who is responsible for the 10% first batch damaged in transit bearing in mind that Windup collected and returned the goods?

2. The first payment occurs after Spiffo's first attempt to make the initial delivery. Who owns the first batch before and immediately after the acceptance test is failed?

3. Are Windup right to refuse delivery of the second batch and can Spiffo claim against Windup for the repeat delivery cost?

4. Does Windup have the right to withhold the September stage-payment?

5. Should Windup have taken redelivery of 90% first batch?

6. Do Windup have the right to refuse the third batch?

7. Are Spiffo obliged to replace the 5% warranty rejects?

8. By November Windup only have 185 working widgets against their requirement for 300 by the end of October. Spiffo have only 75% of their money, 100 widgets made that they cannot deliver and a warranty claim as well. What should Windup and Spiffo do to resolve their mutual problem?

 Analysis

1. Spiffo is undoubtedly responsible for the 10% first batch damaged in transit after rejection by Windup. The contract clearly says that risk does not pass to the buyer until acceptance has taken place. Spiffo could argue that Windup were at fault in collecting the goods in the first place and, as such, how could Spiffo know that the fault causing rejection was not caused by or during transportation? They could also argue that Windup should have advised Spiffo of the acceptance-test failure and required Spiffo to collect the rejected goods. In the former case the contract says that Spiffo are responsible for delivery, in the latter the contract is silent on who transports rejected goods. Neither of these facts would affect the outcome: Spiffo are bound to repair or replace the damaged goods. It is to be hoped that, in signing a contract that includes the responsibility for delivery and in which risk passes to the buyer at a later stage, Spiffo carry the necessary insurance cover against loss or damage in transit. A point to be noted is that it is prudent to check that the insurance does cover rejected goods as well as conforming items.

2. On the question of ownership of the first batch before and immediately after the first delivery attempt, a deficiency in the wording of the delivery clause is discovered. Property, ie ownership, passes to the buyer on delivery but the delivery clause only refers to the timing of physical delivery and the obligation on the seller to effect transportation. Thus it is not clear whether delivery, for the purpose of identifying the passage of property, is physical arrival of the goods or their acceptance. However, the point becomes academic as property passes to the buyer during manufacture in view of the provision in the contract for interim payments. The fact that the initial payment was delayed is not relevant as the contract *provides* for interim payments, ie it does not say that interim payments have actually to be made for property to pass at the early stage. So Windup own the material before and after rejection.

3. The contract gives Windup the right to refuse delivery if no notice is given. Spiffo therefore have no claim in respect of repeat delivery costs. In practice Spiffo would be wise to try and find out more about the refusal to take delivery. On the face of it Windup needed delivery at specific points in time presumably to meet some

production programme. If the requirement for prior notice was included for no more than the convenience of Windup then perhaps there is something more behind the refusal than meets the eye. At this stage in the sequence of events Spiffo would be right to be suspicious and should try to find out more.

4. Without seeing the payments clause in detail it is not possible to say whether Windup had the right to withhold the September payment. Interim payments tend to be discretionary and so Windup may have had the right. Windup would argue that by the beginning of September Spiffo were seriously in default of contract. The first batch all failed the acceptance test and no notice was given for delivery of the second batch and thus payment should be suspended. Spiffo would argue that Windup's collection and sub-sequent return of the first batch may have contributed to the problem, that they had not said that the rejected articles would not be replaced and that the second batch had been refused on a technicality. In any event interim payments were a fundamental feature of the contract and should not have been withheld.

5. There was nothing to stop Windup from taking redelivery of 90% of the first batch. They would have been entitled not to take delivery as the contract clearly said delivery in batches. This partial delivery could not be used as evidence by Spiffo that Windup were acknowledging responsibility for the 10% damaged in transit.

6. Windup had the right to refuse the third batch because it was late. Some sympathy lies with Spiffo. They have had payment delayed or withheld three times and yet they have successfully delivered 90% of batch 1, 100% of batch 2 and were ready to deliver 100% of batch 3. From their point of view Windup has been a fickle customer. Payments have been delayed or withheld, deliveries have been refused, articles that should have been delivered were col-lected and all these have been virtually random events. On top of this the early manufacturing problems – if that was the reason causing acceptance failure of the first batch – have gone away and Spiffo must be desperate to finish the order, take the money and run.

7. The problem of warranty is not clear as the warranty clause is not precise as to when the warranty period commences. Windup have advised the warranty claim within 30 days of the goods passing the acceptance test but beyond 30 days following physical delivery at their works. Windup would argue that as the contract specifically calls for an acceptance test then clearly before that test has been conducted it is impossible to say whether the articles are good or bad and thus warranty must commence following completion of the acceptance test. Spiffo might say that as they have no knowledge or control over when Windup would conduct the test it is only reasonable for the warranty to commence on physical delivery, otherwise Spiffo could carry an indeterminate liability. Windup could respond by saying that the warranty period in itself is irrelevant as clearly the goods are not of merchantable quality and/or reasonably fit for their purpose. Only a court could decide that question and neither party would want to go that far at this stage. In negotiating the contract Spiffo should have tried to close off the risk by agreeing the specific warranty on the condition that it is only warranty, ie undertakings implied by the Sale of Goods Act are excluded.

8. Although the greater sympathy might be with Spiffo, the upper hand is held by Windup. Spiffo must start with the assumption that Windup are not capriciously or maliciously being difficult. On that basis Spiffo should establish what is the maximum that Windup would expect from them such that if Spiffo yielded all those things, Windup would have no excuse for not restoring payments and taking deliveries. The maximum that Windup could want is:

a) An agreement from Spiffo to replace the 10% first batch damaged in transit by a specific date at no cost to Windup.

b) An acceptance of the warranty claim, giving Spiffo a commitment to replace the defective goods quickly, if not within the 15 days, at no cost to Windup.

c) Delivery of the third batch.

d) Agreement that warranty commences at successful completion of the acceptance test, rather than on physical delivery.

e) Compensation from Spiffo for delays caused by non-delivery, late delivery and rejected goods.

Assuming that the third batch will not fail the acceptance test, the 10% damaged units and 5% warranty claim actually means that Spiffo only have to replace 15 units out of 300. This may be an acceptable penalty in order to get the final 25% of their money. Provided Windup agree not to delay final payment Spiffo should make an offer to accept liability to replace 15 units such that delivery of the third batch can go ahead. If Windup insist on a retention until at least the 10% of the first batch have been delivered and accepted Spiffo should try to negotiate a much lesser sum than the 25% owed to them. Spiffo may be able to accept that warranty starts from completion of acceptance testing provided Windup agree to do the tests within a specified maximum period following delivery.

It is in Spiffo's best interests to put this type of solution – phrased to say that this is in full and final settlement of their obligations – forward to Windup before they think of, or make a claim for, compensation. Such a claim, were it to be sizeable, could lead ultimately to the unthinkable – a law suit.

The major lessons to be learned are that the contract clauses must be precise and deal with all possible eventualities. It is important that seemingly minor obligations under the contract – the requirement to give notice of delivery – are not ignored in practice. Additionally the supplier must keep in mind the consequences (cash flow, reputation, level of stock, insurance, legal eventualities) of not performing the contract exactly as required.

4

A P P E N D I X

Self-perception inventory

R MEREDITH BELBIN

From *Management Teams: Why They Succeed or Fail*, by R Meredith Belbin.

This inventory was developed to give individuals a simple means of assessing their best team-roles.

DIRECTIONS:

For each section, distribute a total of ten points among the sentences which you think best describe your behaviour. These points may be distributed among several sentences: in extreme cases, they might be spread among all the sentences or ten points may be given to a single sentence. Enter the points in Table 1 at the end.

i.   What I believe I can contribute to a team:
   a)   I think I can quickly see and take advantage of new opportunities.
   b)   I can work well with a very wide range of people.
   c)   Producing ideas is one of my natural assets.
   d)   My ability rests in being able to draw people out whenever I detect they have something of value to contribute to group objectives.
   e)   My capacity to follow through has much to do with my personal effectiveness.
   f)   I am ready to face temporary unpopularity if it leads to worthwhile results in the end.
   g)   I can usually sense what is realistic and likely to work.
   h)   I can offer a reasoned case for alternative courses of actions without introducing bias or prejudice.
ii.   If I have a possible shortcoming in teamwork, it could be that:
   a)   I am not at ease unless meetings are well structured and controlled and generally well conducted.
   b)   I am inclined to be too generous towards others who have a valid viewpoint that has not been given a proper airing.
   c)   I have a tendency to talk too much once the group gets on to new ideas.
   d)   My objective outlook makes it difficult for me to join in readily and enthusiastically with colleagues.
   e)   I am sometimes seen as forceful and authoritarian if there is a need to get something done.
   f)   I find it difficult to lead from the front, perhaps because I am overresponsive to the group.

g) I am apt to get too caught up in ideas that occur to me and so lose track of what is happening.

h) My colleagues tend to see me as worrying unnecessarily over detail and the possibility that things may go wrong.

iii. When involved in a project with other people:

a) I have an aptitude for influencing people without pressurising them.

b) My general vigilance prevents careless mistakes and omissions being made.

c) I am ready to press for action to make sure that the meeting does not waste time or lose sight of the main objective.

d) I can be counted on to contribute something original.

e) I am always ready to back a good suggestion in the common interest.

f) I am keen to look for the latest in new ideas and developments.

g) I believe my capacity for judgement can help to bring about the right decisions.

h) I can be relied upon to see that all essential work is organised.

iv. My characteristic approach to group work is that:

a) I have a quiet interest in getting to know colleagues better.

b) I am not reluctant to challenge the view of others or to hold a minority view myself.

c) I can usually find a line of argument to refute unsound propositions.

d) I think I have a talent for making things work once a plan has to be put into operation.

e) I have a tendency to avoid the obvious and to come out with the unexpected.

f) I bring a touch of perfectionism to a job I undertake.

g) I am ready to make use of contacts outside the group itself.

h) While I am interested in all views I have no hesitation in making up my mind once a decision has to be made.

v. I gain satisfaction in my job because:

a) I enjoy analysing situations and weighing up all the possible choices.

b) I am interested in finding practical solutions to problems.

c) I like to feel I am fostering good working relationships.

    d) I can have a strong influence on decisions.

    e) I can meet people who may have something new to offer.

    f) I can get people to agree on a necessary course of action.

    g) I feel in my element where I can give a task my full attention.

    h) I like to find a field that stretches my imagination.

vi. If I am suddenly given a difficult task with limited time and unfamiliar people:

    a) I would feel like retiring to a corner to devise a way out of the impasse before developing a line.

    b) I would be ready to work with the person who showed the most positive approach.

    c) I would find some way of reducing the size of the task by establishing what different individuals might best contribute.

    d) My natural sense of urgency would help to ensure that we did not fall behind schedule.

    e) I believe I would keep cool and maintain my capacity to think straight.

    f) I would retain a steadiness of purpose in spite of the pressures.

    g) I would be prepared to take a positive lead if I felt the group was making no progress.

    h) I would open up discussions with a view to stimulating new thoughts and getting something moving.

vii. With reference to the problems to which I am subject in working in groups:

    a) I am apt to show my impatience with those who are obstructing progress.

    b) Others may criticise me for being too analytical and insufficiently intuitive.

    c) My desire to ensure that work is properly done can hold up proceedings.

    d) I tend to get bored rather easily and rely on one or two stimulating members to spark me off.

    e) I find it difficult to get started unless the goals are clear.

    f) I am sometimes poor at explaining and clarifying complex points that occur to me.

    g) I am conscious of demanding from others the things I cannot do myself.

h) I hesitate to get my points across when I run up against real opposition.

Table 1: Points table for self-perception inventory

Section	Item a	b	c	d	e	f	g	h
I								
II								
III								
IV								
V								
VI								
VII								

Having completed this table (make sure the points in each row total ten) then transfer each of the individual scores to Table 2. For example, if Table 1 shows 10 points against answer a to section 1 then put 10 in box 1a in Table 2 (in this case under the column headed RI).

Table 2

Section	CW	CH	SH	PL	RI	ME	TW	CF	
I	g	d	f	c	a	h	b	e	
II	a	b	e	g	c	d	f	h	
III	h	a	c	d	f	g	e	b	
IV	d	h	b	e	g	c	a	f	
V	b	f	d	h	e	a	c	g	
VI	f	c	g	a	h	e	b	d	
VII	e	g	a	f	d	b	h	c	
Total									

Now fill in the total box for each column to discover the Belbin scores.

CW	Company Worker	RI	Resource Investigator
CH	Chairman	ME	Monitor/Evaluator
SH	Shaper	TW	Team Worker
PL	Plant	CF	Finisher

The highest score on the team-role will indicate how best the respondent can make his or her mark in a management or project team. The next highest scores can denote back-up team-roles towards which the individual should shift if for some reason there is less group need for a primary team-role.

The two lowest scores in team-role imply possible areas of weakness, but rather than attempting to reform in this area the manager may be better advised to seek a colleague with complementary strengths.

5

A P P E N D I X

Example
of a
contract

1. **Introduction**
2. **The subcontract**
3. **Analysis**
4. **Summary**

Introduction

The subcontract agreement is a proposed agreement between a supplier of engineering consultancy services and a company who needs assistance to satisfy a contract with a client.

The schedules A, B, C and D referred to are not included as the commercial principles can be satisfactorily demonstrated without them.

To assist in understanding, the terminology in the Analysis is varied according to the context. Thus the company buying the services is referred to as the 'main contractor' or the 'buyer'. The consultancy firm is referred to as the 'subcontractor', 'seller' or 'supplier'. The subcontract agreement is referred to as the 'subcontract' or the 'contract'.

2 The subcontract

1. The Agreement

1.1. Background

1.1.1. This Agreement is supplemental to a contract as referenced in Schedule A (hereinafter referred to as 'the Main Contract') made the 28th day of April 19— between Blinkers Ltd (hereinafter referred to as 'the Client') and the Contractor which provides for the provision of Engineering Consultancy on the terms and conditions therein contained.

1.1.2. The Subcontractor has agreed with the Contractor that it will carry out the services and provide the articles and facilities detailed in Schedule B hereto (hereinafter referred to as 'the Services' and 'the Articles' respectively) in the manner and at the time specified therein in connection with the project to be carried out under the Contract (the 'Project') on the terms and conditions herein referred to.

1.1.3. In this Agreement words and expressions shall except as otherwise provided here have the same meanings as are respectively assigned to them in the Main Contract.

1.2. The services

1.2.1. The Contractor shall employ the Subcontractor to carry out the Services and provide the Articles in accordance with the criteria set out in Schedule B and subject to the terms and conditions of the Main Contract so far as they are applicable. In the event of inconsistency or conflict the conditions in the Contract will at all times prevail, unless otherwise expressly agreed in writing. Failure by the Subcontractor to meet the criteria set out in Schedule B shall, for the purposes of Clause 3.14, be constructed as a serious breach.

1.2.2. In addition to supplying the Services and Articles set out hereto the Subcontractor shall carry out other work in connection with the Project as the Contractor shall specify, provided the price is agreed by the Contractor prior to the work commencing and the work to be performed by the Subcontractor will be carried out in accordance with the terms of this Agreement.

1.3. Project management

For the purposes of the smooth handling and implementation of the Main Contract and the co-ordination of the Project, the Contractor shall appoint a project manager (the 'Project Manager') to whom shall be delegated the day-to-day responsibilities of managing the Main Contract and who shall be responsible for the co-ordination of subcontractors. The Subcontractor shall also appoint a representative through whom contact can be made. The Subcontractor shall obey all reasonable and lawful instructions of the Project Manager as to the manner in which the Services and Articles are to be supplied.

1.4. The project plan

These are shown in Schedule D (attached) and it is agreed that both the Contractor and the Subcontractor will work to these arrangements. The parties to this Agreement will report progress to the other at agreed intervals.

Terms and conditions

2. Pricing

2.1. Price and payment terms

The consideration due (hereinafter referred to as 'the Price') for carrying out the Services and/or supplying the Articles shall be as specified in Schedule C hereto and shall become due and payable by the Contractor to the Subcontractor in accordance with the provisions therein contained.

2.2. Delay in payment

Payment by the Contractor to the Subcontractor may be delayed as a result of the Subcontractor's failure

a) to send on the day of despatch for each consignment, advice of despatch and invoice,

or

b) to send a monthly Statement of Account quoting the invoice numbers applicable to each item thereon,

or

c) to mark clearly the Contractor's Project Number/Main Contract Reference on any packages, packing notes, advice notes, invoices, monthly statements and all other correspondence relating thereof.

3.   General

3.1. Assignment

a) The Subcontractor shall not assign the whole or any part of the benefit of this Agreement nor shall the Subcontractor sublet the whole or any part of the Services and Articles without the prior written consent of the Contractor.

b) 'Subletting' in this Clause shall include placing an order for the supply of the articles and/or services in connection with the Services and/or the Articles.

3.2. Duration

This Agreement shall start on the Commencement Date and shall continue until *either* all the obligations of both parties have been fulfilled *or* the Agreement is terminated in accordance with Clause 3.14 *or* by mutual written Agreement, whichever occurs first.

3.3. Liability

a) The Contractor shall indemnify the Subcontractor in respect of any liability for death of or personal injury to any person caused by the Contractor's negligence.

b) The Contractor shall not in any circumstances be liable to the Subcontractor whether in contract, tort or otherwise for any consequential or indirect loss or damage howsoever arising and of whatsoever nature including (without limitation) loss of profit, loss of contracts, loss of operation time, loss of computer-held data, loss of use of any equipment or process or any other form of loss whatsoever (whether or not similar to some or any of the foregoing) suffered or incurred (directly or indirectly) by the Subcontractor.

c) The liability of the Contractor to the Subcontractor for direct loss or damage whether in contract, tort or otherwise arising out of or in connection with its performance of or its total or partial failure to perform in accordance with the terms of this Agreement shall in respect of any one incident or series of incidents attributable to the same cause be limited to and shall not in any circumstances exceed the lesser of the sum of £300,000 (three hundred thousand pounds sterling) or twice the Price under this Agreement.

3.4. Indemnity

a) The Subcontractor *hereby acknowledges* that any breach by it of this Agreement may result in the Contractor committing breaches of and becoming liable for damages under the Main Contract and other Agreements (in like form to this Agreement and otherwise) made by the Contractor in connection with the Project and all such damages, losses and expenses are hereby agreed to be within the contemplation of the parties as being probable results of any such breach by the Subcontractor against all such breaches and damages as aforesaid.

b) Without prejudice to the indemnities above in favour of the Contractor, the Subcontractor shall take out all necessary public, product and professional liability insurance with an insurance company or companies of repute to cover the liabilities assumed by it hereunder and shall on request make available such policies for inspection by the Contractor or the Client as the case may be.

3.5. Intellectual Property Rights

The Subcontractor recognises that all software listing and associated documentation and manuals supplied, are the Contractor's confidential information and all Intellectual Property Rights therein are and shall remain vested in the Contractor. The Subcontractor shall not, without the Contractor's prior consent in writing, adapt, modify, or make any copies of or divulge to third parties other than the Client the said confidential information and shall so bind its directors and employees, provided that the Subcontractor may for its own use make copies as may be necessary for the proper operation or security of its business.

3.6. Ownership of results

All rights in the result of the work performed by the Subcontractor in the course of this Agreement shall forthwith be communicated to, and shall belong exclusively to, the Contractor. If requested by the Contractor, the Subcontractor will agree to do all things necessary at the Contractor's sole cost to obtain where possible letters patent, registered designs, copyright or like industrial property in relation to any process, product, concept or writing developed or produced by the Subcontractor in the performance of such work.

All Articles prepared or developed by the Subcontractor under this Agreement, including maps, drawings, models and samples, shall become the property of the Contractor when prepared, whether delivered to the Contractor or not, and shall, together with any Articles furnished to the Subcontractor by the Contractor, be delivered to the Contractor upon request and in any event upon termination of this Agreement. This provision will also apply to work completed after the date of termination of this Agreement, but restricted solely to work which forms part of the Project. Rights in concepts, products, processes or writings already developed by the Subcontractor prior to the date of this Agreement, remain the property of the Subcontractor.

3.7. Drawings

All drawings, specifications and similar data issued in connection with this Agreement are to remain the Contractor's property and must be surrendered to the Contractor upon completion or termination. They must be used solely by the Subcontractor in aid of the manufacture and supply of the Articles and for no other purpose whatsoever excepting with the Contractor's prior written consent.

3.8. Delivery

a) The Articles shall be delivered not later than nor more than 28 working days prior to any dates specified in Schedule D and delivery shall not be deemed effected until the Articles have been received at the destination specified.

b) The Contractor reserves the right to terminate this Agreement or any part thereof and to claim damages in the event that the Articles or any part thereof are not received by the Contractor or the Services are not completed by the date or dates agreed in Schedule

D or the Articles or the Services are not in accordance with this Agreement or any part thereof.

3.9. Poaching staff

Both parties agree that, during the period of this Agreement and for 18 months after its conclusion, they will not directly employ any of the staff of the other party at any time engaged in the pursuance of this Agreement without prior written consent by that other party which shall not be unreasonably withheld.

3.10. Confidentiality

3.10.1. Each party undertakes to keep and treat as confidential and not disclose to any third party other than the Client any information relating to the business or trade secrets of the other nor make use of such information for any purpose whatsoever except for the purposes of this Agreement provided that the foregoing obligation shall not extend to information which is:

a)   in or comes into the public domain other than by breach of this Agreement;

b)   in the possession of one party prior to receipt from the other party;

c)   received bona fide by one party from a third party not receiving the information directly or indirectly from the other party.

3.10.2. However, nothing in this Agreement shall operate so as to prevent either party or any of its staff from making use of know-how acquired, principles learned or experiences gained during the execution of the Agreement. This Clause is binding on all parties during the Agreement and for a period of three (3) years after termination and each party shall so bind its directors and employees.

3.11. Force Majeure

Neither party shall be under any liability to the other party for any delay or failure to perform any obligation hereunder if the same is wholly or partly caused, whether directly or indirectly, by circumstances beyond its reasonable control.

3.12. Publicity

No publicity or advertising shall be released by either the Contractor or the Subcontractor in connection with this Agreement without the prior written approval of the other which shall not be unreasonably withheld.

3.13. Alteration of Agreement

No alteration, modification, or addition to this Agreement, nor any waiver of any of the terms hereof shall be valid unless made in writing and signed by the duly authorised representatives from both parties.

3.14. Termination

If either party commits any serious breach of its obligations hereunder and fails within sixty (60) days of written notice to remedy the same, the other party may forthwith, by notice in writing, terminate this Agreement without prejudice to any other rights which may have accrued to it hereunder.

3.15. Notices

All notices shall be in writing and shall be directed to the Contractor or to the Subcontractor each at its respective address shown on the face of this Agreement or to such other address as the recipient may from time to time specify in writing.

3.16. The Agreement

a)   The entire Agreement between the Subcontractor and the Contractor with respect to the subject matter herein is contained in this Agreement and Schedules hereto and supersedes all previous communications, representations and arrangements, either written or oral, and the Contractor hereby acknowledges that no reliance is placed on any representation made but not embodied in this Agreement.

b)   The Agreement shall be construed and governed in accordance with English Law.

Signed ....   Signed ....

For and on behalf of   For and on behalf of

....

Date ....   Date ....

③ **Analysis**

1. **The agreement**

1.1. **Background**

1.1.1. It is helpful to both parties to the contract for a little of the background to be included by way of introduction. Theoretically it is irrelevant and should not be included as the contract in itself should be sufficiently clear and precise as to the obligations of and benefits to each side such that a question of interpretation can be settled by an independent third party – an arbitrator or court perhaps – regardless of the context. However, the buyer in including reference to his customer is beginning to build a connection between his supplier and customer.

1.1.2. Here again a long, rambling legalistic sounding sentence is saying that the supplier will perform the subcontract in line with the requirements of the main contract. Theoretically unnecessary, as the subcontract should be self-sufficient, but the buyer will include it in case there is some aspect of the main contract which he has unwittingly failed to cover in the subcontract. The seller should avoid all this if he can.

1.1.3. This provides further emphasis that the subcontractor is hooked into the main contract. It may be all very well in principle that the end-customer, main contractor and subcontractor share common expressions and meanings but in practice how can the subcontractor know what meanings are understood between the main contractor and end-customer? The expression 'except as otherwise provided' means that this general rule (of meanings from the main contract) can be varied by specific statement(s) within the subcontract.

1.2. **The services**

1.2.1. On the face of it this is a reasonable enough clause providing as it does that the two parties must agree a price for additional work before that work is put in hand – and if so that it will meet the terms of this agreement, ie that it will meet the needs of the main contract. Read carefully, it can be seen that the clause effectively puts an obligation on the subcontractor to carry out additional work if the main contractor requires it. In practice this may not suit the subcontractor in terms of allocation of resources, etc, when he has no idea what extra might be required and when. The subcontractor could always delay discharging the obligation by arguing over the price.

1.3. Project management

This clause is fair enough. It establishes that points of contact and communication channels will be identified to ensure smooth working. In practice all will depend upon the reasonableness of the two project managers and their staff. Taken to the extreme the main contractor project manager could make discharge of the subcontract difficult, although the subcontractor would rely on the phrase 'reasonable instructions'.

1.4. The project plan

The wording here causes no difficulty. The subcontractor must make sure that the project plan is sufficiently clear as regards his activities as, once again, the main contractor is incorporating main contract obligations into the subcontract. Both sides will seek to ensure that the rate and content of progress reporting provides adequate communication within tolerable cost limitations.

2. Pricing

2.1. Price and payment terms

In principle this clause is perfectly acceptable. By reference to Schedule C, the main body of the subcontract is identifying and *linking* price and payment. Too often, people are concerned with getting the price agreed without giving thought to the timing and mechanism of payment. One interesting point is that the clause makes it clear the consideration comprises solely of the price. That is, if there are other obligations upon the buyer of value to the seller these would not be deemed to form part of the consideration.

2.2. Delay in payment

From the main contractor's point of view all of this is entirely necessary. The clause identifies those things which in practice will identify and verify to the main contractor's payment systems that payment claimed under the subcontract is valid. If his system cannot make this identification and verification he cannot pay, although the subcontractor may indeed have fulfilled the primary obligation of providing goods or services.

What the clause neglects to say is how quickly payment will be made once the subcontractor has remedied the defect in these minor respects. Indeed, the clause also fails to oblige the main contractor to promptly notify the subcontractor that payment has been delayed for one or more of these reasons.

3. General

3.1. Assignment

The effect of this clause is to say that the main contractor has let the subcontract to the particular subcontractor and that he wants no other party involved without first giving his written agreement. That is, the subcontractor cannot further subcontract the work or promise the benefits (the money) of the subcontract to anybody else.

3.2. Duration

This is an even-handed statement saying, in conjunction with 3.14, that neither side can get out of his obligations unilaterally. This is slightly unusual as the buyer frequently reserves the right to bring the arrangement to a premature end for his own convenience.

3.3. Liability

a) Ostensibly this is a generous provision for the main contractor to include. In practice it is only a statement of the fact of law. The main contractor is liable if his negligence causes death or personal injury and that liability could not be eliminated by a statement of exclusion in the contract.

b) Here the main contractor is saying that he will not be liable to the subcontractor for the long list of possible *indirect* losses mentioned. Legally this is acceptable although the subcontractor should seriously examine all of the categories and decide which are both likely and serious and attempt to negotiate their removal from the list of exclusions.

c) This clause relates to the main contractor causing direct loss to the subcontractor: for example, a main contractor vehicle damaging subcontractor property in collecting goods. The financial limitation is likely to be driven by the insurance cover held by the main contractor. The lesser of the sum of £XXXX or Y times the price of the subcontract is a common arrangement and is acceptable. Of course where the price of the subcontract is not known at the outset, it is a question of judgement and negotiation as to the size of the Y factor.

As a whole this clause sets out to protect the main contractor by eliminating or limiting (where these are permitted by the law) his liability to the subcontractor for his negligence or other deficiencies. The subcontractor may seek to agree that the clause is revised to give it mutuality in effect.

3.4. Indemnity

a) Following on from 1.2.1 this clause really hammers it home that the subcontractor is only there to help the main contractor perform its contract and that the subcontractor is fully and solely responsible for main contract breaches caused by the subcontractor.

On the principle of 'for want of a nail the battle was lost' the main contractor is right to be very concerned that, having taken the decision and the risk to subcontract, he will not be seriously let down. On the other hand, the subcontractor can argue that he cannot possibly know sufficient of the main contract, that he is only the subcontractor (ie not enjoying the benefits of the main contractor) and that he is working at the instruction of the main contractor's project manager, so he cannot take on that liability.

b) This is a natural and reasonable precaution for the main contractor to secure. If his subcontractor fails in certain ways it is one thing to have the right to sue him, but if this does not yield recompense – because the subcontractor simply goes bankrupt – the right is of no commercial value. Thus the main contractor will want to know that the subcontractor is protected by adequate insurance policies. If the concern is great enough the main contractor may look to the subcontractor to have him identified in the insurance policy itself as having an interest.

3.5. Intellectual Property Rights

The key words here are 'supplied' in the second line and 'are and shall remain' in the fourth line. Together it can be interpreted that the clause is addressing rights in documentation issued by the main contractor to the subcontractor for the purpose of the work under the subcontract. As the clause invites interpretation it is wise for the subcontractor to seek confirmation of this interpretation. Assuming this is correct the subcontractor may seek an indemnity from the main contractor against legal action by third parties in respect of IPR infringement. After all the subcontractor only has the main contractor's word that the IPR belongs to him. If the main contractor is telling the truth there should be no problem in him giving that indemnity. If he will not readily give the indemnity then the subcontractor would be right to have some concern.

3.6. Ownership of results

Provided that the subcontractor is content as a matter of policy to have no rights in design work performed under contract then this clause is acceptable to him. In practice the difficulty is in the merging of ideas and information and thus the separability of intellectual property belonging exclusively to each of the two parties is impossible to achieve.

3.7. Drawings

The important point to make is that this clause is addressing ownership physically of the drawings and other material rather than the intellectual property enshrined within them which is covered by 3.5.

3.8. Delivery

a) This relatively brief clause is to some degree unclear insofar as it is not certain whether the main contractor or the subcontractor is actually responsible for delivery to destination. It only goes so far as saying that for contractual purposes delivery has not occurred until goods have been received at their destination. Transportation and insurance in transit are not mentioned.

b) Unless the contract says so specifically (as it does here) the buyer may not be entitled to terminate if the supplier fails to deliver *exactly* on time or *exactly* to specification. That is, in the normal course of events, late supply and/or delivery of goods not exactly to specification would entitle the buyer only to sue for the resultant damages (if any) for non-conforming performance in terms of time or specification. It is for the supplier to judge how likely these possible events are and to react accordingly. For example, if he believes that late delivery is a distinct possibility and that resulting from that the buyer is likely to suffer real damage (ie of genuine financial impact) then he may wish to negotiate a liquidated damages arrangement. The advantage to the supplier is that, worded correctly, such an arrangement would introduce an absolute maximum liability for late or non-delivery. On the other hand he could find himself making liquidated damages payments to the buyer in circumstances where, in practice and although the supplier was late, the buyer would not actually pursue the defaulting supplier for redress.

3.9. Poaching staff

This type of clause tends to be seen where the type of work involves a fairly close technical relationship between the parties whereunder each may identify in the other's employees potential recruits. It should be noted that such a clause can only go so far as to restrict the activities of the parties insofar as recruitment processes are concerned. It is probably illegal – or at least unenforceable – if the clause were to seek to prevent the parties from actually employing members of each other's staff.

3.10. Confidentiality

3.10.1. These days, such statements of restriction are quite common. In practice they place upon the other party's employees obligations equivalent to those upon employees of the company under each employee's contract of employment. That is, each employee must keep confidential the secrets of his employer and the secrets of those firms with whom his employer contracts.

Subparagraph (*a*) is there to point out that information already available to the public at large cannot suddenly be made confidential simply by the wording of a contract between two parties.

Subparagraph (*b*) similarly points out that if firm *X* already holds certain information, that information cannot become subject to the conditions of confidentiality simply because it is re-transferred to them from *Y*.

Subparagraph (*c*) covers the final permutation of events whereby one party might independently and legitimately receive information from a third party which, had it not been so received, the other party might have had some claim that it should be held in confidence.

3.10.2. The first sentence is quite reasonable and equitable although, in permitting the subcontractor freedom to use knowledge gained, it conflicts with clause 3.6. This is something which the subcontractor should query. Clearly it is in his best interests to have the former statement prevail.

The second sentence is probably meant to apply to the whole of clause 3.10 rather than just the first sentence of 3.10.2. It is

important for the subcontractor to establish exactly and unequi-
vocally what his rights and obligations are.

3.11. Force Majeure

Always the two questions that each party should ask itself in
considering going for the inclusion of a Force Majeure clause are (i)
how likely delay/default is and its potential consequence on the
buyer and (ii) the degree to which it is desirable at the outset to argue
out what precisely are the circumstances which, for the purposes of
the clause, provide excusable reasons for delay/default.

From the seller's point of view he must also decide whether to
propose liquidated damages.

To agree at the outset what the buyer's maximum damage
could be is to limit the seller's exposure. However, in practice he
could find himself making liquidated damages payments to the
buyer in circumstances where, but for the inclusion of liquidated
damages, the buyer would not actually have pressed the seller for
recompense for the delay.

At least this particular Force Majeure clause is mutual in its
effect.

3.12. Publicity

This is an even-handed clause which is designed to prevent
one party from stealing a publicity march on the other. In practice
the two sides would probably agree to a joint release of information.

3.13. Alteration of agreement

This brief clause covers two crucial points. A contract or an
amendment to contract can be made orally. It is usual in business
transactions to make contracts in writing. The purpose here is to
exclude oral variations to the contract. This makes for certainty and
ease of administration. Secondly, it is made clear that only properly
authorised personnel can enter into contractual commitments. In
practice each party should enquire of the other as to which individuals are so authorised. It should be noted, as well, that any
amendments, to be effective, are to be signed by both parties. This
is distinct from the common arrangement of separate offer and
acceptance of contract amendments. The advantage of this approach is that it forces the parties to come to an unequivocal
agreement on the content of the amendment before it can be
effective and therefore before any work is put in hand.

3.14. Termination

Under contract law, serious breach (which we must assume equates to fundamental breach) entitles the innocent side to summarily terminate the contract. In this clause the defaulting party is given 60 days in which to put the problem right before the contract can be terminated. Interestingly the word 'may' (terminate) is used rather than 'will' giving the buyer the discretion to continue with the contract even if the problem has not been rectified. The possibility of termination, or notification of serious breach, are weighty matters and it should be noted that advice of either must be given in writing.

Depending on the nature of the work under the contract the subcontractor may ask the main contractor to consider including words placing an obligation on the main contractor to minimise the direct or consequential effect of the breach and to render assistance to the subcontractor, at his cost, as necessary in correcting the problems.

The reference to the right of termination not affecting (referred to as 'without prejudice') other rights is there to convey that, for example, the obligation on the subcontractor to hold the main contractor's information in confidence does not disappear because of the termination. These termination clauses sometimes end by saying '…without prejudice to any other right or remedy'. This has the more general effect of saying that termination does not affect other rights accrued under the contract or under the law at large.

3.15. Notices

Again this emphasises the formal nature of the contract in saying that matters relating to it must be committed to writing. It is also there to assist in contract administration.

3.16. The agreement

a) Most importantly this clause explains that only the contract and its attachments constitute the entire arrangements between the parties. Read in conjunction with clause 3.13 the effect is to say, for example, that a written agreement between the two chief engineers in relation to the work would not be enforceable unless both were nominated as authorised representatives and their agreement had been incorporated in the contract.

b) This standard statement is included to eliminate any possible doubt of the appropriate jurisdiction in the event of a dispute arising over the contract.

④ Summary

The questions in the mind of the subcontractor in reviewing the offered subcontract are:

    a) Is the type of subcontract offered appropriate to the work?

    b) Is it adequately even-handed?

    c) Are the conditions acceptable?

    d) To what degree of risk am I exposed if I accept conditions which are not favourable to me?

    e) To what extent will I be successful if I seek to negotiate some of the conditions with the main contractor, and will this in itself cause dissatisfaction in him?

    f) If I choose to comment, to what level of detail should I go?

These questions are largely intertwined and commercial judgement will dictate the answers. In this case the answer to question (*a*) is probably no. The contract is stated to be for the provision of engineering consultancy and yet much of the document alludes to the supply of goods. This clearly is inappropriate, but on the other hand if the clauses cannot in practice apply they cannot cause a problem or expose a risk and so perhaps it is better not to object simply on a matter of principle.

Naturally enough a contract prepared by the buyer will be most favourable to him and typically the subcontractor will accept this principle. Subject to one or two changes only, the offered document is reasonably fair.

The conditions are mostly acceptable although there is considerable risk to the subcontractor if he acknowledges all the main contractor's obligations to satisfy the client and accepts that he could be liable for the consequences of breach of the main contract. After all the consultancy might in straightforward value terms be worth only a pittance compared to the value of the main contract. However, if the individuals who will provide the consultancy are top class or it is known that the area in which the main contractor needs help is not critical or key to the end product then perhaps the degree of risk exposure is very small. On balance such clauses are ones to which the subcontractor should seek some revision. The comment regarding prompt payment following rectification of a defective invoice is also worth pursuing. Cash flow is all important and it is unacceptable to leave the main contractor with the contractual right to delay payment indefinitely. All points of clarity, such as the question relating to IPR, should be resolved.

The question of success or failure, disaffection or not in seeking to negotiate contract conditions depends largely on custom and practice, the respective positions and strengths of the two sides and, most importantly, the personal relationship between the two negotiators.

As to the level of detail into which comments on the conditions should go, all the same principles as above apply. For example, the document is less than perfect insofar as it switches between alphabetic and numeric subparagraph nomenclature but this hardly matters since clarity is not compromised and the document is consistent throughout.

Acknowledgements

I am indebted to Michael Bentley, Seminars Director at Hawksmere Ltd for the opportunities he has given me to speak at national and international business seminars. I am also grateful for his encouragement and for that of Neil Thomas, Managing Director at Hawksmere, in producing this publication and my earlier book *The Commercial Engineer.*

I am grateful for kind permission to reproduce extracts and quotations from the following books:

An Introduction to the Law of Contract, P S Atiyah 1990
    by permission of Oxford University Press
English Law, K S Smith and D J Keenan
Dictionary of Law, L B Curzon
    by permission of Pitman Publishing
What is Intellectual Property?, The Patent Office
    by permission of the Controller of HMSO
Management Teams: Why They Succeed or Fail, R Meredith Belbin by permission of Heinemann